RETROSPECT
The Origins of Catholic Beliefs and Practices

RETROSPECT
The Origins of Catholic Beliefs and Practices

John Deedy

THE THOMAS MORE PRESS
Chicago, Illinois

Much of the material in this book appeared in different form in the Newsletter of the same title published by the Thomas More Association.

ISBN 0-88347-260-0

CONTENTS

ABOUT THE AUTHOR
John Deedy is a veteran Catholic
journalist and the author of a number of
highly regarded books including *Your
Aging Parents*, *The Catholic Fact Book*
and *The Catholic Book of Days*. His
articles have appeared in many papers
and magazines including the *New York
Times*, *The Critic* and *U.S. Catholic*.

To friends from Paradise . . .

Miriam and Tom Curnin
Mary Jane and Fred Feuerbach
Mary and Ray O'Connell
Lee and Bill Reynolds

INTRODUCTION

FOR generations, Catholics lived by the assurance that theirs was a church that had never changed and never would change.

It was a proud boast and a perpetual consolation, and it related to the continuity which the church claimed for its teachings. At the same time it was an assurance that did not always bear close scrutinizing. In several areas—among them slavery, usury, church and state, and salvation outside the church—church teaching has taken on different contexts, if nothing more. Did the church change? Yes and no. Pope Paul VI's was the most politic response. He handled the issue of change by maintaining time and again that "the church is consistent with itself."

Which may be another way of saying that if the church does not change, it does evolve. Cardinal Newman used to speak of the "development of doctrine." Father Avery Dulles, the modern Jesuit theologian, uses the word "reconceptualization." Whichever term is the more correct, this much is certain: if the church doesn't change, its teaching does take on mighty different hues at times.

John Deedy

It could not be otherwise. The church is not shut off in some time capsule, frozen at some point in salvation history. Again, it evolves—and no generations of Catholics know this better than those whose Catholicism goes back to pre-Vatican Council II times. The new generations of Catholics know no other church than the one into which they were born, but Catholics of the older generations have experienced ecclesiastical evolution—radically and directly—in their own worshipping lives.

The church's doctrines may be the same, but so much else has changed, in attitudes as well as practices, as to make this postconciliar church virtually unrecognizable in comparison to the church that existed just a couple of decades ago. A Catholic Rip Van Winkle, dozing off for those twenty years, would have trouble on awakening in believing he belonged to the same worshipping community. Things are that different in Catholicism, that changed. The church is the same founded by the Lord and Savior Jesus Christ, but it has evolved.

But then this is the story of Catholicism. The church has been forever evolving. Once upon a time, the sacraments of baptism and confirmation were commonly conferred at the same time; they are not now, at least not generally. (The Eastern churches continue the practice of conferring baptism and confirmation together on infants, and the same is true in much of the Hispanic culture, including Spain. Otherwise in the West, the practice is pretty much confined to the Rite of Christian Initiation of Adults, RCIA). Also once upon a time, Latin was the language of the mass throughout Roman Catholicism;

10

today, the language is that of the local body of believers. Once upon a time, one fasted from midnight before receiving communion; subsequently this was reduced to three hours, then one hour. Once upon a time, the eating of meat on Friday was a matter for the confessional; now Catholics can wolf down porterhouse steaks on Friday in good conscience—if not also, alas, in good health.

There have been numerous other changes in the way the faith has been lived. My grandparents, for instance, were compulsive church-goers, but approached the altar infrequently for communion. It had been such for centuries for Catholics. Why? Partly out of feelings of unworthiness; partly not to risk sacrilege. The divine presence was held in such awesomeness that the prevailing impulse was to adore the sacred host rather than partake of it. That changed like so much else. The reform of the church calendar resulted in the elimination of old saintly favorites like Philomena and Christopher. The restoration of the old Holy Week liturgy was accomplished at the expense of popular Holy Week devotions, like the Tre Ore services of Good Friday and the adoration devotions of Holy Thursday. Remember when the streets of Catholic cities would be jammed Holy Thursday evenings with people making foot pilgrimages to churches (seven, ideally) to pray before elaborately decorated eucharistic altars? Today even during Holy Week many Catholic churches are locked, if not immediately after scheduled morning services, then before dark in order to protect against vandals.

None of these changes, dramatic as some might be, has

altered the substance of the faith. Mostly the changes relate to matters of discipline and custom. They do not relate to doctrines. Nonetheless, even the smallest change can take on large consequences and prove disconcerting to many in a religion which, if not having overstated its claim to changelessness, has not always been successful in acquainting its membership with what is meant by changelessness.

The church does not change in essentials. It changes all the time, however, in accidentals. It is, in fact, in an almost constant state of evolution, obscured though this may be from popular consciousness. The church's story, in a word, takes fascinating, colorful and surprising turns.

The purpose of this book is to trace those turns as it explores aspects of church history. The book will look at the origins and evolution of many of those practices which are part and parcel of modern Catholicism. Was celibacy always a requirement of Catholic bishops and priests? Was the mass always the carefully structured liturgical ceremony it is today? Have devotional practices, like novenas, the praying of the rosary and the saying of the stations of the cross, always been a part of the Catholic experience, or were they devotional appendages born of particular historical circumstances which could be expected one day to fall into religious and spiritual disuse?

RETROSPECT: The Origins of Catholic Beliefs and Practices will examine subjects and questions such as

RETROSPECT

these. The book will focus on dozens of topics in presenting a picture of how Catholics and their church came to be what they are two millennia into salvation history. The net result, it is hoped, will be something of a lesson in church history, and perhaps a better understanding of how Catholicism has adapted to a changing world.

1.

THE BLESSED VIRGIN MARY:
From Total Exaltation to Partial Eclipse

An Obscure Figure

THE surprising thing about Mary, the mother of Jesus, is how little is really known about someone so professedly well known.

Mary is prefigured in the Old Testment, as early as Genesis 3:15, where the Lord says to the serpent, "I will put enmities between you and the woman, and between your seed and hers; she shall crush your head and you shall lie in wait for her heel," but the most pointed reference comes in Isaiah 7:1-17, in conjunction with the confirmation of the messianic promises to the House of David: "The Lord himself will give you a sign. Behold a virgin will conceive and bear a son, and his name shall be called Emmanuel."

In the New Testament, however, one finds precious little about Mary. There are the nativity narratives, and the recounting of a few familial scenes. Eight times Mary is referred to as the mother of Jesus, and of course she's at the foot of the cross when Jesus dies. The historical settings are in place, but there is a sparseness of historical detail. Mostly Mary is just located at one place or another. Except for what can be read into the incident at the wedding at Cana in Galilee, the scene of Jesus' first miracle (John 2:1-11), Mary for all practical purposes is left in obscurity as a person—a matter so unusual as to be the subject of detailed study by Saint Peter Canisius and to be remarked upon by Cardinal John Henry Newman in his famous correspondence with Dr. Edward Pusey of Oxford and Christ Church.

Nor did Mary's image sharpen much after the crucifixion of her son. It was Mary Magdalene who discovered the empty tomb on the first Easter, not Mary the mother of Jesus Christ. Mary, in fact, is not mentioned as being present in the gospel accounts of Christ's several appearances to his disciples or at the Ascension; it is only pious presumptions which have her included at the various happenings. Further, there is no certainty about what became of Mary after the Pentecost, how she died and where; it is tradition alone, rooted in the Middle Ages, which says she died at Ephesus allegedly of love, "her great desire to be united to her son either dissolving the ties of body or soul, or prevailing on God to dissolve them." Nor is there more than the rare direct mention of Mary in the earliest liturgical formulas.

But piety and matriarchal instincts have more than filled in the gaps. However obscure the details of the historical record, so far as Catholics are concerned Mary is no bit player in the salvation story. In Catholic tradition, Mary is exalted above all who have been born of the natural union of man and woman, ranking immediately behind Jesus Christ himself, who Catholics believe, of course, to have been born of the Spirit operative through a virginal Mary.

Still, this was a tradition that had to nurture and grow. It did not spring full blossom into Catholic theology or creed.

Saint John, it is noted, never even used Mary's name, speaking rather of the "mother of Jesus," although no detachment, discounting or distancing is read into this. John's practice is situated within normal familial conventions. In the usual course of events, children do not address their mothers by their given first names. Some exegetes thus see John's literary mode confirming the mother-son relationship which Jesus established between Mary and John from his cross. But if Mary was more ethereal than intimately knowable in the Scriptures, the scenario was quickly to change.

The Seeds of Devotion

By the second century, Saint Irenaeus and Saint Justin were proclaiming Mary as the "new Eve," the specific female corollary to Christ as the "new Adam."

As that and other insights gained currency, whole new vistas were opened for the development of Marian doctrine and worship. Marian representations began to appear in the art of the catacombs, in mosaics and in the adornment of sarcophagi, and references to Mary began to crowd pious literature, much of them uncanonical and, as time went on, wildly extravagant. At the same time, Mary's name was being introduced into the

17

John Deedy

church's liturgy; a second-century baptismal formula, for instance, included the phrase "born of the Holy Spirit and the Virgin Mary."

By the fourth century, churches were being dedicated to Mary, and she was becoming a veritable fixture in the church's prayer life. As an example, a manuscript fragment of the period finds the "mother of God" being petitioned for protection. The fragment was in Greek, and is thought to be the ancient form of the Latin prayer *Sub tuum praesidium confugimus,* "We fly to thy patronage, O holy mother of God," a wording which in due course inspired the medieval prayer the *Memorare:* "Remember, O most gracious Virgin Mary! that never was it known that anyone who fled to thy protection, implored thy help, and sought thy intercession . . . etc."

The exceedingly popular Hail Mary, incidentally, was not of particularly early origin. There is little or no trace of most of its invocations before 1050, and the formula of the prayer as known today traces only to 1495, when with the exception of a single word it appeared at the head of a work by Girolamo Savonarola, the fifteenth-century Dominican reformer, who ended up executed as a heretic. Originally, the Hail Mary seems to have been a salutation rather than a prayer.

Come the fifth century, theologians were speaking of the divine motherhood of Mary (*theotokos*)—and indeed in 431 the church confirmed the concept at the Council of Ephesus, thus directly repudiating Nestorius, who had denied Mary the title *theotokos,* mother of God, calling her merely *Christokokos,* mother of Christ. Reportedly

18

there was "an explosion of joy" over the Council's action, and to the chant "Mary is *theotokos,* she is truly the mother of God," the people of Ephesus escorted the Council Fathers to their dwellings with a torch-light parade.

Beginning to root itself about the same time was the doctrine of Mary's assumption "body and soul, to heavenly glory." Earlier, Saint Epiphanius had expressed doubts that Mary had even experienced death, his theory being that she had been accorded the honor of being assumed bodily into heaven while still alive. That opinion never gained wide acceptance, however. In the sixth century, Saint Gregory of Tours articulated the more common view: "The Lord took Mary's holy body and conveyed it on a cloud to paradise; there it was united with her soul, and glorified with the elect, it enjoys the eternal blessings that shall have no end."

Whatever, by that century's end the feast of Mary's assumption was being observed churchwide, and the cult of the Virgin Mary was bounding ahead with assurance and color—lots of color. For building within the cult was a treasure of *Marienlegenden,* "Mary-legends" or stories of the Virgin Mary, and these won enormous circulation. Ordinarily, "Mary-legends" are associated with the high Middle Ages, but actually they were making their appearance as early as the fifth and sixth centuries. One ancient manuscript, *Transitus Mariae,* contains the following testimony of Christians at Rome:

"Often here in Rome she [Mary] appears to the people who confess her in prayer, for she has appeared here on the sea when it was troubled and raised itself and was going to destroy the ship in which they were sailing. And the sailors called on the name of the Lady Mary and said: 'O Lady Mary, Mother of God, have mercy on us,' and straightway she rose upon them like the sun and delivered the ships, ninety-two of them, and rescued them from destruction, and none of them perished."

Typically "Mary-legends" accented the intercessory powers of Mary, as demonstrated by another story of the time: "She [Mary] appeared by day on the mountain where robbers had fallen upon people and sought to slay them. And these people cried out saying, 'Oh Lady Mary, Mother of God, have mercy on us.' And she appeared before them like a flash of lightning, and blinded the eyes of the robbers and they were not seen by them." In time authorities would discourage such exotic narratives as these, but that was much later. In the meantime, the cult of Mary had solidly established itself as a hallmark of the Catholic Christian faith.

Paintings, Proclamations and Pilgrimages

A vast Marian literature of prayers, sermons, proclamations, offices and masses took shape, and doctrinal trends continued to evidence themselves.

One popular doctrinal proposition of the twelfth century focused on Mary's compassion on Calvary and the interpretation of Christ's words from the cross, "Woman, behold thy son" (John 19:26), which were seen as dramatizing the spiritual motherhood of Mary over the whole Christian family. Another centering on the Assumption, as yet not formally promulgated as doctrine, further underscored belief in the availability of Mary's spiritual assistance for those petitioning her help.

In the thirteenth and fourteenth centuries Marian devotion found expression in the dedication of the great cathedrals of Europe, and in the writings of saints like Bonaventure, Thomas Aquinas and Duns Scotus. The invention of printing from movable type in the fifteenth century made the Bible more accessible to Christian peoples, but the printing press was also put to work early to assist in the dissemination of Marian literature, such as the sermons of Saint Bernardino of Siena, said to be "at once tender and terrible."

Popes added to the swell of Marian devotion by proclaiming and enriching feasts in Mary's honor, such as the Presentation of Mary (November 21) and the Visitation (May 31), both designated in the late fourteenth century. In 1477, Pope Sixtus IV (1471-1484) gave limited approval and indulgenced a Feast of the Conception of Mary, a feast that Saint Bernard, a man noted for his Marian piety, had actually opposed in his day (the twelfth century) as an innovation.

Countless pilgrimages were arranged in Mary's honor; Marian associations sprung into being; the Dominican Order propagated the rosary; and the Franciscans pushed for the formalization of the doctrine of the Immaculate Conception, the proposition that Mary was born free of original sin. Inevitably enthusiasms caught up craftsmen and artists, some of whom celebrated Mary as priest, seemingly the ultimate honor. Church officials of course wanted as little of the latter as possible. Yet, whether historically and theologically accurate or not, the Church of St. Praxedes in Rome contains a painting of the Eucharist being celebrated by women of the second century, and a fifteenth-century painting of the same genre was good enough artistically to make it into the Louvre—a painting entitled "Le Sacerdoce de la Vierge" depicting Mary, Christ-child at her feet, dressed in alb, stole, cincture and chasuble, and attended by acolytes in the form of diminutive angels carrying cross, chalice, an open book and censer . . . every detail, in a word, suggestive of priesthood and preparation for the saying of mass.

The glorifications of Mary seemed limitless. Mary's virtues—her purity, virginity, obedience, faith—were celebrated near and far in sermon, song and sonnet, and from a hilltop in the Vosges Mountains in northeast France in 1493, a site known subsequently as the Three Ears of Corn, word spread that Mary had actually appeared to a group of men, warning that God was about to visit his wrath on the world. On the eve of the Reformation (to which the Vosges apparition came to be tied) Marian devotion was full-blown, and Marian impetuses appeared inexhaustible.

Protestant Challenge

The Reformation was to have a profound effect on the Marian perceptions of those Christians who embraced Protestantism, although not instantly.

RETROSPECT

Even Luther himself did not immediately reject Marian devotion outright. In fact, one of the most moving treatises of his transition period was *Translations and Commentary on the Magnificat,* a work in which he invoked Mary's intercession at its open and close, and in which he discussed Mary's virtues with what is now conceded in Catholic circles to be fervor and accuracy. In that work Luther did deplore the excesses of those who turned to Mary rather than God, saying "She gives nothing; God is the only giver." But no one could argue too strongly with that bit of theology, for Mary's power was of course operative through her son.

Over time, though, Luther's perceptions altered and eventually prejudiced Marian appreciations among many people. Though Luther venerated Mary, he rejected the idea that in becoming mother of the Savior, Jesus Christ, she thus became by divine ordination an intimate part of the divine plan, source of grace, and mediator, cooperator or, as some by then would have it, co-redemptrix of the human race; God was the unique mediator, the one source of grace. Luther's views set the stage for reformers with the unequivocal proposition that any reverence accorded Mary was blasphemous and depreciatory of the triune God. Protestant passions on the subject may be less strong today than they were then, but to this day the cult of Mary is a sticky ecumenical problem.

The Council of Trent (1545-1563) did nothing to lessen these Marian disagreements. Council Fathers were, in fact, almost defiant, energetically supporting prevailing

Catholic concepts of the spiritual motherhood of Mary by confirming as salutary the second half of the Hail Mary ("Holy Mary, Mother of God, pray for us sinners now and at the hour of our death, Amen"), and explaining by way of emphasis that "we should piously and suppliantly have recourse to her in order that by her intercession she may reconcile God with us sinners and obtain for us the blessing, we need both for this present life and for the life which has no end." Trent thus not only affirmed the cult of Mary, but also hardened a point of division between the two churches.

In the four hundred years between Trent and Vatican Council II (1962-1965), and as if to counterbalance Marian neglects and declines within Protestantism, Catholic devotion to Mary intensified and rose to new heights and enthusiasms. Marian lay associations and sodalities flourished, beginning with the Sodality of Our Lady founded by the Jesuits in 1563. In the seventeenth and eighteenth centuries, there was a great flowering of Marian scholarship, notably in France and Spain. The nineteenth century spawned other phenomena, including the Marian apparitions of 1846 and 1858 at La Salette and Lourdes, respectively, in France, and at Knock, in Ireland, in 1879—preludes of a sort to the early twentieth-century apparitions of Fàtima, Portugal, in 1917, and Beaurang, Belgium, in 1932-1933 and probably later apparitions as well. New religious orders, such as the Marists and Oblates of Mary Immaculate, invoked the name of Mary in their very titles by way of authenticating their Marian dedication and commitments. Pope after pope wrote Marian encyclicals, convened Marian congresses, designated Marian years, and established yet additional Marian feasts, such as that of the Queenship of Mary on May 31, set in 1945 by Pius XII. And, of course, there was the formal, explicit promulgation of new Marian doctrines—in 1854 of Mary's Immaculate Conception, by Pius IX (acting well in anticipation of 1870's infallibility decree), and in 1950 by Pius XII of Mary's assumption into heaven.

Vatican II added its emphases to the cult of Mary with dozens of references in several conciliar decrees celebrating the Virgin Mary, confirming her gifts and her charisms, and reinforcing her role as model and exemplar, "the perfect example of . . . spiritual and apostolic life" (*Decree on the Laity,* 4). The Council urged that "the entire body of the faithful pour forth persevering prayer" to Mary (*Constitution on the Church,* 69), assuring that "by her maternal charity, Mary cares for the brethren of her son who still journey on earth surrounded by dangers and difficulties, until they are led to their happy fatherland" (*ibid.,* 62).

Recent Decline

A funny thing happened in the years after the Second Vatican Council.

Mary devotion suddenly experienced an eclipse. Feasts were discounted or ignored; practices of devotion of centuries' standing, like May altars, the praying of the rosary, and the wearing of medals and other symbols of

John Deedy

Marian devotion, went into mothballs. She, in sum, who for centuries had been the very personification of goodness, the ideal of sinlessness, was no longer on her pedestal.

Could the turn-around have been in reaction to Marian excesses and extravagances? Doubtful. Although many such existed, the situation was nothing like it was in the Middle Ages, when unbalanced mysticism and outrageous symbolism characterized so much of what passed as authentic Marian devotion. In Germany, for instance, statues of Mary were made with shutters in the stomach, which when opened showed the baby Jesus in his mother's womb, and in the old French province of Franche-Comté there was a graphic representation of a *virgo parturiens.* In France and Spain, meanwhile, forms of "slavery of Mary" were promoted as pious practices, complete to the wearing of chains.

The exotic had passed, though it must be admitted that excesses and extravagances lingered about in measure such as to provoke cautions from a succession of popes. In 1954 Pius XII on two occasions called for a correct balance in Mariology and Marian devotion. John XXIII in 1961 repeated warnings against "particular practices or devotions, which may be excessive in their veneration of Jesus and Our Mother," adding with assurance that neither Jesus nor Mary would be "offended by these words of ours." Paul VI at least three times urged a Marian devotion that was sound, biblically and pastorally oriented, and faithful to tradition. "It is in the his-

tory of salvation, in the Gospel, that you will find Mary,''
he declared in his 1964 encyclical, *Ecclesiam suam*.

Yet, despite all these warnings and the correctives
which they produced, Marian devotion went into a severe
decline, and nowhere more so than in the United States.
How come?

One explanation is that many traditional forms of
Marian devotion found themselves vulnerable to the reforms of Vatican II, and the broadened forms of piety
which the Council encouraged. For instance, instead of
mourners kneeling and praying the rosary at wakes, they
were now expected to take part in Bible vigils conducted
around the bier. The Bible vigil undoubtedly helps reflect
the stronger emphasis which the Council wanted to bring
on the scriptures, if not also on church and Christian
community, but it does so at the expense of what was
long a particularly popular Marian devotion, the rosary
prayed for the deceased person at the coffin itself. And
that is only one example; there are many such. Devotion
to Mary, in a word, has suffered greatly as a result of the
innovations and greater liberties allowed in practices of
personal piety, occurring with and through the Council's
general reassessment of scriptural, pastoral and ecumenical concerns. The consequence may not exactly be what
was intended, but it is a consequence nonetheless, and
this is paradoxical to say the least given the lavish, un-
qualified praise heaped on Mary in the Council's documents.

Another explanation for the decline in the popularity

of Marian devotion traces to changed social values, and thus to secular rather than ecclesiastical causes. The reference is to the women's movement. Among some people Marian devotion has been undercut, however obliquely, by "women's lib"—the women's liberation movement.

Traditionally Mary has been exalted in Catholicism as the model of all virtue, her qualities of person cited as ideals to be striven for by all females: Mary's gentleness, for instance, her deference, compliance, docility, dutifulness, submissiveness, etc. From time immemorial in the church, qualities such as these made Mary the model of the perfect woman, the sum and substance of femalehood and true feminism. The problem is that with "women's lib" ancient valuations of female perfection went out the window, and new ones began to take form.

Mary in the 80s

Today Catholic women quite generally continue to honor and reverence Mary, but for large numbers of them Mary's virtues (to the extent that they ever existed in the idealized forms of their projection) are no longer necessary.

Their ideas of female perfection are quite different, and this has affected not only the way in which the so-called new woman looks on Mary, but also how she exercises devotion to her. It is, to state the obvious, to remark that the prayer life of a strongly independent career woman is less likely now than in the past to lock onto one whose role was defined primarily as that of instrument in the will of another and in a plan outside herself.

Undergoing change, too, is the idea of Mary as the anchor of the model Christian family, the woman who personified maternal love and familial holiness and dedication, and whose life was largely lived for others in both the immediate and extended sense. Trouble is, that old and honorable concept does not play well in a society where women are encouraged to strive for maximum personal and professional fulfillment, and where wives commonly have places and careers beyond motherhood and the home.

This is a radically new situation, one which is an obvious threat to a religious and cultural value system, essentially Christian, which has been in place for two millennia. Popes know it. Thus, in his 1974 apostolic letter *Marialis cultus* calling for a "right ordering and development of devotion" to Mary, Paul VI included passages on anthropology and on Mary in the context of women's rights, a subject he returned to the following year in proposing Mary as the "way of beauty" complementing the "way of the intellect." Thus, too, in his 1987 encyclical *Redemptoris mater,* John Paul II cited Mary's life as an image of obedience and freedom, and held her up as a model of "femininity with dignity" and a point of reference for all humanity, particularly women.

Whether reminders such as these are going to make any difference is impossible to say. The indicators may be that for some the magic presently is gone from the name and the cult of Mary, but that is not to say that the old appeals will never return. The church is as committed as ever to Marian doctrine, and it has not diluted or deviated from its essential understandings of Mary as model and exemplar of love, affection and piety. Similarly, Marian associations and study groups continue to foster devotion to Mary. There may even be something of a revival of interfaith interest in Mary in the founding in England in 1967, and the introduction of the United States in 1976, of the organization called the Ecumenical Society of the Blessed Virgin Mary. Singularly or in combination, forces such as these could turn things around.

But not everyone is too sure about that. A few Catholic theologians, for instance, are even speculating about a Catholicism of the future which would be largely devoid of special homage paid to Mary. They may not see that as exactly imminent, given the large residues of devotion to Mary in the motherhood of the faith, which are still to be found among Catholics. But the fact that some theologians are even thinking along that line is indication of how real they consider the possibility, sad though the thought may be for many. Should their fears be realized, the faith, needless to say, would not be any less authentic. But it certainly would be different in much of its expression. The future holds the key, of course. Meanwhile, the church endures if not one of the strangest evolutions of piety in its history, then certainly its most surprising.

2.

THE MASS:
It Is The Mass that Matters

The Spoken Word

ASK the average person in the pew to name the change in
the church resulting from Vatican II that most affects her
or him, and chances are the answer will be by the adoption of the vernacular for the mass.

There should be nothing surprising about that. The
mass is the central act of worship in Catholicism, and any
change affecting it would be bound to have major impact
on the body of Catholics, even one so incidental to the
central mystery of the ritual as the language in which it is
celebrated.

Deep and impassioned emotions were—and for some
still are—bound up with the use of Latin in the mass, the
valid ones mostly having to do with aesthetics. Some
Latin diehards also cite tradition, but their ground is not
strongly tenable. As the famed Father H. A. Reinhold
would insistently remind, Latin was not the language of
the first mass, the Last Supper; Hebrew and Aramaic
were. Similarly, Latin was not the language of the masses
of Saint Paul; Greek was. Latin was not even the lan-

31

guage of the mass of the early Roman church; for a couple of hundred years Greek was.

Latin was actually a third-century innovation to the mass, and why was it adopted? "One, because it was the vernacular of Rome," said Reinhold in an interview shortly before his death. "Two, because it was the language of commerce, law, literature, the army, and the administration of western Europe. In a word, it was the language of the people. If the people were to be reached, it had to be in words they understood."

Father Reinhold wasn't around to see his kind of logic carry Vatican II. If, in fact, he had an input into the council, it was merely in helping create a climate for change. Nonetheless, his words certainly anticipated the Council's action. The Western or Roman Catholic Church went from Latin, no longer the vernacular anywhere for anything, to polyglot. Local vernaculars are now being used everywhere for the mass. The results have been mixed, to say the least, but, if nothing more, they demonstrate that change of a kind can come even at this late date to the oldest and most important of the church's liturgies—the liturgy performed in memory of Christ, the liturgy that incorporates the Eucharist. The mass, like so much in the church, isn't frozen in time either.

Vatican Council II's return of the vernacular to the mass was only one of the changes brought to the ceremony. The altar was turned around so that the priest faced the people; the priest's vestments were simplified; the readings of the mass were reorganized and made more flexible; laity appeared on the altar as lectors and eucharistic ministers; the congregation was encouraged to raise its voice in song—and gone were several appendages to the traditional Latin mass, beginning with the prayers at the foot of the altar, which, it was decided, obscured the entrance rite.

More noticeable, however, to many Catholics was the dropping of two appendages to the end of mass. The first, a favorite of many, was the prayer which followed the final blessing as a kind of blessing of its own, the beautiful opening verses of the Gospel according to John. The second, far less a favorite, were the Leonine Prayers recited in the vernacular at the end of all low masses—the unsung, so-called private masses as distinct from the sung, high masses. The excising of these appendages helped simplify the mass and return it to its original state. But the fact that an excising was at all necessary pointed up that not even so sacred a ceremony as the mass was above tampering with at given points in the church's history.

How did the opening of John's Gospel and the Leonine Prayers ever get to be a part of the mass? Much of the church's history might be lost in antiquity, but not the answer to that question.

The Latin mass, however unlike the mass of the early church, had been fairly stable since the reign of Pope Gregory I (590-604). But in the thirteenth century the Dominicans began to recite the first fourteen verses of John's Gospel ("In the beginning was the Word, and the Word was with God, and the Word was God. . . .") at the end of privately celebrated masses, and the practice grew such in popularity that recitation was eventually made obligatory by Pope Pius V (1566-1572). He ordered the passage included in the *Missale Romanum* of 1570, the ordo which gave the mass its uniform shape for almost 400 years.

The Leonine Prayers, on the other hand—the three Hail Marys, the Hail Holy Queen (*Salva Regina*) and the prayer to Michael the Archangel, said at the foot of the altar before the priest departed for the sacristy—were of much later origin. These prayers were in use in the Papal States from 1859; then after the loss of the Papal States their recitation was mandated after low masses throughout the universal church by Pope Leo XIII (1878-1903). The mandating came in 1884. In 1904 the concluding prayers to low mass were embellished further with the introduction of the ejaculatory prayer to the Sacred Heart ("Most Sacred Jesus, have mercy on us," said three times), this on the directive of Pius X (1903-1914). The Leonine Prayers seemed to have been rendered superfluous by the Lateran Treaty of 1928 which settled the issue of the Papal States, but liturgical trappings obviously can be as difficult to get rid of as any other. Thus, Pope Pius XI (1922-1939) retained the prayers while switching their intention to the conversion of Russia.

From Ceremony to Ritual

As would be expected, the mass was a relatively simple ceremony in the early church.

RETROSPECT

The disciples gathered weekly for a meal of fellowship, and they broke bread and shared wine not merely as devout Jews carrying ahead the Jewish concept of a sacramental meal, but also as followers of Christ, Christians, committed to the memory of their risen savior. There appears, however, to have been a marked informality about these gatherings, to the degree that Paul in a letter to the community at Corinth warned that the meetings were becoming "not profitable but harmful." The problem, as seen by Paul, was that some were getting drunk on the wine and some were going hungry, as people were not sharing with others the food brought to the gatherings (1 Corinthians 2:17-34).

Gradually, the fellowship aspect of the gatherings was brought into line and the ritualistic came into dominance. The words of institution or consecration of the bread and wine remained constant to those of the Last Supper, but stylistic variations became common. Prayers were freely added to stress lessons in the life of Christ and links to the Old Testament, and ceremonial flourishes multiplied, such as the formal presentation of the gifts of bread and wine for consecration, the processional often including deacons waving fans to keep flies and other insects away from the gifts. Ceremonies such as these—celebrated in the local vernacular as language diversified and incorporating many local customs—helped spawn the church's many rites, including a few, like the Ambrosian and Lyonnaise Rites, that exist yet within pockets of the Western church itself. At the same time, rituals tended to become lengthier and more elaborate, particularly after the emperor Constantine declared Sunday, hitherto a work day, a day of rest in 321.

For Christians, worship became the focus of the day. At first, however, the ritual of memory in honor of Christ was not called the mass. In the beginning it was known commonly as the *Eucharist,* a Greek word, used in the sense of giving thanks. The word "mass" was almost three centuries in developing, its first certain use being credited to Saint Ambrose (c. 339-397). Curiously, the word has no sublime origin. It derived from the twin dismissals of the evolving ritual—first, the ceremony of dismissal of catechumens after the lessons of instruction (opening readings), and second, the dismissal of the initiated after the eucharistic service, the *Ite, missa est.* Missals usually render this Latin phrase in translation as "Go, the mass is ended," but the more literal translation is "Go, the dismissal is made." The ritual accordingly came to be referred to as the *missarium solemnia* or "ceremony of dismissals," and this in time was telescoped to *missa* or mass. The word mass, incidentally, is of strictly Western or Latin Rite usage. It was never adopted by any of the Eastern Rites. There the corresponding word is "Liturgy," a term coming into increasingly common use of late in the Western church with the postconciliar return to the mass of emphases of the early church.

As mentioned, during the reign of Gregory I, at the turn of the seventh century, the mass acquired the form it would essentially hold for centuries thereafter. There were fewer lessons or readings in the early part of the mass, and those used now more directly reflected the relevant liturgical season or feast day. Dropped were the prayers for catechumens, and also the ceremonial of dismissal of catechumens. Dropped too were the prayers of the faithful before the offertory—lately restored, of course—and the invocation of the Holy Spirit (the *epiklesis*). The canon of the mass was recast, and the Our Father was shifted from the end of mass to before communion.

Although the format of the mass was set, over the centuries minor additions nonetheless crept into the ceremony. The Nicene Creed was added after the Gospels by Benedict VIII (1012-1024), and working their way in during the Middle Ages were three prayers said by the celebrant before his communion for peace and for his personal worthiness to partake of the body of Christ. The prayers at the foot of the altar were originally part of the priest's preparation for mass and were said in the sacristy as he vested for the ceremony. Paul V (1605-1621) ordered that the prayers be said before the altar itself.

This is the same pope, incidentally, who forbade evening mass as an attempt to pervert the ancient custom of the church—a directive which the *New Catholic Encyclopedia* cited as an instance of the church losing its historical memory since, in the early church, evening mass was the rule, not the exception. Its faulty reasoning notwithstanding, Paul V's directive was not relaxed until the 1940s. The relaxation was made to accommodate the requests of military ordinariates, who wanted a change so that chaplains could minister more effectively to troops fighting World War II. In 1953, Pius XII (1938–1958) allowed evening masses to be celebrated on holy days of obligation, First Fridays and occasions of religious solemnity, and in 1957 he relaxed the rule further, granting to bishops the authority to allow evening masses anytime. Paul VI (1963-1978) broadened the bishops' authority in 1963, so that they could approve the celebration of mass at any hour of the day.

The Sacred Meal

With the mass in more or less definitive form from the seventh century onward, professional attention relating to the mass tended to center on understanding and interpretations—in the main, esoteric points of a highly theological nature, notably the changing of the bread and wine into the body and blood of Christ.

How was it accomplished and at what precise moment? After much debate, theologians settled on the concept of transubstantiation, meaning that the whole substances of bread and wine of the Eucharist were changed in their totality into the body and blood of Christ with the traditional words of consecration during the canon of the mass, with only the externals of bread and wine remaining. The term transubstantiation, so familiar today with Catholics of a given age, did not originate until the thirteenth century, however.

At the same time, the settling of format and points such as transubstantiation did not preclude the mass's developing in other ways, some of them ahistorical and not exactly felicitous. To begin with, despite the precedents of the patristic period and the fact that the mass's structure closely resembled that of a meal, there was a gradual suppression of the concept of ritual or sacred meal and a concomitant emphasis on the mass as sacrifice, unbloody to be sure, but nonetheless the sacramental reenactment of Christ's death on the cross at Calvary. It was an understanding confirmed in 1562 by the Council of Trent, and one that was to prevail until Vatican Council II, when the notion of thanksgiving and the shared eucharistic meal were returned to the ceremony in measure balanced to that of sacrifice.

The loss of the concept of a communal sacred meal and the growth of emphasis on the mass as sacrifice, with Christ being literally present in the Eucharist, contributed over time to the evolution of many unusual practices. The mass had traditionally been a public rite, and one of limited frequency, particularly during those centuries when only one mass was allowed in a church on a given day, no matter how many priests were present; in such circumstances, priests concelebrated rather than offer masses of their own. This changed as priests came to prefer separate, private celebrations of the mass, and on a daily schedule—a development, incidentally, which made necessary the construction of many altars in a church to handle the demands of priests for altar accommodations. Hitherto churches had one, central altar.

The private mass resulted in another notable development. In the interests of haste and simplicity, the low mass (*missa privata*), originally offered for small, local congregations, became common and eventually was regularized alongside the sung high mass (*missa solemnis*), historically a reenactment of the pontifical mass. In the streamlined low mass, the server (altar boy) took the place of the choir and of assisting ministers, and various ceremonials were omitted, including the kiss of peace and the use of incense.

The low mass contributed also to the phenomenon of assembly-line masses—masses offered one upon another by clerics, many of whom were ordained to do nothing other than say mass, *seriatim.* These clerics were known as "altar priests" or "massing priests," and they would stand at the altar celebrating mass after mass, sometimes telescoping the ritual in order to increase the production. One method was by way of what became known as the *missa bifaciata* or *missa trifaciata*—a ceremony in which the priest-celebrant would recite the first part of the mass, from the Introit to the Preface, two or three times, then join these recitations to one canon, thus satisfying several mass intentions with the one action.

The need for so many masses was created by the demands of the faithful. So strong was belief in the powers and graces of the mass that the faithful besieged the clergy with mass offerings for special intentions, requests far more than the average priest could meet in the normal course of duties. The most common intention at the time was for the release of souls from purgatory.

Obviously the system was prone to abuses, and they occurred, in fashion more shocking even than the *missa bifaciata* and *missa trifaciata* travesties. For instance, some priests were known to multiply production by reducing the mass to the words of consecration. Several medieval councils condemned mass abuses such as these, but the problem was not brought fully under control until Pope Alexander II (1061-1073) outlawed the celebration of more than one mass a day for a stipend, a regulation still in effect.

Private Devotions

By the fourteenth century the privatizing of mass had effectively transformed the ceremony from an act of public worship to a kind of personal clerical prayer.

Stress on the mass as sacrifice did not help the situation. The priest, alone empowered to say mass, became a kind of religious superstar, a God figure of a sort. He celebrated mass facing a crucifix, his back to the congregation and he himself largely oblivious to the worshippers in the church except for those few common prayers that necessitated his turning around to address the people —in Latin—as at the *Orate, fratres.* The mass became for the most part the priest's private devotion, and this contributed in turn to the parallel development of the mass becoming the devotional setting for those present at the ceremony. Instead of following the mass, people began to finger rosaries, recite novena prayers, or even move up and down the aisles making the stations of the cross as the priest was busy at mass. So disconnected were the faithful from the mass—indeed, so anxious were some priest-celebrants not to disrupt the mood of the mass as sacrifice—that communion was often distributed before or after mass, rather than within the context of the mass itself, a practice which eventually became one of convenience. And of course there were those solemn occasions—funeral masses, for instance—at which no one was expected to receive communion except the priest-celebrant.

Other distortions of emphasis resulted in infelicities of additional kinds. There was, for example, the preoccupation with worthiness and the stiff admonishment that an unworthy communion could lead to one's judgment and damnation. The priest prayed at every mass that the partaking of the body of Christ would not turn to his judgment and condemnation (*"Perceptio corporis tui . . ."*), and if a priest had to be concerned about worthiness, how much more so the person in the pew? In any instance, the net effect was to reduce the number of communicants—reduce them so drastically, in fact, that the church had to stipulate the necessity for periodic reception of communion, a stipulation which survives in the Easter Duty regulation. The emphasis on worthiness and the resulting decline in the numbers approaching the altar rail had one further consequence: it was no longer necessary to obtain in a loaf of bread for mass; a small wafer made from flour and water would do.

There is more. Emphasis in the Middle Ages on the mass as sacrifice and reenactment of Calvary tended to discount the importance of a sermon. The mass spoke for itself. Accordingly, sermons at mass were regularly omitted, and when priests did preach, the homilies often had no relation to the readings or lessons of the mass itself—although the latter was of limited consequence, since the mass was in Latin and no one understood the readings in the first place; they were lost on the congregation. The neglect of the sermon may have created a condition from which the church is yet not fully recovered.

Most of the emphases current at the time were confirmed by the Council of Trent. In 1551 the Council reaffirmed the principle of transubstantiation, declaring that ". . . Our Lord Jesus Christ, true God and man, is truly, really and substantially contained under the appearances of bread or wine." In 1562 the Council endorsed the evolved custom of receiving the Eucharist under one species, that of bread, a practice which Protestant reformers had brought under fire. Finally, again in 1562, the Council reiterated the concept of the mass as unbloody sacrifice made present under signs and symbols, preeminently the bread and wine transubstantiated into the body and blood of the Second Person of the most Holy Trinity. That was pretty much it until Vatican Council II.

Restore and Renew

Vatican I (1869-1870) had other things than the mass on its mind, most notably, the subject of papal infallibility.

In fact, the only truly major development to come to the mass between Trent and the renewals of the twentieth century was the dialogue mass, which originated in Belgium late in the nineteenth century and achieved wide popularity, even in the United States, by the middle decade of the next century.

Though the format of the mass was generally in a fixed state for many centuries, theologians nevertheless continued to probe its meaning and history. The famed French Jesuit Pierre Teilhard de Chardin (1881-1955), for instance, saw the mass as the extension of the Incarnation of the Word, the promise of the world's transfiguration, the channel by which the risen Christ was perpetually renewed in the world. For Teilhard, the mass was thus the vital energizing element in the ultimate convergence of the world on the God of evolution.

Intriguing as Teilhard's theory might have been, and influenced though many of the Fathers of Vatican II undoubtedly were by Teilhard, when it came to the mass the Council Fathers were elementary rather than esoteric. What they did was to go back to the beginning. Well, not exactly the very beginning, for then the mass was, as said, an extremely simple ceremony consisting of the consecration of the bread, the consecration of the wine, the breaking of the bread, the communion of bread, and the communion of wine. But they did revert to the mass of the church's earliest centuries.

Thus it was that the Fathers of Vatican II restored the vernacular, again as mentioned, so that the mass could be celebrated in the "mother tongues" of Catholics worldwide and be understood. They turned the altar around, so that the priest again faced the people. They specified that the sermon was to be "highly esteemed as

part of the liturgy itself," and they stressed its importance for conveying "the mysteries of the faith and the
guiding principles of the Christian life." They reinstated
the "common prayer" or the "prayer of the faithful"
after the Gospel, and they revised the ceremony of the
"kiss of peace" so that the entire congregation would be
taking part. The congregation, in sum, was to be composed not of silent worshippers separated from the
priest-celebrant by an altar railing and thus looking on
from a distance, but of people with an intimate role to
play by virtue of their "royal priesthood" through their
participation in the one priesthood of Christ. They were
expected to participate in direct, meaningful ways. Lay
persons were brought into the sanctuary as lectors or
readers of the lessons of the mass, and those in the pews
were not only expected to respond aloud to prayers, but
also to raise their voices in song. The silent mass was suddenly clamorous. Also, its new flexibility would open the
door to imaginative adaptations, as for children and
teen-agers.

But most significantly, by accenting the biblical and
eucharistic elements of the mass through renewed emphasis on the Scripture readings and the availability of
communion, the Fathers of Vatican II returned the concept of the mass as sacred meal, as "paschal banquet."
The idea of the mass as sacrifice was not suppressed, but
rather was combined with the notion of Eucharist, or
thanksgiving. In fact, a common term for the mass in
conciliar documents is "eucharistic sacrifice." Indeed,
one is hard pressed to find the word mass in any of the

Council's sixteen decrees. A check of a dictionary of the Council finds no index entry at all for mass. The preferred word is liturgy, the word that Eastern Rite Catholics had used all along.

Will the new mass be in place as long as the old Latin mass was? Who knows? The only thing that seems certain is that as the mass saw change in the past, so is it likely to see change in the future.

3.

MARRIAGE, DIVORCE, ANNULMENT:
Assuming Authority That Was Originally the State's

Bond, Law, Sacrament

CATHOLIC tradition celebrates marriage in the ethereal sense as sign and symbol of the union which exists between Christ and his church, and in the temporal sense as the social contract which is the very bedrock of the properly ordered society.

The church classifies marriage as a sacrament and surrounds the sanctity of the bond it seals with rules and regulations which, even for so codified a faith as Roman Catholicism, are amazingly explicit and detailed. No less than 111 canons of the Code of Canon Law are concerned with matrimony and the related topics of divorce and annulment.

Catholic tradition holds further that the sacrament of marriage was instituted by God during the creation process itself, and specifically in the Garden of Eden when God provided Adam with a "helpmate," saying, "It is not good for man to be alone; let us make him a suitable partner" (Gen. 2:18). The problems with this tradition are several, as the creation story is assuredly more metaphorical than literal. We're not sure there actually was a

John Deedy

Garden of Eden. We're not even sure that the human race originated with an Adam and an Eve—that is, with one pair of humans—or, as some modern scientists hold, with several pairs of humans who, rather than being in the one place, were likely widely scattered over one continent or more.

What we do know is this: matrimony is implied, but not explicitly mentioned, in the New Testament as a sacrament. Jesus himself said very little about matrimony, and when he did it was generally in the context of divorce. The church did not come to regard matrimony as a sacrament in the same exalted sense as, say, baptism, the Eucharist or holy orders, until the twelfth century. Finally, once included in the roster of sacraments, matrimony's doctrinal justification rested less on Scripture than on tradition and the infallible teaching authority claimed by the church. The Council of Trent was particularly insistent on the point, pronouncing in its final sessions in 1563: "If anyone says that Matrimony is not truly and properly one of the seven sacraments of the New Law, instituted by Christ our Lord, but was invented by men in the church and does not confer grace, let him be anathema." The anathema was hurled at reformers like Martin Luther and John Calvin, who believed that marriage was not a sacrament, but rather a human contract whose terms were essentially under the jurisdiction of civil authorities.

Their contention was not entirely without merit, for matrimony was a discipline under the governance of community and state long before it was made to yield to that of church.

RETROSPECT

By the time of Christ's arrival on earth, society had largely passed through the social male/female stages of concubinage (mating without contract), polygamy (one husband, several wives), and polyandry (one wife, several husbands)—not necessarily in the order given—and none of them was considered necessarily licentious in all historical time frames. In fact, by the time of Christ's arrival, society had long since arrived at the male-female bonding stage—state supervised, since legal inheritances were involved—that we know yet. In Christ's time, monogamy (one husband, one wife) was the accepted bonding arrangement, though there was yet no parallel rule on permanency etched in stone.

One Flesh

The problem with which Jesus had to cope was that of divorce—for which, in fact, a certain justification existed in the Old Testament.

Divorce was taken for granted and at least tolerated as existing custom in Deuteronomy and in Malachi—though, admittedly, it was a custom which the Scriptures sought to amend. "For I hate divorce, says the Lord, the God of Israel. . . . You must then safeguard life that is your own, and not break faith" (Malachi 2:16).

Jesus, too, was dogmatic on the subject in the New Testament, saying in Matthew 19:3-9, Mark 10:2-12 and Luke 16:18 that marriage made husband and wife two in one flesh, and that what God had joined together, no one was to divide or put asunder. Further, Jesus added, one who divorced and married another committed adultery against the original partner.

Jesus drew on Genesis for these principles. However, in using the Old Testament as his bridge to the New Law, Jesus had to grapple in direct measure with Moses who, in challenging the Pharisees, had actually permitted divorce. Confronted with a seeming moral dichotomy, Jesus responded—depending on the translation in use—that the exception existed only because of the Israelites' "stubbornness" or "hardness" of heart.

The opposition to divorce would seem to be unequivocal—except that Matthew quotes Jesus, not once but twice, in a fashion that would appear to leave the door ajar for both divorce and remarriage, at least for the husband. The instances are located in Matthew 5:31-32 and 19:3-9. In both places extramarital lewdness (or fornication, again depending on one's translation) is identified as a factor that is a legitimate consideration in equations affecting the permanence of a marital bond. Some biblical exegetes interpret the qualification in Matthew to pertain to individuals who, before their conversion to Christianity, had married within the prohibited degree of blood relationship and therefore were involved in an illicit sexual union (Leviticus 18:6-18 and Acts 15:20). Whether the exegetes are correct or not, Matthew's comments are not easily reconciled with the absolute prohibitions against divorce that are found in Mark (10:11-12) and Luke (16:18).

By the same token, Paul accepted the possibility of divorce, and his prescriptions in 1 Corinthians 7:12-16 and

RETROSPECT

2 Corinthians 6:14-18 allowing a believing spouse to separate from an unbelieving partner ("The believing husband or wife is not bound in such cases. God has called you to live in peace") became, of course, the basis for what is known as the Pauline Privilege—the dispensation granted unbaptized persons to seek the dissolution of a legitimate, consummated marriage and remarry in the Catholic Church. Similarly, there is the dispensation known as the Petrine Privilege—a dispensation reserved to the pope, freeing a person in a legitimate, consummated marriage to marry again, whether the person be baptized or unbaptized.

The invocation of the Pauline Privilege and the Petrine Privilege is today very much more the exception than the rule in Catholicism. As for the comments in Matthew's Gospel, some churches—the Orthodox Church and those of the Reformation—use them to allow divorce and remarriage in various circumstances. Within Catholicism, however, the strictest interpretation of Jesus' remarks applies. Divorce is absolutely prohibited.

Toward a Christian Ceremony

As for marriage itself, there is no question but that Jesus brought radically new emphases to the way marital life was to be lived.

But he did not create the ceremony. Matrimony was a fact of life, a long-established social institution before he came along. Apart from tightening the reins over divorce and stressing the mutual responsibilities of partners

51

within marriage, Jesus did not seek to remake marriage as a social or religious contract. Nor did the early fathers of the church. The state regulated marriage, as it did divorce, whether the parties were baptized Christians or not, and it remained that way for at least three centuries. To be sure, the early fathers viewed marriage as an important element of Christian life, but they did not lay claim to its regulation and control as an ecclesiastical prerogative, even where the baptized were concerned.

Even so, marriage was regarded by Christians of the time as more than a civil agreement between two persons, and marrying couples increasingly asked the blessing of the church on their union. Initially, church authorities in the West seemed content so long as marriages were contracted publicly (thus eliminating the many abuses inherent in secret marriages), and so long as they were not in conflict with Christian tenets. Still they regarded marriage as a sacred contract, and were anxious to preserve its integrity. This was no less true in the East. The writings of St. Basil, Gregory of Nazianzus and John Chrysostom, for example, indicate that by the third and fourth centuries Catholics of the East commonly married in ceremonies taking place before a priest. Before the fourth century closed, Pope Siricius (384-399) directed that priests and deacons have their marriages solemnized by a priest, and Innocent I (401-417) repeated the directive. Neither of these papal decrees applied to lay persons, however. As late as the seventh century, lay Catholics could still become validly married in ceremonies that were totally secular in character. Nevertheless, it was obvious that, so far as marriage was concerned, the church was steadily moving in a new direction.

As it did, so did the marriage ceremony itself, evolving from a simple exchange of vows in the home between the two parties entering the marriage compact (then as now marriage was contracted by expression of mutual consent) to a more elaborate ceremony in a church setting involving liturgical activities and the official witness of a priest. Interestingly enough, the Christian ceremony borrowed strongly from the secular rite, which had taken form during Roman times. The bridal procession, for example; the giving away of the bride in marriage by her father; the unveiling of the bride; the joining of hands; the garlanding of the marrying couple with flowers; the wedding feast—customs such as these were incorporated from ancient, so-called pagan ritual. The Christian difference was that the ceremony as a whole was solemnized by the presence of the priest, by Christian prayer and sometimes by the liturgy of the mass. The union was thus not just legalized; it was blessed before God.

An Early Misreading

There was no real talk of marriage being a sacrament until the eleventh century and the discovery—relocation, actually—of the writings of Augustine (354-430), which referred to marriage as a *sacramentum.*

Augustine's usage of the term sacrament was based on his reading of Paul's Letter to the Ephesians, 5:32, wherein Paul spoke of marriage between a man and a woman as a "great mystery" or "great foreshadowing" symbolizing the union existing between Christ and the church. The irony is that Augustine, if not himself inexact, was then misinterpreted.

The complication is without great mystery. Paul wrote in the Greek, and he used the word *mysterion* to describe what he called this "great mystery," this "great foreshadowing." Augustine, on the other hand, read Paul in Latin translation, where *mysterion* was rendered as *sacramentum.* It seems clear, therefore, that in the context of marriage Augustine was not using the word "sacrament" in the same, strictly dogmatic sense that later came to be standard. As Joseph Martos remarks in his 1981 book *Doors to the Sacred,* to Augustine marriage was *sacramentum* much the way that a soldier's pledge of loyalty was *sacramentum;* "It was a sacred pledge of fidelity." Nonetheless, it was on the basis of Augustine's usage that within Catholicism the belief became common that marriage was a sacrament in exactly the same sense that baptism and the Eucharist were sacraments. It is a paradox of history that one day would make it easier for critics—Protestant reformers in the main—to argue that Rome elevated marriage to the status of a sacrament in order to complete ecclesiastical control over this social institution, a control which had gradually grown stronger as the state's power waned in the voids created by the disintegration of the Roman Empire.

Creation history, Roman history and the Augustine problem all aside, however, Rome's sacramental claims for marriage were theologically tenable, for it was readily able to situate marriage within the family of sacraments. The sacramental marks were all in order. There was the first condition of divine origin—the originator being the first person of the Trinity, God the Father, acting in the instance of Adam and Eve. There was the second condition of the outward sign—the sacred contract, freely entered upon by male and female in becoming husband and wife. There was, finally, the sacramental endowment— the mutual sanctification of the lives of the contractors through the bestowing of grace on those pledging their love to one another. Lingering talk about marriage being merely a social or civil contract was put to rout by Trent, which provided the conciliar equivalent of *Good Housekeeping*'s "Seal of Approval." Christian marriage, Trent pronounced, was a divine institution, a holy state superior to all other forms of male/female pairing; Christian marriage was a sacrament!

The basic sacramental question thus settled, the church's attention could be turned to other issues, notably the ends of marriage as an institution.

The Tainted Act

The issue of the ends of marriage had long been a theologically sticky issue in Catholicism since, from the beginning, suspicions had been widely harbored that sexual intercourse was not and could never be a holy act, whatever the circumstances.

Fathers of the patristic period, for instance, tended to regard sexual intercourse, even within marriage, as at best a necessary evil. Most believed sexual intercourse to be a tainted act. John Chrysostom and Gregory of Nyssa, among others, held sexual intercourse to be explainable only in terms of the fall of Adam and Eve from God's grace; if that hadn't happened, the claim was that God would have devised some more decorous way for the populating of his world. Similarly, since sexual intercourse inevitably involved lusty arousal, an individual like Augustine—who "knew" two mistresses and fathered a child by one of them before getting religion—would maintain that even its legitimate expression involved some slight, though excusable, sin. Excusable, that is, provided the intention was to beget a child.

Thus it was that the primary end of marriage was held to be the propagation of the human race. But the book could not be closed at that point, for the effect would be to reduce the matter of marriage to begetting, an overly one-dimensional concept even in a period which so exalted virginity as a state of virtue. Obviously there was more involved in the sacrament of marriage than just baby-making. So a second end was introduced to support efficaciousness—namely, that of the mutual help of husband and wife. Marriage, in sum, provided the grace for husband and wife to bear one another's faults, to raise their children properly, and *to love one another faithfully*.

The last sacramental benefit is underscored, for it clued to a constant preoccupation of church authorities: the "problem" of sexual attraction between the sexes. Committed to virginity as the ideal state in life, and prejudiced against sex from the beginning as something tainted, if not actually dirty, marriage became the answer to both a demographic and moral dilemma. Like it or not, sex was necessary if life on earth was to continue and earth itself was to be populated. Hadn't the Lord God himself in Genesis (1:28) commissioned Adam and Eve to increase and multiply, to fill the earth and subdue it? Toward this end, the Lord God had made sex attractive —indeed, seductive. The act of sex was therefore tolerated. But its essential sacramental justification was decoded as "safety valve." Marriage was the individual's release from concupiscence, a his-and-hers outlet for sexual expression, itself the root of so much that was evil in the world.

John Duns Scotus (c. 1265 - c. 1308) had viewed sexual intercourse between husband and wife as a good, an expression of love which actually protected and enhanced the marriage bond. But little of his thought took deep root in Catholicism in his lifetime or during several centuries to follow. Most theologians—St. Thomas Aquinas (1225-1274) among them—approached marriage not so much as a religious and social growth experience, but rather as a natural and necessary social phenomenon. This was understandable, since as we have seen from the beginning of recorded history marriage was an important civil contract shaping, if not governing, much of society itself. Lawful marriages determined blood lines, and they helped settle such urgent questions as regency and familial succession, property and inheritance rights. Inevitably, therefore, the focus of early theologians and secular legalists would center on nuances connected with the validity of the marital contract. Were the two parties free to marry? Was the consent exchanged free and deliberate? Were any impediments involved? Were the proper procedures followed in a mixed marriage? Did the marriage ceremony take place before a duly authorized witness? (Here again, the persistent worry connected to secret marriages, which could be used as an excuse for concubinage or as an easy exit from an existing union.)

Most of the theological concern, in other words, was on legality and licitness. Given the context, it was virtually inevitable that ecclesiastical emphases would be more on the correct regulation of marriage within the sacramental situation than on such intangibles as the graces and blessings that flowed from the sacrament itself to those entered upon it. The marriage ceremony might have been sacramentalized, but considerations of legality continued to dominate. This was a condition which was to exist well into the twentieth century.

Modernizing Eros

Paradoxically, it was not so much Vatican Council II as the debate beyond the Council over the possibility of change in the church's laws on artificial birth control that ultimately produced within Catholicism a new outlook on marriage and its purposes for those embraced by the sacrament.

Uprooted was the medievalist view of marriage—essentially legalistic and fundamentally suspicious of sexual expression even in its marital context—and in its place there took form a view of marriage infinitely more personalist in focus.

Conceded, in effect, was that sacramental marriage was not merely a procreative and rearing experience anchored within a contractual situation, but also a physical and, yes, spiritual adventure in behavioral and religious growth, nourished both by the graces and blessings flowing from the sacrament, and by erotic sexual contact itself as an expression of love on the part of the married couple.

This was a revolutionary development. For a thousand years and more, the church had justified marital sexual relations primarily for purposes of procreation. Now a new element was entered into the equation: genital expression as a fact of healthy marital love and of positive spiritual growth. Once this was conceded, out the window went the traditional distinctions between the primary and secondary ends of marriage.

The church has never officially disowned the distinctions between primary and secondary ends of marriage. It just stopped talking about them, assimilating in the meanwhile the new person-centered thought into the psychology, if not theology, of the sacrament. As an example, in 1975 the Congregation for the Doctrine of the Faith issued a document—"Declaration on Certain Questions Concerning Sexual Ethics"—reaffirming Catholic teaching on such issues of sexual morality as premarital sex, artificial birth control, homosexual acts and masturbation. There were no surprises in the document—except for its introduction, where the function of sex was acknowledged to be a morally valid determining factor in human personality and, it followed, a basic element in the spiritual maturation of those bonded within sacramental marriage.

This acknowledgment, of course, altered none of the church's moral criteria governing sexual conduct. Quite the opposite. If the rest of society was in a sexual revolution, the church was not. But culturally and sociologically it had shifted ground ever so subtly on the matter of sexual expression within sacramental marriage, and there has been no reverting back since. Indeed, the modernist viewpoint of the wholesomeness of marital sex has been carried with such clarity through the reign of Pope John Paul II, and been accompanied with an appreciation so factual and realistic, as to feed rumors, unfounded to be sure, that John Paul II had either been married or widowed before entering the priesthood.

The Annulment Clause

Though the church has moved away from certain ancient legalistic conceptions about marriage to an understanding more personalist and psychologically sound, it has not budged on the issue of permanency.

Except for the death of a spouse, the church holds a validly contracted marriage to be indissoluble by both church law and divine law, and it tolerates civil divorce strictly as a legal arrangement, which does not affect the bond of a valid marriage. It allows aggrieved parties in troublesome marriages to obtain a civil divorce out of such considerations as family, health, custody of the children and property, but these people are not free to remarry in the church, for spiritually the original bond is still in effect. Pressure has been building in recent years in some Catholic circles for the validation of "good conscience" second marriages, mainly on the premise that marriages that are emotionally and psychologically dead are dead in fact. The church, however, shows no sign of evolving soon to that position.

The one concession to impermanency is the granting of annulments. In some circles "annulment" is a code word for "divorce," but the church rejects this. The church takes pains to emphasize that, rather than being divorces, annulments are ecclesiastical acts based on findings that no marital bond of a sacramental kind ever existed because of the presence of an impediment rendering null and void the very attempt to marry. In sum, there never was a marriage.

The grounds for annulments were spelled out with great specificity at the Council of Trent, and included such factors as fear, coercion, impotence, consanguinity, etc. For long years the interpretation of annulment laws and the spirit of the proceedings were dictated by the letter of that sixteenth-century convocation. Lately, however, new pastoral and psychological understandings have come into play, greatly broadening the grounds for annulments and relaxing the procedure itself in the process—or at least making it less of a test and trial. In 1968, Catholic Church marriage tribunals in the United States issued 450 annulments; in 1981, the number was in the tens of thousands. What was once extremely difficult to come by has obviously become more of a possibility for those willing to petition.

Are the grounds for annulment likely to broaden further? Quite possibly, particularly as insights into the human psyche themselves broaden.

Will the church one day accept civil divorce? Doubtful, even though in annulment proceedings grounds often duplicate those for granting divorce in civil courts.

Will the church's essential view of marriage as a sacramental rite ever change? Never. Changing lifestyles may bring new forms, new emphases to marriage, but marriage will forever be that sacred covenant between man and woman, husband and wife, modeled on the covenant that has existed from the beginning of the Christian era between Christ and his church.

4.

SACRAMENTS—THE OTHER SIX:
The Resonances Reach Beyond
Christianity Itself

Sacramentum—Mysterion

SACRAMENTS, as most of us can recite from the old *Baltimore Catechism,* are outward signs instituted by Christ to give grace.

They are the primary channels of grace in the church, and they receive their power to give grace from God through the merits of Jesus Christ. They total seven in number. We have already looked at the sacrament of marriage. Here we look at the remaining six and their evolution: baptism, confirmation, holy Eucharist, penance (now known as reconciliation), extreme unction (now the anointing of the sick), and holy orders.

The most immediately striking thing about the sacraments is that, though instituted by Christ and hallowed by Christian history, none is without a ritualistic precedent rooted in another religion or culture, and none is without its evolutionary chapters. Even the word "sacrament" has resonances from beyond the boundaries of Christianity.

In its broadest sense the word "sacrament" translates as an external sign of something sacred. It comes from the Latin, of course—*sacramentum*—a word used originally to signify an external thing endowed with a meaning and purpose beyond itself. In Roman law, it was the money, *sacramentum*, deposited by litigants to a suit with a priest or in a sacred precinct—the winner getting his money back, the loser forfeiting his to the winner or to the gods. In the Roman military, *sacramentum* was the oath which soldiers took pledging not to desert or otherwise abandon their responsibilities. The word had other meanings. The Roman naturalist and writer Pliny, for instance, spoke of *sacramentum* as the oath by which the Christians of Bithynia bound themselves not to commit acts of wickedness at their solemn gatherings, Christians of the time being commonly suspected of indulging after love feasts in what was labeled "the sacrament of infanticide," a grisly libel once widely believed.

In the Christian understanding, the term sacrament was used from the beginning to indicate a sacred rite. But so also was the term used by others at the beginning of the Christian era, both monotheists and polytheists. The oaths and offerings, festivals and devotions, oracles and divinations of the people of so-called pagan Greece and Rome were known as sacraments. Similarly, though Judaism is not generally considered a sacramental religion, Jewish life then as now centered about acts of worship, purifications, symbolic meals, temple traditions and the like, which can be said to comprise a sacramental tradition.

Christianity, therefore, was not instituting anything

unique with its sacramental system, only something that was different by way of detail. Even then, early Christians did not adopt the word *sacramentum* as a generic term identifying its basic rituals of faith. Christians of Greek background spoke of "mysteries," *mysteria,* or *mysterion,* and, as noted in the chapter on marriage, this led to a certain confusion as *mysterion* came to be rendered dually as *mysterium* and *sacramentum,* thus obfuscating the linguistic distinction between mystery and sacrament. But that came later. Most of the time in the early church sacramental rites were known simply by their generic name—baptism, the eucharistic meal, etc.

It may surprise many Catholics to be told that it was not until the twelfth century that the sacraments of the church were standardized and their number fixed at seven, but such is the case. Until then, the number of sacraments ranged from as few as five to as many as thirty, depending on the source. For instance, Pierre Abelard, the celebrated French philosopher and theologian, who died in 1142, listed six sacraments, leaving out that of holy orders, (an omission which for some probably hints more at the solidness of Abelard's love for Heloise than of his theology).

Whatever, the number of sacraments was pared to seven, as theological scholarship sorted out distinctions and agreed on the elements which determined what was sacrament and what was not. The initial codification of the sacraments is credited to Peter Lombard (c. 1100-1160), who was known as the Master of the Sentences.

John Deedy

An Italian theologian whose professional career was spent mostly in France, Lombard produced the first manual of systematized theology.

Baptism

Together with holy Eucharist, baptism is the most clear cut of the sacraments, one thoroughly documented in the Scriptures for Catholics and Protestants alike.

In Matthew 28:19, Christ told the Apostles, "Go, therefore, and make disciples of all the nations, baptizing them in the name of the Father, and of the Son, and of the Holy Spirit." The sacrament makes use of water, of course, both as essential matter and as sign. Christians, however, were not the first to adopt water for ritualistic purposes in such a way. Water being a natural element of cleansing, refreshment and regeneration, from the beginning it was used in religious ways. Ritualistic washings and bathings were common to ancient, pre-Christian religions, and Judaism too had its rites of purification employing the use of water.

What made the Christian use of water unique was what it was intended to affect in baptism: a new birth in the spiritual order—a new life, in sum, corresponding to the resurrection of Christ himself. With baptism the individual became a new person, a new creation, reborn of water and the Spirit, dead to original sin, and alive in Christ and his church.

The paradox is that, though Christ underwent a ritualistic baptism at the hands of John the Baptizer in the river Jordan, there is no record that Christ himself baptized people, or that Christ submitted himself to the Christian baptism he charged his Apostles to administer. Nor is there evidence that the Apostles ever received Christian baptism either. The first recorded baptisms occur in Acts 2:37-41, when the Apostles went out and baptized three-thousand on the day of Pentecost.

The matter and form of baptism have remained constant from that day to this, although emphases have varied from time to time, as have the means of administration. At one time the sacrament was connected to the observances of Easter and Pentecost, and immersion of the whole body in water was a common baptismal mode. Also, in the first centuries the ceremony usually took place in the early morning hours so as to avoid inciting the persecutory instincts of Romans. That necessity ended with Constantine's edict of 313 extending religious tolerance to Christians.

Still, for centuries baptism was largely an annual ceremony, a circumstance which provoked continuing theological debate. If baptism was essential for entry into heaven, why should any delay at all be countenanced in its administration? This was an especially pertinent question in days when mortality rates were high among the new born, and when theological opinion consigned unbaptized babies—individuals, therefore, still stained by original sin—to limbo, that lately-discovered place of *natural* happiness (as distinct from *supernatural* happiness) on the border (*in limbo,* in the Latin) of heaven. The upshot of the debate was that between the eleventh and thirteenth centuries baptism became a ceremony administered soon after birth, preferably within days and, accordingly, a sacrament available at all times of the year.

There were other questions to be worked out, like baptism of blood (for the unbaptized who were martyred) and baptism of desire (for the millions who were suddenly found by explorers to be living beyond the known Christian world), and nuances such as who can baptize and under what circumstances (in times of necessity, anyone). Anointings and blessings became part of the ceremony but generally baptism has come down over the ages much as it was in the beginning.

The renewals of Vatican II have sought to return the sacrament to the rich personal and communal experience that it was in the ancient church, and accordingly the ceremony now stresses not only the values of faith and belief, but also that of community. The sacrament thus becomes, now as it was in the beginning, a ceremony of Christian initiation.

Confirmation

Confirmation is the problem sacrament in the Catholic registry—the sacrament, as the saying goes, in search of a theology.

Traditional teaching relates confirmation to baptism, in the sense that confirmation "makes-fast," *confirms,* as it were, the sacramental seal of baptism and adds the sacramental dimension that makes individuals perfect Christians and soldiers of Jesus Christ.

The historical reality is that confirmation did not exist as a separate sacramental rite until the third century; that the very term "confirmation" was not used until the French Councils of Riez and Orange in 439 and 441; that confirmation was not a common ecclesiastical rite until after the fifth century; and that well into the Middle Ages there was still argument about the sacrament's origin. Theologians such as Hugh of St. Victor and Peter Lombard held that confirmation was instituted by the Holy Spirit through the instrument of the Apostles; the Dominican school argued that Christ himself was the immediate author of the sacrament; the Franciscan school said that the Holy Spirit had indeed instituted the sacrament, but with the Spirit acting through the Apostles or through the church after the death of the Apostles.

To this day no one knows for sure, for precise scriptural documentation for confirmation does not exist, though some see the sacrament's institution in Christ's promising to send the Paraclete. Further, as Joseph Martos notes in *Doors to the Sacred* (1982), several key historical documents providing confirmation with a lengthy sacramental lineage were ninth-century French forgeries aimed at protecting French clerical prerogatives against claims of emperor and nobles. The Second Council of Lyons in 1274 named confirmation among the seven sacraments of the church, but later councils were less dogmatic. The Council of Trent held confirmation to be a sacrament and anathematized those who held it to be a useless ceremony, but otherwise gave the sacrament perfunctory treatment. Vatican II was ambiguous. Its references to confirmation were brief, and were framed in the context of the Holy Spirit or confirmation's link to baptism.

In point of fact, it was baptism that provided confirmation its liturgical *raison d' etre*. In the early church, baptisms were performed by bishops, and the ceremony concluded with an anointing and imposition of the bishop's hand, which many saw as a receiving of the seven gifts of the Holy Spirit (wisdom, understanding, counsel, fortitude, knowledge, piety, fear of the Lord). As Christianity grew and baptisms multiplied enormously, baptism became less and less an episcopal rite, but one presided over by a priest. For a time it was common to take the newly baptized to a bishop for the postbaptismal anointing and imposition of hands that theoretically completed and sealed the sacrament of baptism, but this practice too ended, as much for reasons of logistics as anything else. It wasn't exactly easy to travel about in the old days.

The separation of confirmation from baptism did nothing for the sacrament's popularity. In some places confirmation fell into serious disuse, such that ecclesiastical sanctions up to and including excommunication were threatened against those who continued to neglect its existence; in other places, the sacrament was reduced to incidental administration, such as a bishop's passing through town on horseback, anointing as he rode by.

RETROSPECT

Things are not that bad today for the sacrament. Nevertheless, for some sacramental theologians confirmation continues to present problems. They all see confirmation as sign, but many are hard pressed to see it also as cause of grace. For them the sacrament reduces to a kind of ecclesiastical equivalent of the initiation which accompanies a person's acceptance into some secret society or select group. Even so, confirmation must be accounted an experience of the Holy Spirit. As such it remains an important religious rite.

Holy Eucharist

There is no problem among Christians about the roots of the Eucharist as sacrament.

Scriptural documentation abounds—John 6:48-58, Matthew 26:26-28, 1 Corinthians 10:16, 11:27, etc.—such as to satisfy any doubter.

Along with baptism, the Eucharist is in fact the surest of sacraments. Protestant reformers themselves had little hesitancy in retaining the Eucharist as a sacrament, although to be sure they did so with a variety of understandings. In 1577, Christopher Rasperger counted up some two-hundred differing interpretations of the Eucharist.

The Catholic understanding, which itself went through a long process of discussion and debate, began to lock onto belief in the Eucharist as the transubstantiated body and blood of Christ with the ninth-century teachings of the monk Paschasius Radbertus. The issue was addressed dogmatically at Trent, with eucharistic principles being particularized at Sessions XIII, XXI and XXII. Trent ruled, in essence, that in the Eucharist the body and blood of the God-Man are truly, really and substantially present for the nourishment of our souls, by reason of the transubstantiation of the bread and wine into the body and blood of Christ; and that further, in this change of substances the unbloody sacrifice of the New Testament is also contained.

When its turn came, Vatican II acted to restore pre-Trentian emphases on the Eucharist as *agape* (love-feast) and communal celebration—the emphases, in a word, of the early church. Vatican II's action has been remarkably effective, for the focus of the eucharistic liturgy, the mass, has indeed shifted from the Trentian view of the mass as act of sacrifice (the unbloody reenactment of the events of Calvary) to the patristic, scriptural view of the mass as sacred meal, traditional among all people. The net result has been to make the mass more the community act of worship that Vatican II wanted.

But whatever the emphases of the mass, the belief in transubstantiation is retained, and this continues the Eucharist as the most solemn and exalted of Christian mysteries.

Reconciliation (Penance)

No Catholic sacrament is so scripturally documented, while at the same time none has gone through such an evolution as penance, now known as the sacrament of reconciliation.

John documents the institution of the sacrament: "Whose sins you shall forgive . . . etc." (20:22-23). So does Matthew: "Whatsoever you shall bind on earth . . . etc." (16:19). There's more, as in Acts 19:18: "Many who had become believers came forward and openly confessed their former practices."

The problem is that although Christ pointedly conveyed the power of forgiveness to his church, he left no formula for the process itself. The sacrament actually began as a public ritual, and did not become the essentially private ritual it was to remain until its introduction in Ireland by Saint Patrick in the fifth century. Irish missionaries then carried the ritual to the continent, where it took hold in the larger church.

Similarly, the sacrament passed from being a once-in-a-lifetime ceremony to one of monthly or even weekly frequency, then to general neglect on the part of huge numbers of the faithful—its present state. In the meantime, penances meted out to penitents passed from the severe (denial of public office to civil leaders; denial of marital intercourse to a husband or wife) to the symbolic ("three Our Fathers, three Hail Marys").

At various times refinements were made to meet problems. In 1614, for instance, the confessional screen was mandated to protect the privacy of confessees, and also to blunt criticism that the confessional was being used by unscrupulous priests as a place for solicitation of women whose confessions suggested sexual impulses which might be exploited.

After Vatican II, the sacrament was completely over-hauled—given a new name to reflect new emphases (reconciliation rather than absolution) and offered to the faithful in three forms, one private, one public and the third a combination of the two. For whatever reasons, the new product hasn't sold, making it likely that the sacrament's past is only prelude to its future: further evolution.

Anointing of the Sick (Extreme Unction)

The Anointing of the Sick is a sacrament rooted in healing and anointing traditions that go back to Christ and the Apostles.

The specific sacramental promulgation is based on the letter of James 5:14-15: "Is anyone among you sick? Let him ask for the presbyters of the church, and let them pray over him, anointing him with oil in the name of the Lord. . . ." In 416, in response to an inquiry from a Bishop Decent of Gubbio, Pope Innocent I referred to this anointing with oil as "a kind of sacrament." Still it was not until the ninth century that a formal rite is found to exist for the sacrament's administration.

In a way, the anointing of the sick is the effort to make sense out of those mysteries and problems—sickness, disease, untimely or painful death—which disorient the rhythms of what we would like life to be. Societies have grappled with questions born of those mysteries and problems since primitive times, and they have responded with solutions ranging from the magical to the mystical. The church's answer is the sacrament known variously as extreme unction, the last rites, and anointing of the sick.

Initially, as practiced in the early church, the sacrament was one of physical and spiritual health. It had a clear medical dimension, bringing health to body as well as to soul. In medieval times, however, as liturgical emphases shifted and took on strong penitential understandings, the sacrament shaped into a rite of passage to one's final reward. The rite came thus to be regarded as a sacrament of the dying—the last anointing (*extrema unctio*), as it were, before one met one's Maker—acquiring, coincidentally, its obvious new name. The sacrament now came to be known as extreme unction, or the last rites. Trent confirmed this end-of-life understanding of the sacrament, and it prevailed until several centuries later, when the renewals set in motion by Vatican II returned the sacrament to the understandings and name—anointing of the sick—used in patristic times.

The sacrament is still one for the dying, but now, as in the early church, it is again administered to those for whom danger of death is not necessarily imminent, such as the aged, those with spiritual worries, and those with serious physical and emotional problems from which they might be expected to recover. This practice revives the healing dimension of a sacrament whose primary effects had long been associated in the main with forgiveness of sin and so-called "happy death."

The sacrament may be administered in a communal

ritual—once again, as in the early church—and the anointing is now usually only to the forehead and hands, rather than as of old to the five senses, all extremities of the body, as well as the area of the body in need of healing.

Holy Orders

The priest as mediator of the sacred has existed in Catholic theological concepts since the Last Supper, when the power and grace to perform the cultic duties of the priesthood is held to have been conveyed by Jesus Christ.

The priesthood as Christians came to know it, however, evolved comparatively slowly, and it was not until the end of the third century that the office would begin to assume the complex organizational shape that would be its form from early medieval times until the reforms of 1971 and 1972.

At the start it was fairly simple. The priesthood was the episcopacy, and bishops presided over the liturgy. As the church grew, the bishops could not be everywhere and do everything, so various responsibilities had necessarily to be delegated—and were, to people designated as presbyters and deacons. These responsibilities depended largely on the whim of the bishop. If a bishop were jealous of his prerogatives as arbiter of the word, for instance, or fearful of the spread of heresy, he might allow his presbyters and deacons to minister to the community, short of preaching to its members.

RETROSPECT

Gradually a network of clerical offices came into being, some dictated by pragmatics as much as anything else. Persons who could read well were named lectors; persons with what came to be called a "vocation" served as acolytes. Thus a hierarchy of ministry came into being, and one advanced to the priesthood through a series of ordinations to major and minor orders, seven steps in all. The major orders were priest, deacon and subdeacon; the minor were porter, lector, exorcist and acolyte.

Eventually distinctions were made, informal or otherwise, within the orders themselves. For example, as presbyters came to be known more commonly as priests, bishops, also priests of course, came to be called "high priests." There were also two classes or categories of deacons: permanent deacons, and those for whom the order was a step en route to the priesthood—a distinction which carried through the sixth century, when the permanent diaconate disappeared for fourteen centuries before being revived again.

This seven-step road to the priesthood was radically revised during the pontificate of Paul VI, when the church came to grips with the fact that some of the orders had fallen into disuse—like that of exorcist—or involved functions which plainly did not require ordination, like that of acolyte. The orders of porter, exorcist and subdeacon, accordingly, were abolished. Acolyte and lector survived, but persons were henceforth to be installed rather than ordained to those ministries. Suppressed too was the ceremony of tonsure, which in the past had symbolized admission to the clerical state. Now one enters the clerical state on ordination to the diaconate. Earlier —in 1967—the office of permanent deacon was restored by way of implementing Vatican II's desire for a return to emphases originally associated with the diaconate; the move also helped alleviate problems in countries plagued with vocations shortages.

Not changed is the exclusion of women from the church's ordained ministries, although there is considerable pressure to include women, as a matter of justice and personal rights, and also on the historical precedence that before the Council of Nicaea in 325, in some Christian places, women were actually considered members of the clergy.

5.

MIRACLES:
What Wonders Has God Wrought?

The Old and the New

A MIRACLE, quite simply, is an effect or extraordinary event in the physical world which surpasses all known human or natural powers and is ascribed to a supernatural cause and, ultimately, to God.

A common impulse with many Christians is to connect miracles essentially to the life of Jesus Christ and to his agents of divine revelation—saints, for instance—and this in a sense gives Christian believers a corner on the miracle market. It is a mite presumptuous. The fact is that the Old Testament contains many recorded miracles, such as Moses' parting of the sea in Exodus (14:21ff), Elijah's multiplication of the flour and cooking oil in 1 Kings (17:11ff), and Elisha's multiplication of the loaves, along with other miracles, in 2 Kings (3-9). The objection has been made that these and similar wondrous events of the Old Testament belong more to the realm of natural phenomena than they do to the category of true miracles. But then the same thing can be alleged of certain miracles of the New Testament and of the history of Christ's church. In its own evolution, science had furnished natural explanations for phenomena that one day would have been looked upon as supernatural, a point to be returned to later.

The miracles of the New Testament are generally of a substantially different kind from those of the Old. Still there is no question but that the supernatural element permeates the Old Testament—in God's guidance and guardianship of his people, and further in the leadership provided by the prophets. Concomitantly, it is the supernatural element—the moral quality by which an event or happening corresponds with the character of God, and thus is arguably connected with some point of divine intent or reasoning—which essentially defines a miracle. At the least, it establishes grounds for distinguishing the serious from the coincidental or the frivolous: for setting a bona-fide miracle apart from a "miraculous" circumstance, such as a person's surviving a disaster in which others die, or from "miraculous" finishes, like a Catholic school's football team gaining a last-minute victory as its cheerleaders kneel in prayer on the cold, cold ground. "Miraculous" finishes, like "miraculous" circumstances, involve luck rather than divine intervention.

During the thirty-three years of his incarnation, Christ worked some thirty-five miracles that we know of, and seemingly many more that went unrecorded in the gospel stories.

The most dramatic of Christ's miracles—the raising of the dead to life (Matthew 9:18-26; Luke 7:11-17; John 11:1-44), the multiplication of the loaves and fishes (Matthew 14:13-21; 15:29-39), his own resurrection—are viewed as actions placing a divine seal on his life and

80

message. In a word, these are miracles accenting his own divinity. The miracle of the loaves and the fishes, for instance, relates to the Eucharist as much as to divine power to provide for human needs.

Other miracles—making the blind see, cripples walk, lepers clean, the deaf hear (Matthew 11:4-5, etc.)—are seen as special manifestations of God's mercy and love for humankind, and also as works confirming in one way or another some point of his teaching. The miracles of healing, for instance, are related symbolically to the power of Christ, and subsequently his church, to cure the spiritual sickness of sin.

' Christ's miracles, in sum, are demonstrations of God's goodness and interest in humankind's welfare and happiness, and of his concern for the eternal salvation of his creatures. The miracles of deed complemented the wonder of the total comprehensiveness of God's concern, made clear in Christ's answer to John the Baptist's query from his prison cell: "Are you he who is to come, or shall we look for another?" Christ responded to John's disciples with the words, "Go back and report to John what you have heard and seen: The blind see, the lame walk, lepers are cured, the deaf hear, the dead rise to life, and the poor have the good news preached to them" (Matthew 11:1-5).

Skeptics and Scientists

The power of miracles might belong to divine prerogative, but miraculous events were not to end with Christ's mission on earth.

John Deedy

Christ promised the power of miracles to the church as a sign of its divine mission: "Signs like these will accompany those who have professed their faith. They will use my name to expel demons; they will speak in new tongues; they will be able to handle serpents; if they drink a deadly poison, it shall not harm them; and the sick will recover upon whom they lay their hands" (Mark 16:17-18).

Miracles can be said, therefore, to continue to occur. Certainly throughout its history the church has regarded miracles and other wondrous happenings as reasonable manifestations of God's concern for his people. At the same time, however, the church's understanding of miracles had undergone something of an evolution. The theology of miracles does not preoccupy ecclesiastical scholars in ways that it did Thomas Aquinas, for example. Vatican Council II mentioned the subject hardly at all, and then only in the context of the public life of Christ.

Similarly, the church itself is no longer so quick as it used to be in accepting at full face value claims involving events that on the surface seem miraculous. A case in point would be the Marian apparitions which are alleged to have taken place at Medjugorje, Yugoslavia, since 1981. In June 1985, the Vatican discouraged pilgrimages to Medjugorje, while the principle prelate of the area, Bishop Pavao Zanic of Mostar-Duvno, publicly discounted the purported visions as "collective hallucination."

What has rendered the church cautious is, of course, science. It is easy enough to respond to philosophical objections to miracles, like those of theists or deists, who regard miracles as being in opposition to God's immutability and wisdom since they imply interventions by God in his original divine plan in order to redirect nature or correct some course ordained by nature for his creatures. (The Catholic answer to that objection is that miracles do not change the divine plan by correcting some defect therein, but rather that miracles complement the divine plan by building on nature and moving it to a higher perfection. The further argument, however narrowly parochial, is that God in his divine wisdom would not cause or allow any miracle unless it were intended as a sign of the supernatural.)

In science, though, the theology of miracles comes face to face with a branch of learning presenting difficulties that cannot regularly be countered and overcome by some nifty syllogism or use of the logic of scholasticism. Science has not, and—the believer has to be convinced—science cannot disprove the possibility of miracles. Much less can science debunk miracles as so many fables and myths. But science is in a position of producing explanations for phenomena which were once thought to be without explanation, except for divine intervention of a specific kind. What was thought for centuries, for instance, to be a form of demonic possession, often can now be demonstrated to be a case of epileptic seizure, routinely controlled by medication. No petition to God for relief is particularly necessary—although Christians do believe in the power of prayer and do pray to God for relief from afflictions or problems of such a sort. The point is that one should pray when one encounters complications of health. But one should also see his or her physician.

The church is fully aware that science can produce its own miracles—and even explain miracles that once upon a time could only be thought to be of divine attribution. This accounts for the care, indeed the scrupulosity, which the church exercises today before accepting the authenticity of miracles. The healing miracles of Lourdes, as an example, are subjected not only to the usual points of investigation, such as the visibility of the cure, the characters of the person cured and his or her sponsors, the testimony of reliable witnesses and the like, but also to rigorous clinical examination and confirmation. A true miracle of healing, in a word, must be beyond the explanation of the family doctor.

This stringency, which extends to all types of miracles, is traceable partly to the pressures of eighteenth-century rationalism and nineteenth-century scientific determinism, but also to twentieth-century practicality. The net result has been to reduce, if not belief in miracles, then their expectation and the concrete claims of their occurring. The insistence on verifiability and certitude has had a dramatic effect. Miracles are in short supply these days —so short, in fact, that the church itself is no longer so insistent as it once was on a specific number of miracles before a person is canonized, and indeed has been known to waive old numerical requirements in order to move the process along for a particular beatus or saint.

Fantastic Facts

The church is prudent in accrediting phenomena as miracles for the additional reason that an event which might seem a miracle could allow of a perfectly logical explanation. It's the stuff of history—and of fiction.

For instance, Russell Janney's 1946 novel *Miracle of the Bells* tells of a Pennsylvania coal-mining town thrown into a religious fervor by heroic-sized marble statues of Michael and the Madonna in a local parish church, which pivoted on their bases toward the center aisle and the coffin of the book's heroine, a local-girl-made-good brought home from Hollywood (where else?) for burial following a sad and premature death. It turned out that the pivoting of the statues was caused not by divine intervention but by a shifting of the support columns because of settlement in the mining shafts deep beneath the church.

Janney's story was pure invention, of course, though not cynical in the least. It was not debunking of religion; it was not a derogating of believers. Quite the opposite. The point of Janney's book was the positive transformation that took place in the lives of those experiencing the supposed miracle of the repositioned statues. A town and people of spiritual poverty had turned to gladness, community and holiness. The "miracle" was eclipsed, overshadowed, overwhelmed by the changes that took place in the hearts of people. A happening with a remarkable but totally natural explanation had resulted in profound, far-reaching religious effects.

Life, they say, imitates art. So it is that Janney's book, saccharine as it was, comes to mind in the context of a happening in Chicago, beginning in December, 1986, when a painting of the Blessed Virgin in St. Nicholas Albanian Orthodox Church suddenly began to weep. The event brought throngs to the church. "They came by the hundreds of thousands," said *Newsweek,* "crippled children in tow, lips whispering prayers." Stories of weeping icons of Mary are not exactly new, many icons over the centuries having taken to tears, according to pious accounts. But not in Chicago, and not in a setting so challenging to scientists—"ever the skeptics," in *Newsweek*'s words.

Shawn Carlson, a physicist at Lawrence Berkeley Laboratory in California, produced a possible answer. Two years before, Carlson had been told of weeping icons by a seminarian and asked if such "miracles" could be produced naturally. After what *Newsweek* described as some "fiddling," Carlson made a nude painted by his grandfather weep. He pursued his paint-into-tears alchemy more industriously upon hearing of the Chicago icon, and soon came up with what he said were "six ways to gimmick a painting and make it cry." *Newsweek* carried a picture of Carlson and a copy of Leonardo's "Mona Lisa," which, it said, was made to cry with the use of crystal salts. "We're not saying the Chicago icon is a fake," Carlson was quoted, "but you'd think a 'sign from God' would not be so easily duplicated by natural means." Carlson, who claims to be able to make statues as well as icons weep, and weep fragrant tears to boot, kept secret from the magazine his precise formulae, but he did say the methods were "very simple, requiring no detailed knowledge of physics. It could have been done hundreds of years ago."

It likely will be done hundreds of times in the future,

and in contexts varying by the hundreds, for Carlson plans to patent his discovery. ("He thinks that a teary-eyed Tammy Faye Bakker, mascara turned to dirty rivulets, would be a fine way to launch the line," commented *Newsweek*.) But that still leaves questions behind for religion. Is every weeping icon a fake? Could some weeping icons be accidents of an artist's creation, for conceivably the elements which Carlson entered into his compositions to make icons weep could have been used earlier in innocence of effect? Is the weeping Chicago icon a fake? Carlson is right in saying that real miracles cannot be distinguished from fakes unless researchers are permitted to examine them. But Bishop Isaiah of the Greek Orthodox archdiocese in New York is also right when he says that the final determination of the authenticity of an unusual event, such as Chicago's weeping Marian painting, is "what people feel and experience" in the context of the happening.

Of course that's the essential meaning of miracles— "what people feel and experience"—going all the way back to the God of the Old Testament and the Christ of the New. Whatever miracles prove by way of the existence of a God and the sanctity of those who are his instruments in the working of miracles, their meaning and import are defined primarily in terms of the effects they work on people. For miracles are not an exercise in divine stuntsmanship, but signs of the larger, indeed supreme power that controls the universe, someone more powerful than anyone to be conceived on earth.

John Deedy

Gradations of Twilight

Does it follow that, with the expectations and claims of miracles today being fewer, the day of miracles is closing, if not already over?

Not necessarily. Christian belief in the efficacy of prayer as a connecting link between God and the believer obviously presupposes a feeling on the part of the person praying that God can work effects in the life of the individual beyond his or her own power. One prays, for instance, for a safe journey, or for recovery from an illness, or for relief from a drought, and in the praying is an implicit concession that God can interfere in the life of the person and the very laws of nature. One prays, too, for restoration of lost bonds of love with a spouse, or for reconciliation among family members, or for reinvigoration of a waning faith, and in those prayers is recognition that miracles can also be subtle things. They don't have to be huge, dramatic displays of divine power.

Curiously, however, though saints have traditionally been considered instruments of divine intervention in the human order, Catholics do not pray to them—nor to the Blessed Virgin, for that matter—as fervently as once they did for signs of a miraculous kind. For example, pilgrimages are fewer to those shrines festooned with crutches, surgical boots, rosaries, crosses, scapulars and other deposited symbols of earlier days to prayers answered, requests granted. Similarly, devotions such as that to Mary under the title of miracle worker, Our Lady of the Miraculous Medal, have waned, and it is almost impossible to conceive of a high church figure loading a plane with sick and handicapped persons and flying off with them to Lourdes in hopes of a miracle, as Boston's Richard Cardinal Cushing once did.

Developments such as these would appear to concede the old objection that, remarkable as miracles ascribed to the saints and to Mary might have seemed, they nonetheless lacked the *a priori* (cause to effect) probability that could be credited to the scriptural miracles on account of their connection and congruity with divine revelation. Accordingly, they could be discounted because the *a posteriori* (effect to cause) evidence for these wonders, both with respect to moral and religious quality, was inferior to the evidence for the miracles of Scripture.

But even to concede that does not explain the lowered expectations of many of the faithful and sometimes, it seems, of the church itself for great signs and wonders from on high. Has a large cynicism taken root with respect to miracles?

Not necessarily. As far back as the sixteenth century, when the age of faith was still in full flower, the Spanish Carmelite mystic St. John of the Cross was expressing distrust of post-scriptural miracles and cautioning that there were natural explanations likely for such phenomena as visions, the experiencing of the stigmata, the hearing of voices, wondrous signs and other seemingly magical interventions of the divine in the course of human affairs. John of the Cross's caution does not deny to God the power to work miracles directly or through instruments of his will, such as Mary and the saints. But it does suggest that, rather than look for wonders, the wise person should look to self and his or her surroundings, since in the normal course God speaks to individuals through the persons and places, situations and events, which form the context of their everyday lives.

Obviously something of this logic has coalesced in Catholics of the twentieth century. They are less credulous, less predisposed to credit God than are Catholics of earlier times when confronted with the remarkable and the seemingly unexplainable. Nor are they ahead of the leadership on this. The church itself, which one day would have been quick to accept an astonishing happening as a miracle of God, is cautious about coming to a conclusion directly relating the wondrous and unexplainable to the divine. Today, in a Rome that, if not skeptical, is realistic and far more demanding that miracles be beyond all natural explanations before being accepted as the work of God, many would have a hard time taking "miracles" seriously.

Thus it is that, though it still holds miracles to be possible, the modern church would not anathematize, as did the church of Vatican I (1869-1870), "him who says . . . that by miracles the divine order of the Christian religion is not rightly proved" or that "miracles are impossible." Vatican II a century later was content to speak more narrowly of the miracles of Christ, and for the most part in the context of their being external proofs of divine revelation, confirmation that "the kingdom has already arrived on earth" (Dogmatic Constitution on the Church,

5). It was the only explicit use of the word "miracles" in all of Vatican II.

The Ultimate Sign

De-emphasis of the notion of miracles as a continuing integral part of the divine presence and power in the natural order relieves the church of certain problems of explanation.

Some of these are happenings having the aura of genuine miracles, but occurring in churches other than the Catholic Church and thus vitiating the church's claims of exclusivity on God's favor; and the rationalization of prodigies performed by so-called evil spirits. The second difficulty is easier to handle than the first.

The power of evil spirits is strictly conditioned and readily identifiable, as in Exodus 8:14, when the "magicians" sought to bring about an infestation of gnats by their magic arts, and Apocalypse (Revelation) 9:14-15, when the four angels of the abyss tied up on the banks of the "great river Euphrates" were released to kill a third of humankind. In the words of the old (1913) *Catholic Encyclopedia:* "Granting that these spirits may perform prodigies—i.e., works of skill and ingenuity which, relatively to our powers, may seem to be miraculous—yet these works lack the meaning and purpose which would stamp them as the language of God to men (sic)."

Less easy to handle, and far more delicate ecumenically, is the problem of miracles occurring outside the

Catholic Church. Traditionally the church regarded miracles as being largely, if not exclusively reserved to the one, holy, catholic and apostolic church (*unam, sanctam, catholicam et apostolicam ecclesiam*), the Holy Catholic Church, the Church of Rome, as proof of God's favor and confirmation of the truth of Catholic Christian revelation. Even as late as the publication of the *New Catholic Encyclopedia* several years after Vatican II, the claim was being maintained that true miracles could only be so-called Catholic miracles.

"Fact," says the *New Catholic Encyclopedia*'s entry after positing the theory of extra-Catholic miracles: "Whether or not there have been certain miracles at all outside the Catholic Church is debatable. The vast majority of supposed cases on record are open to question from one standpoint or another—e.g., unreliable or insufficiently detailed testimony, the possibility of a purely natural explanation, and in some instances strong indications of a diabolic origin." The "Miracles" entry proceeds to recommend L. Monden's 1960 book *Le Miracle, signe du salut* as a "comprehensive survey and evaluation of the best-known claims in miracles outside the Catholic Church."

The problem with the *New Catholic Encyclopedia*'s reasoning is that if God works through other churches, as Vatican II said he did, then there is no question but that God could work miracles in connection with another church or religion besides the Catholic one, and do so at the same time without diminishing the Catholic Church's claims of priority on divine favor.

RETROSPECT

But whatever conclusions one reaches about the nature and existence of miracles, they are of no cosmic importance, for after everything is factored in and totaled up, the bottom line is that miracles are not the sum and substance of religion. Certainly, in these latter centuries of the church's life, miracles (barring those of the Scripture) need not and, better, should not be the basis of one's belief—unless, maybe, one is talking of the "miracle" that happens at every mass, the miracle of the transubstantiation, or conversion of the bread and wine (their sensible appearances alone remaining) into the body and blood of Christ.

In theological terms, the transubstantiation is not an observable event and therefore not a miracle in the proper sense, belonging rather to what are called "miracles of faith"—supernatural events in the material order knowable only by divine faith.

On the other hand, if the hallmark of a miracle is the exceptional manifestation of God's care and concern for the salvation of his people, it follows that nothing could be more genuine a miracle than the eucharistic sharing of communicants in Christ's divinity. For nothing more clearly is a sign of the supernatural world and the believer's connection with it than the Eucharist. In that context, this one "miracle of faith" that is the Eucharist may be said to be greater than all the physical miracles of Christian history.

On the matter of physical miracles, the church's attitude is far more nuanced than in the past and, of course, nothing like it was to be found in ages when almost any striking phenomenon was referred to supernatural cause. The church's attitude toward miracles today may even border on the skeptical, and to the extent that it does, it is understandable. When much is involved—in this instance, the credibility of faith—it is better to be doubtful than credulous, to be prudently cautious than impulsively foolish.

The "miracle of faith" that is the transubstantiation is something entirely different, however. On that there is no need for nuance, for doubt, for prudent caution. The transubstantiation is what it always was: the miracle of the Last Supper continued into time for as long as the world will last. On that, the official thought and teaching of the church have evolved not one iota.

6.

INDULGENCES:
Is Anyone Counting Quarantines Anymore?

Tickets to Heaven

IN Graham Greene's 1954 short story "Special Duties," businessman William Ferraro of Ferraro & Smith, an exceedingly busy man deeply concerned about his personal salvation, had delegated to his assistant confidential secretary, a certain Miss Saunders, the special duty of amassing indulgences on his behalf, thus to cut down time he might have to do in purgatory if he up and suddenly died, as he almost did three years before of pneumonia.

It was right after that scare that Miss Saunders was hired to shop around for quality, richly endowed indulgences, and in the time since she had amassed a total of 36,892 days on Mr. Ferraro's behalf—or so he thought. It turned out that Miss Saunders was bedding down with a boyfriend in Bayswater instead of kneeling down at shrines like Walsingham. Mr. Ferraro had been had.

Greene's story was fiction, to be sure. Still, it is—or was—an old Catholic custom to store up indulgenced time as an offset against the time-sentence to purgatory in the afterlife. Actually, Greene's William Ferraro was a

95

small-timer as far as harvesting indulgences went. In the thirteenth century the pious elector of Saxony, Frederick the Wise, laid up in just one twelve-month period a grand total of 127,799 years' worth of indulgences, surely a good start in offsetting the time anyone, Palatine elector or ordinary guy, would be expected to do in purgatory.

Of course, no one knew precisely how time was calculated in the afterlife, but relative assessments could be made, and the common calculation in Frederick the Wise's day was that even a forgiven sin required the equivalent of seven years of suffering in purgatory before one's soul qualified for admission to heaven. That's a lot of heat for just one sin. Figuring that most folks don't get through life with just one sin against their record, the average Joe (and Josephine) faced the prospect of a long stretch in purgatory. Frederick the Wise was wise, it would seem, to build up points—meaning, indulgences.

What's an indulgence? Pure and simple, it is the remission before God of the temporal punishment due in the afterlife for sins committed and already forgiven on earth as far as guilt is concerned. So the church says. An indulgence can be gained for oneself or can be applied to one of the faithfully departed. There are conditions, naturally, and proper disposition is required, but the time is there for the taking, and it is obtained through the intervention of the church.

That's the traditional teaching. Emphases, however, are quite different now from what they were in Frederick the Wise's time, or as recently as twenty-five years ago for that matter. But first the background.

Absolve and Commute

The idea of indulgences has its roots in early Christian history, and is probably most accurately traced to those Christians who defected during the Roman persecutions.

Those subsequently desiring to be restored to the church's good standing would present a memorial (*libellus pacis*) to a bishop, that the bishop, in consideration of the martyrs' suffering, might grant absolution, and thus release them from the punishment which they had incurred before God. The logic was that the merits of the martyrs could be applied to the less worthy by what was known as vicarious satisfaction.

Contributing, too, to a notion of indulgences was the stiffness of penances handed down in the early church for sin, notably among Celts, who saw to it that the penance was proportionate to the transgression. Often this resulted in penances of such "astronomical proportions," in the words of the *New Catholic Encyclopedia,* that penitents were known to die before the penances could even be completed. That seemed unfair, so confessors were given commutation powers; penances could be met with prayer, pious practices and almsgiving, the latter being applied with increasing frequency.

The commutations or substitute penances were indulgences of a sort, and formed the basis of a new tradition in the church. By the ninth century, popes and bishops were concluding letters with grants of absolution in the form of solemn prayers petitioning God through Christ and his saints to absolve the sinner of all penalties due to sin. By the eleventh century, indulgence grants—as Catholics of today's senior generations came to know them— were making their appearances. They were obtainable for acts as easy as a visit to a particular church, and as difficult as the joining of a crusade. In 1095 Pope Urban II (1088-1099) decreed that anyone who joined in "the liberation of the Church of God at Jerusalem" could reckon himself relieved of all penance due to sin.

In time a complex system was in place. There were plenary indulgences and partial indulgences, the difference being the remission in whole (plenary) or in part (partial) of the temporal punishment due to sin in that place called purgatory. There were universal indulgences (obtainable anywhere) and local indulgences (obtainable only in a specified place, such as Rome or Jerusalem). There were perpetual indulgences and temporary indulgences; in other words, indulgences which could be gained at any time of the year (perpetual) and indulgences obtainable only on certain days or in certain periods (temporary). There were real indulgences, such as those attached to the use of certain religious objects (rosary, medal, crucifix), and personal indulgences, which were reserved to persons belonging to particular associations, such as a religious order or confraternity. There were indulgences granted in behalf of the living, and indulgences that could be applied to the souls in purgatory for their earlier release. There were also apostolic indulgences, indulgences attached to religious articles by the blessing of the pope or those having special faculties.

Most of the indulgences were calculated in time frames (commonly years, days and that favorite ecclesiastical measuring period, quarantines, or forty days). Even though the church made no claim to absolute exactness in the relation to time on earth of time in the hereafter, alleging only a relative value, it still had to account for the empowerment it assumed. In providing indulgences that were in effect time bonuses, it could only give away that which it possessed. It had to draw on something, but what and how? Hugh of Saint-Cher came up with the answer around 1230. The church was drawing on its treasury.

An Infinite Treasure

The treasury of the church was that accumulation of superfluous and unspent merits and good works built up by Mary and the saints, both those living and dead, undiminished by any penalty due to sin, and free to be drawn upon by the church in its wisdom.

These merits and good works were added to the treasury of the church as a secondary deposit, not independent of but rather acquired through the merits of Christ, which formed the primary deposit. Hugh of Saint-Cher built his principle on that of Christian solidarity in the Mystical Body of Christ.

Pope Clement VI (1342-1352) liked Hugh's proposition, and on January 27, 1343 issued the bull *Unigenitus Dei Filius* dogmatically declaring the treasury of the church to be infinite and inexhaustible. Clement's words on the subject: "Upon the altar of the Cross, Christ shed of his blood not merely a drop, though this would have sufficed, by reason of the union with the Word, to redeem the whole human race, but a copious torrent . . . thereby laying up an infinite treasure for mankind. This treasure he neither wrapped up in a napkin nor hid in a field, but entrusted to Blessed Peter, the key-bearer, and his successors, that they might, for just and reasonable causes, distribute it to the faithful in full or partial remission of the temporal punishment due to sin."

Saint Bonaventure and Saint Thomas Aquinas developed Hugh of Saint-Cher's theory, and echoing Clement VI held that an indulgence was not so much the remission of the debt of temporal punishment but a payment of the debt from the church's treasury. In 1476 Pope Sixtus IV (1471-1484) followed with the declaration that indulgences could be applied to the souls in purgatory, though he hedged the proposition a bit, saying that they applied by way of suffrage (*per modum suffragii*), a qualification which suggested to some that the efficacy of indulgences in cases involving the dead was not so certain (absolute) as in cases involving the living (where indulgences applied *per modum absolutionis*).

There were conditions attached to the gaining of an indulgence, such as being in the state of grace and the fulfilling of certain terms, usually devotional in character. Confession and contrition would be two. However, the notions of treasury and of being able to qualify for an indulgence through alms-giving were inopportune and infelicitous, as gradually many indulgences became too closely associated with hard cash. To be sure, the money was intended for noble ends, and indeed much of it went for holy and wholesome causes—as for the construction and maintenance of cathedrals, churches, universities, hospitals and social programs, including some state-neglected projects such as the building of bridges and dikes. The church in France, for instance, was substantially restored in the aftermath of the Hundred Years War thanks to money collected for indulgences.

But the system was open both to popular misinterpretation and easy exploitation, and it encountered each in abundance, with effects that contributed to the Protestant Reformation and the divided Western Christendom which exists to this day.

From Skepticism to Revolt

There was to begin with confusion over the phrase *indulgentia a poena et culpa* attached to plenary indulgences, and out of this grew the misconception that plenary indulgences freed sinners not only from the temporal punishment (*poena*) but also the guilt (*culpa*) of all the sins themselves.

It was a misconception that fostered skepticism—cynicism too—and eventually considerable doubt about the intrinsic value of indulgences generally.

Then too, there was the problem of preachers who re-

John Deedy

garded indulgences as downpayments on salvation, and who taught quite literally that by spending now one could take out a mortgage on a place in heaven. In such a context indulgences took on the aura of a magical quality, and in Germany this gave birth to the popular jingle: *Sobald das Geld im Kasten klingt/Die Seele aus dem Fegfeuer springt* ("As fast as the money rattles in the box, the soul [on whose behalf it is given] leaps out of purgatory"). Some preachers were outright exploiters, like the Franciscan at Besancon who in 1486 was promoting his order's interests by telling people that if they wore the Franciscan habit, Saint Francis of Assisi himself would come and collect them from purgatory.

Indulgenced time also got out of hand. In 1456, recitation of a few prayers before a church crucifix could earn an indulgence of 20,000 years *toties quoties* (as often as the act was done), and in England the early reformer John Wycliff (1320?-1384) remonstrated against indulgences that provided 2,000 years for the saying of a single prayer.

There was a whole lot more of such nonsense, but crisis did not come until after Pope Alexander VI (1492-1503) issued a bull in 1499 granting plenary indulgences to individuals, applicable to themselves or to souls in purgatory, in return for contributions of money for the restoration of St. Peter's Basilica in Rome, the precise amount of the individual contribution to be fixed by priests according to the means of the person. The indulgences were continued in 1506 by Pope Julius II (1503-1513) and in 1514 by Pope Leo X (1513-1521). By 1517 it was the most important indulgence preached in Germany, and one Augustinian monk took exception. His name was Martin Luther, and he issued his great challenge to the whole idea in Wittenberg on October 31, 1517.

October 31, it will be noted, was the day before the Feast of All Saints, the festive prelude to one of the church's great feasts, and so observed in Wittenberg. In fact, energetically so. For All Saints was the feast during which each year in Wittenberg the exotic collection of relics of the late Frederick the Wise, the very same as mentioned earlier, was removed from the storerooms of the Schlosskirche and displayed for the edification of the faithful. For decades upon decades, people had flocked to Wittenberg during All Saints to gaze with pious awe on such remarkable religious artifacts as the complete corpses of saints, nails from Christ's crucifixion, rods from his flagellation, part of the child Jesus' swaddling clothes, chips of wood from his crib, and, yes, that most rare of relics, drops of milk from the breast of the nursing Virgin Mary. In addition to the thrill of the spectacle, there were valuable indulgences to be gained from the veneration of these and the several thousand other relics on exhibition.

In the carnival atmosphere of Wittenberg on the morning of October 31, Martin Luther hurled down the gauntlet, so to speak, on the issue of indulgences. But Luther's challenge was directed not so immediately against Rome as against Brother Tetzel, the famous Dominican preacher of indulgences, who was peddling "passports to cross the sea of wrath and go direct to Paradise" throughout the area, although not in Wittenberg itself. Though the "offerings" for these "passports," or indulgences, could in fact be very small, almost trifling in many cases—once again, the amount being scaled to fit the resources of the believer—Luther took exception. He hammered to the doors of the Schlosskirche, the castle's chapel, a manifesto, a document of ninety-five theses that he offered to defend against all comers.

There were no immediate debaters; written in scholastic Latin, the manifesto could in fact be read by only a handful in the largely unlettered crowd at Wittenberg, illiteracy being common at the time. But the knowledgeable few who could read the Latin sensed the importance of what was before their eyes, and they were anything but wrong. Those ninety-five theses were to form the basis for the Lutheran revolt that grew into the Protestant Reformation.

Correcting Abuses

In those ninety-five theses Luther made six different assertions about indulgences and their efficacy:

1. An indulgence is and can only be the remission of a merely ecclesiastical penalty; the church can remit what the church has imposed; it cannot remit what God has imposed.

2. An indulgence can never remit guilt; the pope himself cannot do such a thing; God has kept that in his own hand.

3. It cannot remit the divine punishment for sin; that also is in the hands of God alone.

104

4. It can have no efficacy for souls in purgatory; penalties imposed by the church can only refer to the living; death dissolves them; what the pope can do for souls in purgatory is by prayer, not by jurisdiction or the power of the keys.

5. The Christian who has true repentance has already received pardon from God altogether apart from an indulgence, and does not need one; Christ demands this true repentance from everyone.

6. The Treasury of Merits has never been properly defined; it is hard to say what it is, and it is not properly understood by the people; it cannot be the merits of Christ and of his saints, because these act of themselves and quite apart from the intervention of the pope; it can mean nothing more than that the pope, having the power of the keys, can remit ecclesiastical penalties by the church; the true treasure-house of merits is the Holy Ghost of the grace and glory of God.

As debate heated up, Luther would become blunter, describing indulgences as "pious frauds on the faithful." The church would dispute this mightily, but at the same time it would clean up its act and its theology relating to indulgences. Credit for this goes largely to the Council of Trent (1545-1563) and its decree "On Indulgences" of Session XXV—a decree that energetically supported the concept of indulgences as belonging to the church's divine patrimony, but explicitly acknowledging that abuses existed in the system. Trent anathematized those "who either declare that indulgences are useless or deny that the church has the power to grant them," but added the remarkable codicil:

John Deedy

"In granting indulgences the Council desires that moderation be observed in accordance with the ancient approved custom of the church, lest through excessive ease ecclesiastical discipline be weakened; and further, seeking to correct the abuses that have crept in . . . it decrees that all criminal gain therewith connected shall be entirely done away with as a source of grievous abuse among the Christian people; and as to other disorders arising from superstition, ignorance, irreverence, or any cause whatsoever—since these, on account of the widespread corruption, cannot be removed by special prohibitions—the Council lays upon each bishop the duty of finding out such abuses as exist in his own diocese, of bringing them before the next provincial synod, and of reporting them, with the assent of the other bishops, to the Roman Pontiff, by whose authority and prudence measures will be taken for the welfare of the church at large, so that the benefit of indulgences may be bestowed on all the faithful by means at once pious, holy, and free from corruption."

By way of underscoring its point, Trent abolished entirely the name, method and office of *quaestores,* traders in indulgences, and ordered that bishops publish and bestow gratuitously all indulgences and other spiritual favors, so that, in the paraphrase of the 1913 *Catholic Encyclopedia,* it will be clearly understood "that these heavenly treasures were dispensed for the sake of piety and not of lucre." Not everyone got the message immediately, which prompted Pope Pius V (1566-1572) to add the direct weight of the papacy in 1567, by abrogating "every indulgence . . . for which a helping hand must be offered, and which contains in any way whatsoever permission to make collections." Pius V's decree translated to a serious loss of revenue for many of the church's institutions, but it got the job done. "Trafficking" in indulgences—a practice which actually had been condemned as far back as Lateran Council IV of 1215—became rare, then virtually nonexistent.

In 1807 the Holy See published the *Raccolta,* a collection of the prayers and pious exercises to which the popes had attached indulgences. The book was periodically updated, and it grew in size with each updating. Extravagances of earlier times were carefully avoided, but the inducements were still strong. For recitation of "The Memorare" one received three years' indulgences; a plenary, if recited daily for a month with fulfillment of the "usual conditions" (confession, communion, visit to a church, and prayer for the intentions of the pope). Ejaculations such as "Sweet Heart of Mary, be my salvation" won three hundred days, and the stations of the cross were worth ten years and ten quarantines per station, a plenary for the lot.

Despite the cleaning up, dubious practices of piety persisted. Parochial-school children, for instance, were often encouraged to draw up "spiritual bouquets"— pledges to say large numbers of rosaries, ejaculations, stations of the cross, etc.—and present these as gift offer-

John Deedy

ings to a pastor, say, on his anniversary, or to parents on their birthdays (the church's teaching notwithstanding that indulgences could be gained for self or for the dead, but not for another living person).

Modern Amendments

By the time Vatican Council II (1962-1965) came around, there was what the *New Catholic Encyclopedia* terms "a widespread undercurrent of sentiment toward dropping the function of indulgences entirely."

That did not happen. In fact, Vatican II had little or nothing to say about indulgences; the word does not even rate an index entry in Deretz's and Nocent's *Dictionary of the Council*. Vatican II, however, did have a marked indirect effect on indulgences, through the updating it ordered for devotional practices generally in the church.

Thus on January 1, 1967, appeared Pope Paul VI's apostolic constitution "The Doctrine of Indulgences." In terms of the past it was an astonishing restatement of what indulgences were all about. Gone entirely were old notions of a treasury of the church (*thesaurus ecclesiae*) containing inexhaustible, unspent merits accumulated over the centuries and now available to the faithful. Gone too were precise, descriptive time terms for an indulgence or pardon, like five years, five hundred days, five quarantines. Instead, the document said, ". . . the faithful who perform an action to which a 'partial indulgence' is attached, obtain, in addition to the remission of the temporal punishment acquired by the action itself, an equal remission of punishment through the intervention of the church"—which the 1967-1974 supplement to the *New Catholic Encyclopedia,* with some whimsy, summarizes as "in short, a matching grant." Another surprise was that Paul VI's apostolic constitution did not even cite Matthew 16:18-19, the passage dealing with Peter and the power of the keys, and traditionally invoked in defense of the church's authority to grant indulgences.

More change was to come. Two and a half years later —June 29, 1968—the Holy See replaced the *Raccolta* with a new *Enchiridion Indulgentiarum* ("Handbook of Indulgences"). The new *Enchiridion* was dramatically shorter than the old manual, and the emphases quite different. "In conformity with the changed conditions of present times," the *Enchiridion* placed "greater value . . . on the . . . *opus operantis* [personal contribution] of the faithful . . . instead of [on] a lengthy series of indulgenced works of piety" [*opus operatum*]—in other words, the disposition of the individual took precedent over the mere performance of an act. The *Enchiridion* accredited three "General Grants of Indulgences," and listed some seventy grants of indulgences for devotional acts and exercises, such as prayer and visits to designed churches or shrines. Stressed now, however, was not the beefing-up of one's personal treasury of indulgences by the mechanical or ritualistic fulfillment of some prescribed formula, but instead the spirit of joyful and efficacious participation in the fellowship or communion of the saints and the prayer life of the church—a concept, incidentally, broached by the German Jesuit theologian Karl Rahner, back in 1955. It is there that the theology of indulgences stands today, perhaps awaiting some new evolutionary chapter, some new historical twist of fate.

7.

CLERICAL CELIBACY:
Is the Past Harbinger of the Future?

Holy Continence

ABOUT the time of Pope John Paul II's 1987 visit to the United States, the CBS show "60 Minutes" aired a segment about a priest in an upper Midwest diocese who was living openly in the rectory with the woman of his affections.

Diane Sawyer was the interviewer, and she probed the priest on parish reaction to their arrangement. The priest contended that parishioners regarded the situation as no big deal, adding there was a whole lot more controversy when he proposed moving the organ to a new spot in the church.

That priest is no longer in the clerical fold. He resigned and married, Diane Sawyer declared, five days before "60 Minutes" went public with his story. The implication was that the priest would be a dead duck in the church once his story hit national television, and so he got out while the going was good, or that he could do so gracefully.

Of course the priest was a dead duck so far as institutional Roman Catholicism was concerned, for the church

111

requires celibacy and the unmarried state of life from its priests. The priest's living a noncelibate life might have been no big deal with members of his local parish, but it certainly would be for officials of the larger church. In Eastern Rite churches, candidates for the priesthood may marry before becoming deacons, but the very notion of a noncelibate clergy is one of the great hobgoblins of the Western or Roman Catholic Rite.

Whether the Roman Catholic Church will always require celibacy of its clergy is a matter of speculation, particularly in the light of current pressures for change. But this much is certain: things weren't always the way they are now. A married, noncelibate clergy was once common in the church. Not only were some of the Apostles married, for instance, but there is a theory that Peter even took his wife along on his missionary journeys. What is certain is that as the church burgeoned across the Mediterranean from the Holy Land, many of the new Christian communities were placed in the charge of married men, the practice being to choose family men as leaders. If nothing more, they had a track record on which to base judgments and expectations.

This is not to suggest that a celibate clergy was not an early ideal. Saint Paul celebrated celibacy and virginity as a higher calling, urging the unmarried and widows to "remain as they are, even as I do myself" (1 Corinthians 8-9), and more pointedly telling those in the service of the Lord that they couldn't serve two masters: "I tell you brothers, the time is short. From now on those with wives should live as though they had none. . . . The unmarried man is busy with the Lord's affairs, concerned with pleasing the Lord; but the married man is busy with this world's demands and occupied with pleasing his wife'' (1 Cor. 29-34). Paul's admonitions, particularly the latter, set the tone for much of the latter-day defense of celibacy, though in the short run it seems to have created a problem of a different sort, a warning having to be sounded in *The Apostolic Constitutions* against ditching one's wife under the pretext of piety.

The Base Activity

The concept of a celibate clergy built on the enactments of local councils, beginning with one in Elvira, Spain, between 295 and 302, and including councils at Rome, Turin, Toledo and Carthage, among others.

Initially the objective appears to have been not so much to keep clergy from marrying but, because so many of them were already married, to discourage them from the practice of sexual intercourse, which was considered unholy and defiling. The Council of Elvira was particularly severe, imposing celibacy on bishops, priests and deacons, and ordering deposed those who continued to live with their wives and beget children. But other councils were more lenient, merely denying promotion to those who, while continuing to live with their wives, produced offspring. In any instance, as Joseph Martos points out in *Doors to the Sacred,* the idea of continence gradually evolved into the ideal of celibacy.

Enactments such as these would seem to have reduced

clerical wives to the level of pariahs, but in point of fact clerical wives enjoyed a status not negligible for the times. Those married to deacons received a special blessing on their husbands' ordination. They were accorded a distinctive garb, and were known as *presbyterissae* (*presbyterae*) and *diaconissae* (*diaconae*). As if to emphasize the special character of these honors, they were not permitted to remarry, not even after the deaths of their spouses.

The fundamental hang-up was of course over sexual intercourse, that unclean thing in the view of some. It was a view that extended even to the Eastern church, whose married clergy were directed to abstain from sexual intercourse on days when they celebrated the liturgy (not an impossible hardship since the liturgy was usually celebrated but once a week), and also when they traveled in Latin Rite areas (probably a diplomatic consideration). But the hang-up was particularly pronounced in the Latin Rite, where sexual intercourse was widely regarded as a base activity, however necessary it might be for the very propagation of the human race. Celibacy and virginity, in turn, were exalted ideals—such indeed that Origen (c. 185-c. 254), the Christian theologian, writer and teacher at Alexandria, would castrate himself, believing this an aid to spiritual perfection.

Gradually, a consensus built up in favor of celibacy— to such a degree, in fact, that celibacy became an elitist state, a mark of distinction, with the so-called higher principled. It divided the ranks. The learned elements of the clergy generally supported celibacy; those of lesser accomplishments and gifts seemed on balance to hold fast for a married clergy. The former—theoretically the sophisticated—were to be found in the main in the cities and in the universities, while the latter more likely were to be found serving the peasantry in much more humble circumstances. Much of this categorizing was caricature, to be sure, but the caricature was fostered by various synodal enactments which, despairing of bringing uniformity to the discipline, allowed rural clergymen—again, those men of allegedly modest attainments—to retain their wives.

Harsh Measures

It was not until the turn of the millennium that the church came fully to grips with the issue of clerical celibacy, sometimes not always in a Christian manner.

A rather astonishing early measure was one of Pope Benedict VIII (1012-1024). He not only forbade priests, deacons and subdeacons to marry or to cohabit with a woman, but also declared the children of any such union to be forever serfs of the church, with no rights of property or inheritance. The latter edict was adopted to put an end to the practice of clergymen, bishops as well as priests, transmitting their benefices and other institutional assets to their sons and daughters.

It was during the pontificates of Leo IX (1049-1054) and Gregory VII (1073-1085) that pressures were more effectively exerted for clerical reform, and that the tide was turned, resulting in the enforcement of celibacy as a discipline on all Roman Catholic priests without exception. In both those papacies, however, clerical celibacy was the secondary rather than the primary issue. The larger concerns were the problems of simonaical episcopal appointments (bishoprics bought and sold) and heretical ordinations. It was the latter that Leo IX targeted almost exclusively. Gregory VII, the Hildebrand pope elected by clamor of the Roman mob within 24 hours of the death of Alexander II, factored in the sexuality element. Before his election as pope, when he was *praepositus* (provisor) of the mona⁺ery of Saint Paul Outside the Walls, Hildebrand ended the practice of monks being attended in their refectory by women. His position infinitely strengthened as pope, Hildebrand promulgated a decree at his First Lenten Synod (March, 1074) ordering all clerics involved in sexual incontinence to stop the exercise of their ministry.

Though there was growing support in the church for a celibate clergy, Hildebrand's decree was still not a popular one. It was protested throughout Italy and encountered vehement opposition in parts of Germany and France. The Bishop of Passau, for instance, came close to losing his life for daring to publish the decree. Similarly, the Archbishop of Rouen was stoned and had to flee for his life when he tried to enforce celibacy among his clergy.

Nonetheless, committed as the Hildebrand pope was to the continency issue, simony persisted as the larger and more immediate of his concerns. The conviction was common that order in the house was predicted on the elimination of simony, and that once this was accomplished lesser problems, such as clerical celibacy, would fall into perspective and be easier to grapple with. The unfolding of history supports the logic of that position.

Following Gregory VII's pontificate, the weight of ecumenical church councils began to accumulate on the side of celibacy.

Lateran Council I, convened in 1123 under Callistus II, adopted two canons aimed at the promotion of clerical celibacy. Canons 3 and 21 of the Council forbade priests, deacons, subdeacons and monks to marry or keep concubines, and furthermore declared marriages already contracted by such persons null *pleno jure*.

In 1139, Lateran Council II under Innocent II added five canons on the subject, most of them generally duplicating those of Lateran I and of the synodal gatherings at Clermont in 1130, Reims in 1131, and Pisa in 1135. Once again concubinage was condemned and marriages involving clergymen were pronounced to be without standing; sons of such unions were not to be ordained unless they first became monks or canons regular; and the faithful were enjoined against attending mass celebrated by married priests.

There were other matters, of course, also to occupy the attention of the Fathers of Lateran I—like clerical dress. It was at this Council that a canon was adopted counseling bishops and ecclesiastics to dress in a modest, well-regulated manner lest they scandalize the faithful with the colors, shape or extravagance of clerical vestments.

Dogma or Discipline?

Thus it was that in the Western or Latin church, that which was at first merely recommended to priests came to be imposed by law on all who were to be promoted to sacred orders.

Priests were not to marry. However, the issue of clerical celibacy was obviously not neatly and completely settled, for 400 years later the Council of Trent (1545-1563) was forced to call for the suppression of concubinage among the clergy.

Gradually, though, clerical celibacy became not just the rule, but a fundamental operative principle of the Roman Catholic priesthood. Indeed, clerical celibacy became a given in Roman Catholicism—to such a degree, in fact, that by the time Vatican Council II (1962-1965) rolled around, no railing or exhortation was required in its behalf. It was necessary merely to celebrate celibacy in the terms in which it had commonly come to be understood in the Western or Latin Rite: that is, as the life of perfect chastity undertaken in total dedication to the service of God and people. The Council's Decree on the Ministry and Life of Priests would extol the blessings derivative of celibacy thus: "Through virginity or celibacy observed for the sake of the kingdom of heaven, priests are consecrated to Christ in a new and distinguished way. They more easily hold fast to Him with undivided heart.

RETROSPECT

They more freely devote themselves in Him and through Him to the service of God and men. They more readily minister to His Kingdom and to the work of heavenly regeneration, and thus become more apt to exercise paternity in Christ, and do so to a greater extent"(16).

It should be emphasized that throughout most of church history celibacy was never proposed nor offered as a strictly defined dogmatic principle—although it is true that at times the celibacy notion was advanced by some wildly exotic religious reasoning, particularly in those early centuries influenced by gnostic theory when sexual intercourse and procreation, even in the marital state, were often held to be, if not directly sinful, then barely tolerable morally. Saint Augustine, for one, viewed sexual desire or lust as an evil resulting from original sin, passed on by way of sexual intercourse from one generation to another. In such a climate of thought, celibacy almost inevitably came to be regarded as a vehicle for spiritual perfection. Nor was it just a case of the clergy being urged to be celibate. Widows were discouraged from remarrying; virginity was encouraged among single persons; sexual continence was urged upon those who were married. Begetting offspring was a dirty business.

Once the church outgrew those influences, clerical celibacy came more correctly to be seen as an ideal and was accordingly promoted as a discipline, the observance of which would help in the advancement of the kingdom of God. For church leaders there was the added dividend that with a celibate clergy the church would be spared certain administrative and probate difficulties, like problems of rocky clerical marriages and the willing of church property and other assets by married priests to members of their own family, a not uncommon practice, as mentioned earlier.

A curious development occurred, however, once clerical celibacy was firmly entrenched as a church discipline. With little in Scripture to buttress arguments for celibacy apart from the letters of Paul and the Gospel reference in Matthew 19:12 about eunuchs who make themselves "that way" for the sake of the kingdom (for the word "eunuchs," some modern translations use terms like "those who have freely renounced sex"), defenders of the discipline eventually began to look afield. What did they find? Lo and behold, they found material in a most unlikely place. For there was the testimony, experience and example, pro and con, of non-Catholics to reinforce the Catholic position.

Anglicans and Others

Much was made at one time, for instance, of the fact that celibacy was not a bone of contention with Martin Luther, at least not immediately.

When he broke with the church in 1517, Luther did not denounce clerical celibacy. Seven years later, in a letter dated January 17, 1522, Luther was still in support of celibacy, expressly declining to encourage sacerdotal marriage. He would not come to an actual denunciation of celibacy until near the end of 1522, and he himself would not marry until 1525.

Similarly, the old *Catholic Encyclopedia* (The Gilmary Society, 1908) would bolster its defense of celibacy with citations such as the letter to an Anglican friend of Dr. Johann von Dollinger, the learned theologian and historian who broke with the Catholic Church at the time of Vatican I over the issue of papal infallibility. Dollinger was said to have been "sorely grieved" when his "Old Catholic" followers abolished compulsory celibacy in their sect. He wrote to his friend: "You in England cannot understand how completely ingrained it is into our people that a priest is a man who sacrifices himself for the sake of his parishioners. He has no children of his own, in order that all the children in the parish may be his children. His people know that his small wants are supplied, and that he can devote all his time to them. They know it is quite otherwise with the married pastors of the Protestants. The pastor's income may be enough for himself, but it is not enough for his wife and children also. In order to maintain them he must take other work, literary or scholastic; and they know that when the interests of his family and those of his flock collide, his family must come first and his flock second. In short, he has a profession or trade, a *Gewerbe,* rather than a vocation; he has to earn a livelihood. In almost all Catholic congregations, a priest who married would be ruined; all his influence would be gone."

The old *Catholic Encyclopedia* did not stop with Dollinger. Cited in the same celibacy entry was the comment of the freethinker George Sand (Madame Amandine Aurore Lucie Dudevant) on the departure from the faith of the famed nineteenth-century Carmelite preacher, Pere Hyacinthe Loyson. "Will Pere Hyacinthe still hear confessions?" she asked. "That is the question. Is the secrecy of the confessional compatible with the mutual confidences of conjugal love? If I were a Catholic, I would say to my children: 'Have no secrets which cost too much in the telling and then you will have no cause to fear the gossip of the vicar's wife.'"

Even now the old *Catholic Encyclopedia* was not finished. It continued with other examples of the same genre, and acceptable as these citations might have been in their time and place, they stand out now as caricatures. The priesthood is not so blissful, nor family life so demanding, as the old *Catholic Encyclopedia* obviously sought to portray them. It was near travesty, for example, to include in the celibacy entry an extract from *The Decay of Modern Preaching* by Trinity College Dublin's Professor Mahaffy, a married Protestant clergyman: "From the point of view of preaching, there can be little doubt that married life creates great difficulties and hindrances. . . . The Catholic priest when his daily round of outdoor duties is over, comes home to a quiet study, where there is nothing to disturb his thoughts. The family man is met at the door by troops of children welcoming his return and claiming his interest in all their little affairs. Or else the disagreements of the household demand him as an umpire and his mind is disturbed by no mere speculative contemplation of the faults and follies of mankind but by their actual invasion of his home.''

Maybe Catholic priests were better preachers in Mahaffy's time, the late nineteenth century, but if so, the talent has been lost. In any instance, the inclusion of so inane an observation in support of celibacy in so authoritative a source as a Catholic encyclopedia smacks of defense by smugness—which indeed is what the defense of celibacy became in the centuries between Trent and Vatican II, a period when the discipline was not challenged in a serious or widespread way. If nothing more, current defenders of celibacy, including Pope John Paul II, deserve credit for being aware that celibacy will not be preserved and protected by the setting up of straw men. The emphasis thus is on clerical celibacy as a holier state or, as John Paul II described it in a 1986 talk to Angola's bishops making their *ad limina* visit to Rome, clerical celibacy is a ''treasure,'' a sign of the priest's ''undivided and liberated heart,'' a ''gift of the Spirit,'' a life different from others in that it is lived ''in intimacy with God.''

The Papal Commitment

To be sure, for many celibacy is all of these things—although obviously it isn't for everyone, and this helps account for much of the pressure of recent years for change.

Being a discipline, as distinct from a dogma, the celibacy rule could be changed by a mere papal directive, and once again, as through eleven centuries in the Latin or

John Deedy

Western church, there would be a married clergy existing alongside a celibate one. One day this may happen, but not likely during the pontificate of John Paul II. John Paul is obviously willing to grant exceptions to the celibacy discipline in the cases of Protestant and Episcopalian (Anglican) clergymen who convert to Catholicism and proceed to ordination as Roman Catholic priests. But there is presently no accommodation for others.

Nor does John Paul II appear swayed by the Eastern Rite tradition of a married clergy, one which goes back to the Trullan Synod in the year 692. At Vatican II, the Council Fathers took note of the Eastern tradition, saying in the decree on priestly life: "In these [Eastern] Churches, in addition to all the bishops and those others who by a gift of grace choose to observe celibacy, there also exist married priests of outstanding merit. While this most sacred Synod recommends ecclesiastical celibacy, it in no way intends to change that different discipline which lawfully prevails in Eastern Churches. It lovingly exhorts all those who have received the priesthood after marriage to persevere in their sacred vocation, and to continue to spend their lives fully and generously for the flock committed to them" (16). John Paul II not only recommends clerical celibacy, he insists on it. As he made clear in addressing clergy during his 1984 visit to Switzerland, "Celibacy is not simply a juridical addition to the sacrament of orders. It is a commitment of the person, taken in full maturity, to Christ and the church."

The intensity might be different, but the logic and attitude of John Paul II on the issue of clerical celibacy are

124

consistent with those of popes almost without exception going back a millennium and beyond. Even Paul VI, a pope who upset many traditionalists with his leniency toward priests seeking laicization in order to marry, was firmly committed to clerical celibacy. In 1967, he issued an encyclical on the subject, *Sacerdotalis Celibatus,* in which he admonished those probing the church's celibacy discipline, telling them that "There are better things to do." For one thing, he said, "It would be better to promote serious studies in defense of the spiritual meaning and moral value of virginity and celibacy." Paul VI's words bristled, as do many of John Paul II's today on the subject. Whatever allowances and concessions may be made, celibacy stays! At least for the time being.

No one disputes that clerical celibacy has its place in the church, or at least very few do. The question that many raise is: how necessary is clerical celibacy as a condition for ordination to the secular priesthood and, as some would add, how desirable?

To pose that question here is not to argue one way or the other on the subject, although certain realities cannot be escaped.

Changing apostolates, the clergy drain, modern behavioral modes and new physiological theories—these and other developments work such pressure for change once again in the church's discipline respecting clerical celibacy that it is doubtful the last word has been spoken on the subject.

But that's often the case in the church. Some thought John XXIII spoke the last word on the relationship of language to the faith, when in February of 1962 he issued the apostolic constitution *Veterum Sapientia* celebrating Latin for its "immutable" qualities and noting that it was blessedly spared the liabilities of modern languages, where words are constantly taking on new and different meanings. (He had a point. Look what's happened to the word "gay" and the term "best friend.") *Veterum Sapientia* might have guaranteed Latin's place as the liturgical language of the then upcoming Vatican Council, but it did not insure its historic place as the language of the universal church. The Latin tradition was undone in less than two years' time by the Council's very first decree, the Constitutional on the Sacred Liturgy, which provided for the worldwide replacement of Latin with the vernacular in the mass and at other liturgical services.

8.

CONSECRATED VIRGINITY:
The Virtue of Optimum Chastity

Exalted Purity

WHEN the calendar of the saints was subjected to its great pruning in May, 1969, a national Catholic lay magazine took note with a two-paragraph editorial which focused on the excising of the Feast of Saint Ursula and the 11,000 virgins, reputedly martyred in Cologne by the Huns in hatred of the faith.

The editorial:

Those Dirty Huns

St. Paul the Hermit, St. Maurus, St. Prisca, St. Martina, St. Domitilla, St. Boniface of Tarsus, St. Venantius, St. Pudentiana, St. Modestus and St. Crescentia, St. John and St. Paul, two early Roman martyrs, St. Alexis, St. Symphorosa and her sons, St. Margaret of Antioch, St. Praxedes, St. Christopher, St. Susanna, etc., etc.

"We will miss them all. But most of all St. Ursula and her band of 11,000 virgins slaughtered for refusing the advances of the Huns. Where will we ever see their likes again?"

John Deedy

It is perhaps mildly ironic that the writer of the editorial happened to go on to a career at *Penthouse*. But then sport was being made of the feast well before its striking from the calendar and the editorial in the Catholic magazine. The official church itself had long since informally discounted the tale of the 11,000 virgins, with church historians consigning the feast, sometimes with great levity, to the category of pious romantic legend.

But there was never any levity in the church's regard for virginity itself. From the beginning, the church has esteemed virginity as a special and most exalted virtue. It does so today, although with certain nuances introduced to the appreciation.

The virginity tradition is firmly rooted in the New Testament. Christ himself in Matthew 19:11,12 lauded those who freely renounced sex for the sake of the kingdom, and as noted in another context, Paul in 1 Corinthians 7:8 counseled the unmarried, widows included, to remain unmarried "even as I do." Later, in the same letter (7:34), he contrasted the unmarried and the married woman, to the disadvantage of the latter: "The virgin, indeed any unmarried woman, is concerned with the things of the Lord that she may be holy in body and in spirit. The married woman, on the other hand, thinks about the things of the world and how she might please her husband."

On the basis of scriptural quotes of this sort, it is easy to see how the church would come to view female virginity (and male celibacy, since logically there are two sides to the sexuality coin) as the preferable state in life, superior even to the state of marriage.

In fairness, it should be said that the virginity mystique was inherited rather than initiated by the church. The Greeks worshipped the maiden or virgin Athene, and ancient Rome had its Vestal Virgins, maidens most pure who kept the torches alive, as it were, in primitive Roman agricultural villages—a serious responsibility in days before the match and the pocket cigarette lighter, when along with a water supply a central fire was maintained for the convenience of villagers.

The sacred Vestal fire symbolized the unbroken continuation of the life of the state, and the duty of watching the fire was assigned to unmarried women, exalted in their maidenhood as individuals of esteem and respect, freshness and purity. These women pledged commitments of thirty years and took strict vows of chastity. For this and the fulfillment of other duties, like praying daily for the welfare of the Roman state, Vestal Virgins were accorded great privileges. They enjoyed the honors of semi-royalty, and were given the best seats at theaters and forums. Predictably, their attendance was excluded at nude athletic contests.

Romans too had their version of this "custody-of-the-eyes" prescript. Furthermore, woe to those Vestal Virgins who violated their vows of chastity. They were buried alive at a spot near the Porta Collina known as the "Campus Sceleratus."

The Catholic Church went to other kinds of extremes in its exaltation of virginity.

John Deedy

Taking the Vow

By the fourth century, mention is found in Christianity of a virginity specially consecrated to God (*virgo Deo dicta, famula Dei*), and the Council of Elvira in Spain (c. 306) was imposing canonical penalties on virgins who "consecrated themselves to God" but were unfaithful to their "pact of virginity."

In those early centuries it was not unknown for children to be vowed to virginity before birth or very soon afterwards. By the same token, vows of virginity were accepted from girls as young as ten and twelve years old, and a liturgy evolved for their acceptance. The liturgy endured.

Indeed, the Third Lateran Council of 1179 not only ratified the concept of a consecrated Christian virginity, but authorized the consecration of virgins on all Sundays and, with permission, on other special occasions. According to official rubrics, the ritual was to take place during the celebration of mass. After certification of the worthiness of the candidates, the women were to be asked if they were resolved to persevere in holy virginity. Together they were expected to respond *volumus,* "we are." Each candidate was then to confirm her pledge individually, after which the Litany of the Saints was to be sung "with a double invocation on behalf of the virgins present": *Ut praesentes ancillas benedicere . . . sanctificare digneris,* "That thou wouldst vouchsafe to bless and sanctify thy handmaidens here present." The hymn "Veni Creator" was to follow, after which the consecrated virgin received the veil and donned specially designed and blessed clothing. The ritual then closed with the reading of a lengthy anathema aimed against anyone who would seduce the consecrated virgin or lure her away from her holy commitment.

From the beginning, consecrated virgins wore modest dresses of dark or somber color. Though required to lead an ascetic life of prayer and be available for one form of work or another, early on they were not required, nor even expected, to retreat behind convent walls. It was only after the eighth century that enclosure became the rule for consecrated virgins in the service of God. The movement of women to convents parallelled the monastic development involving men practicing a similar sexual continence and religious asceticism. The male movement evolved, of course, into monasticism; the female counterpart became the religious sisterhood.

Taking shape at the same time in the church was a verbal terminology distinguishing between female and male abstainers from carnal pleasures and sexual relations, one that endures to this day. Males practicing "perfect chastity" would be commonly known as celibates, the women as virgins. Incidentally, on the matter of virginity, the church never insisted on absolute "bodily or physical integrity" of the female individual. Saint Jerome wrote in his twenty-second Epistle to Saint Eustochium: "I tell you without hesitation that though God is almighty, he cannot restore a virginity that has been lost." Nonetheless, the church has always realized that so-called virginal "integrity" could be lost involuntarily, as by accident, surgical operation or rape. That recognition opened moral theology to an understanding of virginity as being most essentially an act of the will, in contradistinction to the mere existence of an accidental bodily element or tissue.

With the twin development of those separate female and male monastic traditions, however, an unusual practice took shape both in the Western and Eastern churches: the cohabitation under one roof of clerics and monks with consecrated virgins. The "pretext," to use the *New Catholic Encyclopedia*'s word, was to assist and protect the women. The arrangement was questionable from the start and inevitably it led to abuses. According to the *Encyclopedia,* the clerics or monks were sharing not only the houses, but also the lives of the virgins. This produced strong condemnations by bishops, preachers such as John Chrysostom (c. 347-407), and local church councils. The end result was the development of ecclesiastical legislation aimed at protecting the virtue of virgins, while assisting them in their fidelity to their holy commitments. At the time most women of consecrated virginity were still living in the world.

That necessary disciplinary adjustment further established women of consecrated virginity as more than some new kind of holy person in the church's ambit. In time they would emerge, almost literally, as "spouses of Christ," individuals in whom was realized a station and holiness parallel to the nuptial union of Christ and his church.

This concept of spousehood was dramatized in the

veiling of the woman at the time of her formal consecration. The veiling, a ceremony actually borrowed from the Roman ritual of marriage, symbolized the mystical marriage of the consecrated virgin with Christ. In the Middle Ages, a ring and a crown were added as further symbols of this mystical union. So serious was the church about the reality of this spousehood that subsequent unauthorized marriage on the part of a consecrated virgin was actually considered an act of bigamy. The bigamy label was assigned by the Council of Ancyra in 314. Earlier (c. 306), the Council of Elvira in Spain imposed its own severe penalties on virgins "who have consecrated themselves to God," then were unfaithful to their "pact of virginity." The women were excommunicated. Those who repented were allowed to receive communion only at the end of their lives.

The Office but Not the Title

The church dealt firmly with its women under vows, yet it honored them, and actually allowed room for some to achieve large measures of power and independence.

In medieval times, it was not unknown for abbesses of large and important communities of women to exercise authority rivaling that of bishops and abbots. The condition was sufficiently widespread for the Capitularies of Charlemagne to sound a warning. Particularly reprobated were "certain abbesses who, contrary to the established discipline of the Church of God, presume to bless the people, impose their hands on them, make the sign of the cross on men, and confer the veil on virgins, imploring during that ceremony the blessing reserved exclusively to the priests.''

The paradox is that, though the church honored its virgins and considered many of them to be saints, it initially tended to reserve its highest recognition, that of sainthood, limiting it to women who were martyrs—persons such as the two Saint Felicitys, and Saints Perpetua, Agnes, Agatha and Lucy—or women held by legend to be martyrs although not actually such, among them Saints Pudentiana, Praxedes, Sabina and Cecelia. That would change in due course, and many women would be raised to the honors of the altar whose reputation for holiness and sanctity was based on spiritual leadership and achievement other than martyrdom. So matters improved in that regard for women of the church. There was devolution, however, on the issue of ministry.

In the early centuries, women of holy state, ''widows'' and ''virgins,'' served in various ministries of the church, and their roles and responsibilities were such that in some places they were actually regarded as members of the clergy. These women prayed for the church; they catechized, assisted at baptisms, visited the sick and the needy, and brought the Eucharist to the homebound. In Celtic countries in the fifth and sixth centuries, ''virgins'' and ''widows'' also assisted in the celebration of masses and in presenting the chalice to communicants, practices which were said to have shocked Gallican bishops.

There is little evidence of women being ordained priests in those years, at least as priesthood is understood today. But women did serve as deaconesses, and as such came to constitute a distinct ministerial group, if not an official separate clerical order. A prayer for the ritual of deaconesses is in fact found in the first *Apostolic Constitutions:* "Look now, Lord, upon this handmaid of yours, called to the work of your service, and send upon her the rich and abundant gift of your Holy Spirit." The ritual sometimes included the laying on of hands, the key element in the ordination of priests. Once "ordained," deaconesses were subject to the usual clerical disciplines as their male counterparts.

Progress for women in the church's ministerial tradition came to a halt, however, with the Council of Nicaea of 325, the Fathers ruling that female deacons were not to be ranked as clergy, but rather as laity engaged in the performance of special missions of service. The ruling effectively killed the tradition of a female diaconate. After the fifth century, one finds little evidence of deaconesses still being around in the Western church, and they were gone entirely from the Eastern church after the sixth century.

Modern Suffrage

The matter of women and the clerical ministry would remain pretty much a dead issue until the twentieth century, when it would resurrect in the context of reform possibilities opened up by Vatican II.

Suddenly there was talk once again of women deacons, and some even dared speak of women priests in the church's not too distant future. The Vatican moved

John Deedy

quickly to control the situation. In 1977 it issued the 6,000-word document, "On the Question of the Admission of Women to the Ministerial Priesthood," the main point of which was that because a priest "truly acts in the place of Christ," there should be a "natural resemblance" between Christ and his minister in keeping with the "sacramental sign" of holy orders. Gender qualification, in a word, was an absolute prerequisite for ordination to the priesthood: one had to be a man.

That same Vatican document, however, did leave open "for the future" the question of women being ordained as deacons, an intriguing possibility which, if it materialized, would return female ministry to what it must have been in the fifth and sixth centuries. Though there has been virtually no official exploration of that opening, other forces have been at work to bring about much that would result from a female diaconate.

Between the twin pressures of feminism and decreasing male vocations to the priesthood, there has been a marked broadening of ministerial activity on the part of women, among other things as acolytes (altar girls), as lectors, as eucharistic ministers, as catechizers (teachers in religious education programs), as spiritual counselors (including in seminaries), as preachers (where permitted), as diocesan officials, as administrators of parishes. Women are in fact so involved in the church's ministries that the situation cannot be much different from what it was before the church's first general council ruled that women, specifically deaconesses, were not to be counted among members of the clergy.

RETROSPECT

But further change of a dramatic kind—the official ordaining of women deacons, for instance—is not likely soon. Indeed, it seems especially unlikely during the pontificate of John Paul II, who has demonstrated little flexibility on the issue of women and the ministry. To be sure, women eucharistic ministers, who were barred from papal liturgies during John Paul II's 1979 visit to the United States, were allowed on his return in 1987. On the other hand, the 1987 Synod of Bishops over which John Paul II personally presided—a synod focused on the role of the laity—could not even bring itself to recognize officially what it obviously acquiesces to unofficially: the presence of female acolytes as servers at the altars of churches throughout much of the world.

Changing Morality

Apart from the issue of female ministry, there is for the official church the problem of maintaining among the faithful popular regard and acceptance of the concept of consecrated virginity as an object of superior good, a state even more excellent than that of marriage.

This may be a large task, but it is not a new problem. In the sixteenth century, the Council of Trent had to confront the contention of Protestant reformers that the conjugal state was to be preferred to virginity or celibacy, a contention which Trent rejected out of hand ("the conjugal state is not to be preferred to the state of virginity, and it is better and more felicitous to remain in virginity or celibacy than to be bound in marriage"). Similarly, in our own century, Pope Pius XII felt himself compelled to speak out against the tendency to exalt the beauty and dignity of marriage at the expense of consecrated virginity, and did so, stressing at the same time that virginity and celibacy were not obstacles to the development and flowering of the individual (*Sacra Virginitas,* encyclical on consecrated virginity, March 25, 1954; "Allocutions to the International Congress of Superiors General of Orders and Congregations of Women," September 15, 1952).

The difference between then and now is the pervasive eroticism of society, and the parallel development of a totally new value system with respect to sexual mores. For many persons, female as well as male, virginity has passed from being the proud and cherished virtue that it once was—the great gift of integrity of body that a woman carried to her marriage bed and the consecrated virgin to religious life and her spouseship with Christ. Many, in fact, consigned virginity, consecrated or not, to the category of behavioral, of not also moral, anachronism. The church does not accept this thinking, of course. It honors virginity, and it continues to celebrate consecrated virginity as a state in life ordered to a divine good.

The old *Catholic Encyclopedia* (1913) says flat out that "perfect integrity of body, enhanced by a purpose of perpetual chastity, produces a special likeness to Christ, and creates a title to one of the three 'aureolae,' which theologians mention. According to the teaching of St. Thomas . . . these 'aureolae' are particular rewards added to the essential happiness of eternity, and are like so many laurel wreaths, crowning three conspicuous victories, and three special points of resemblance to Christ: the victory of the flesh in virginity, the victory over the world in martyrdom, and the victory over the devil in the preaching of the truth."

The *New Catholic Encyclopedia* (1967) is just as lavish in its entry on virginity, and considerably more presumptive about motivation and psychological effect: "Virginity is inspired above all by charity. The virgin vows to Christ an exclusive love that admits of no sharing, and because of this she may call herself spouse, according to a theme already used in the Canticle of Canticles and by the Prophets, and which is adopted and developed in the whole of monastic and spiritual tradition. In this there is no element of unhealthy compensation for a grudgingly accepted chastity or for repressed sexuality. All must be raised to the level of the spirit and of charity. Without an increasingly limpid and pure charity, virginity would in fact involve a risk of repression, or desiccation of the heart. With charity, which it requires and develops, it is an occasion of growth, and brings about a remarkable equilibrium of the affections. Moreover, inspired by charity, virginity disposes toward a mystical union, which is the supreme fruit of charity."

The Future of Chastity

For many reasons, some personal, others vocational, the life of consecrated virginity to Christ does not have the appeal at the present time that it had for centuries. Obviously, many do not regard it as a necessary element in the ordering of an apostolate life or career.

It is, of course, pious rationales of yesterday which are being put to the test today, not so much by secular society—psychiatrists, psychologists, practitioners of the new morality, and the like—but by the very ones who were once open to the logic of those rationales and receptive to their messages; namely, idealistically motivated, devout young Catholic women.

The evidence is in the numbers. Many women have left the convents; fewer are entering them. Between 1966 and 1981, the number of religious sisters dropped twenty-five percent worldwide. In the United States, the figure was thirty-one percent, six points higher than for the rest of the world. In 1965 there were 179,954 sisters and nuns in the United States; in 1989, the number was 104,419, a loss of 75,535. It is a situation which has caused major apostolic and human problems. For one thing, there are fewer persons to continue Catholic apostolates traditionally associated with women religious—teachers in parochial schools and nurses in Catholic hospitals being two of them. For another, the absence of new vocations has created a marked generational imbalance within religious orders of women. In many, indeed most, communities of women religious, the median age of the members is now 62 and 63 years; in a few it rises to 68. Some sisterhoods have virtually become communities of geriatrics, where the care of older members, if not the dominant activity of the membership, is so consuming as to occupy disproportionate amounts of the time and energy of those of younger years.

None of this means that consecrated virginity of a religious kind is in its death throes. Vocations to female religious life, and therefore to consecrated virginity, are not likely to disappear completely and forever. To begin with, virginity as a state of life out of religious motivation is not some Christian invention. Pagan society, as noted, honored female virginity, and though the Old Testament regarded marriage as the normal state for the average man and woman, it nonetheless so respected virginity as to specify harsh penalties for those who trivialized it. For instance, Deuteronomy tells us (22:23-24) that a man and a maiden betrothed to another could be stoned to death for engaging in illicit sexual intercourse—she for not crying out for help; he for violating his neighbor's committed one.

Esteem for virginity mingles with the story of history itself, so much so that in the unlikely event the chapter closed entirely on religious sisterhoods as a prominent part of the church's life, it would not necessarily follow that consecrated virginity would become a total casualty in the process. One has always found numbers of Catholic women choosing to live lives of consecrated virginity in the world, today for instance as members of secular institutes—communities whose members observe the evangelical counsels (voluntary poverty, perfect chastity and obedience) and do apostolic works of special kinds in measure to their talents and the opportunities presented. Secular institutes are not religious communities, and they're probably not the future of the church. However, in their commitment to the evangelical councils, they are witness that historic Christian values have enduring qualities, including that of consecrated virginity.

There are other examples as well. Vatican Council II declared in its Dogmatic Constitution on the Church that the holiness of the church is fostered in a special way by those who "devote their entire lives to God alone with undivided heart" (42). That's one more likely reason why some will forever receive the divine gift of consecrated virginity.

9.

RELIGIOUS GARB:
The Habit of the Habit and Other Things

Decorum and Distinction

IN a postmortem on Chicago's late Cardinal John Patrick Cody, A.E.P. Wall, one-time editor of the *Chicago Catholic* remarked that "to Cardinal Cody, one of the biggest problems in the world was priests who appeared in public without the Roman collar."

In a time and place where so many problems of more substantial kind were facing the church and its leaders, Cardinal Cody's punctiliousness appears preposterous. . . . Except at a similarly momentous time in church history, also soon after Vatican Council II, I can recall the upset of Pittsburgh's late Bishop John J. Wright, himself subsequently a cardinal, when a new priest's picture appeared in the *Pittsburgh Catholic* during my tenure as editor, with the cleric wearing regular shirt collar and tie rather than Roman collar.

The church attaches enormous importance to the wearing of symbolic articles of clothing by those in religious life, and not just on the part of men. Pope John Paul II's repeatedly stated preference that women religious dress as women religious demonstrates the compre-

143

hensiveness of the gender concern. As priests are expected to wear the Roman collar in the normal course of their religious lives, so are women expected to wear the habit traditional to their order, along with such other articles that their rule might call for, like veil, rosary beads, scapular, cross, ring, etc.

Incidentally, the word "habit" in context of religious garb derives from botany and zoology, where the term is used to describe the instinctive actions of animals and tendencies of plants, and also the manner of growth or external appearance of an animal or plant. From the latter usage of the word—that is, to describe external appearances—derives its application to fashions in clothing. A lady's riding dress thus became known as her riding habit; similarly, the garment adopted by members of a religious order became known as his or her religious habit.

The church expects its professed members to dress distinctively. Today the church pleas and exhorts on the point of religious dress. Yesterday it didn't fool around. It not only insisted that religious dress in a manner setting themselves apart from secular persons; it attached severe penalties to those who took the discipline lightly. Pope Boniface VIII (1294-1303) met the matter head on. He issued the bull *Ut Periculosa,* leveling an excommunication *latae sententiae* (automatically incurred) on those who triflingly laid aside their religious habit.

That document remained the basis of church law on the matter of religious garb into modern times. As recently as 1913, the old *Catholic Encyclopedia* said bluntly in its entry on religious life, "if an order has a special habit, the members are strictly bound to wear it, and if any of them puts it off without good cause, he incurs an excommunication not reserved." The *Encyclopedia*'s entry cited *Ut Periculosa* as basis for its statement.

To be sure, the regulation applied directly to priests and monks professed under solemn vows, as distinct from lay brothers and sisters and nuns professed under simple vows, who were not so severely bound, then or now. Furthermore, excommunications were hurled about somewhat casually in the old days, and the fact that this particular excommunication was "not reserved" meant that it was of minor class, so to speak, and fairly simple to remit. In practice, any confessor could absolve from a nonreserved excommunication. Nonetheless, the mere threat of the imposition of penalties on people in religious life for not wearing the prescribed religious habit underscored the significance attached by the church's leadership to the formalities of proper religious dress. Persons in religious life were expected—indeed, mandated—to wear distinctive clothing, and most especially when appearing in public.

Establishing the Tradition

Monks of the very early church did not wear a habit or clothing of a special kind, one reason being that a garb that differed markedly from the dress of the rest of the populace could have subjected them to vituperation or worse.

John Deedy

The fact is that clergy did not begin to dress differently until the fourth century and the reign of the Roman emperor Constantine. The change in dress was largely connected with Constantine's conveying to bishops the authority to act as judges in civil suits. With that authority went to bishops the privilege of wearing ceremonial clothing appropriate to their new station, including cape, head covering, footwear and ring. Since civil judges sat on thrones and were entitled to further honors, such as processional introductions and incensing with fragrant smoking substances, so also now were bishops.

The practices quickly became incorporated into the liturgy, and they continued as established Christian traditions after Constantine and the fall of Rome. Furthermore, there would be embellishments with the years, and expansion of honors of dress to lower clergy and others in religious vows, including consecrated virgins. Individual communities would develop clothing attires peculiar to their institute. But the latter change did not come overnight. In 428 Pope Celestine I (422-432) reprimanded those who sought to introduce the habit as distinctive garb for the clergy of Gaul.

The trend toward distinctive dress, however, was not to be stemmed, and in the fifth century, ordinary clerics were wearing a long robe (cassock) as a symbol of their special status, rather than the short tunic that was common dress of the time. The development of distinctive attires for those in religious life led inevitably to the parallel development of special dress for the celebration of specific liturgical rites. Nothing would be more immediately affected than the mass, the most significant of liturgies. No longer would it be a ceremony celebrated informally in everyday clothing. Solemnity of dress came to be expected, and by the ninth century the rubrics called for an elaborate assortment of vestments. Guiding protocols by then was *Admonito synodalis,* a document of obscure and uncertain origins, but a governing code nonetheless. Among much else, *Admonito synodalis* dictated that the priest at mass was to wear an amice, alb, cincture, maniple (since discontinued), stole and chasuble—all specially blessed, of course, before being first put into use.

These mass vestments are piously said in many histories to date from apostolic times. The truth is that most were introduced well after the Apostles had gone to their respective rewards. Further, though a religious significance was claimed for each of these vestments, in some cases the claim seems to have been overstated. The use of at least a few of the vestments derived from practical and utilitarian considerations having little to do with the religious or the spiritual.

Until relatively recent years special prayers were said as the priest donned the vestments of the mass. Each article of liturgical attire had its own prayer, and prompt cards were commonly tacked to vesting cases in church sacristies for clergy who did not have the prayers committed to memory. The prayers, stylistically stilted and painfully archaic, fell eventually into disuse. The general rubrics of the Missal still called for their saying in 1956, according to a study by Father J.B. O'Connell, but the prayers were not even alluded to in the revised 1969 sacramentary or

John Deedy

guide to the celebration of the mass, based on the apostolic constitution *Missale Romanum* of Pope Paul VI. That sacramentary is still in use. It merely specifies what vestments are to be worn at mass, and continues: "The priest and the ministers put on their vestments and, when the people are assembled, go to the altar. . . ."

Vestments of the Mass

The history of the vestments of the mass provides an interesting glimpse into the evolution of ecclesiastical attire, how church officials—or those celebrating the Eucharist, at an rate—came to dress the way they do, and for what holy or plainly secular reasons.

Taking each of the mass vestments in order (and including for quaintness sake the English for the old vesting prayers), they are:

Amice: A piece of white linen cloth covering the priest's shoulders and throat. In the old days it was donned with the prayer, "Place, O Lord, on my head the helmet of salvation, that I may overcome the assaults of the devil." The amice served vague purposes of vanity, like hiding the bare throat and providing a neat, smooth base for the vestments to be worn on top. But the real reason for its adoption seems to have been utilitarian. The amice protected the more beautiful and expensive exterior vestments against—well, if one must know, ring around the collar.

Alb: A long, white linen tunic with close-fitting sleeves. Worn over the priest's regular clothing, it

148

reaches to the ankles, and was donned with the prayer: "Purify me, O Lord, from all stain and cleanse my heart, that washed in the Blood of the Lamb, I may enjoy eternal delights." The origin of its use is somewhat vague. The alb could derive from the clothing of the Jewish priesthood, specifically the kethonet, the white linen tunic mentioned in Exodus 28:39. On the other hand, a white linen tunic was part of everyday secular dress for early Romans and Greeks. As worn by the priest, the alb came to symbolize self-denial and chastity. By the year 818, the alb was considered a formal article of attire for the mass.

Cincture: This is the cord or girdle with tassled ends, which is worn around the waist. It was fastened in days of yore to the words, "Gird me, O Lord, with the cincture of purity, and quench in my heart the fire of concupiscence, that the virtue of continence and chastity may remain in me." Though considerable liturgical significance is read into the wearing of the cincture, and though some religious orders once industriously promoted the wearing of cinctures (Cord of Saint Francis, Girdle of Saint Augustine, etc.) as a profession of allegiance to a particular institute, the reality is that the cincture was adopted for the pragmatic purpose of confining the loose-flowing alb. It enabled the wearer to move about more freely. The cincture has been used liturgically since the ninth century, but probably saw its most useful service in the sixteenth century, when voluminous garb was the vogue and some albs had a circumference of seven yards.

Maniple: This was the ornamental narrow strip of

cloth that the priest at mass wore on his left arm, and which was fixed in place with the vesting prayer, "Let me deserve, O Lord, to bear the maniple of tears and sorrows, so that one day I may come with joy into the reward of my labors." Originally, the maniple was a cloth of fine quality for the wiping away of perspiration, but that usage ended as the maniple grew elaborately decorative and took on the colors of the liturgical season.

Once upon a time the maniple was the liturgical sign of the subdiaconate, and one was placed on the subdeacon's arm by the bishop at the time of his ordination as subdeacon. The subdiaconate was suppressed as a separate clerical order during the liturgical revisions of 1971 and 1972, but the maniple was gone before then. It was eliminated during the vestment modifications of the 1960s.

Stole: This is the long silk band, sometimes heavily embroidered, which fits around the neck and is crossed over the breast of the priest. Traditionally, the priest kissed the stole before putting it on and recited the prayer, "Restore to me, O Lord, the state of immortality which was lost to me by my first parents, and although unworthy to approach thy sacred mysteries, grant me nevertheless eternal joy."

Some trace the stole to the Jewish praying mantle. There is also speculation that the stole is the remnant of a more elaborate vestment that disappeared, leaving only the trimming. There are various other theories. What is agreed is that the stole is one of the chief liturgical vestments. It is the symbol of authority, the mark of office of deacons, priests and bishops (though not at the same time a mark of parochial jurisdiction). The stole is mentioned in council proceedings of the fourth and fifth centuries, and so dates from at least that time. The stole was once such a remarkable badge of honor that priests of the Frankish Empire were directed to wear it constantly, and particularly when traveling.

Chasuble: This is the most conspicuous and colorful of liturgical vestments. It is worn over all the other liturgical vestments, and when vesting prayers were in vogue it was put on with the prayer, "O Lord, who has said, 'My yoke is sweet and my burden light,' grant that I may carry it so as to obtain thy grace." It is the liturgical vestment with the least question as to origin. The chasuble derives from secular attire common to the early Roman Empire. Liturgically, it was the equivalent of the priest's best suit, the garment reserved for special occasions, and thus the mass. The vestment's name came from its shape. The chasuble was a square or circular piece of cloth, with a hole in the center through which the head passed. When the arms hung down, the vestment covered the whole body. The appearance then was of a cottage or little house (*casula*), complete with chimney hole. *Casula* evolved to "chasuble."

The chasuble tended to take on great weight as heavily embroidered brocades, jewels and other decorations were added to it. Chasubles took on such weight, in fact, that deacons and subdeacons were ceremonially assigned to roll back or hold up the flaps in order to relieve the weight of the vestment on the priest's shoulders and arms. Eventually the chasuble was lightened and stream-

151

lined, principally by paring away shoulder areas and opening up the sides. It thus became more manageable— or endurable. Chasubles come now in a variety of styles and weights. Still, they have retained much of their traditional shape. They also come in colors appropriate to the liturgical season.

Clothes for Every Day

The vestmental history of the church did not end with the dress rubrics relating to the mass, or with the decreeing of clothes to be worn at other ecclesiastical liturgies.

Those in religious life were to dress distinctively even aside from ceremonial occasions. Clothes make the man, they say. In the church, the intention was that clothes should identify the man—and the woman—religious. It is still the case.

As religious communities multiplied, each tended to adopt a distinctive garb, generally a modest, somber costume of the period of its founding. Monks and mendicant friars, for instance, put on hooded cloaks, the hooded cloak being a popular article of clothing in the Middle Ages with both men and women, religious and lay. Sisters and nuns followed suit (pardoning the pun).

In the secular world, clothing fashions change from season to season. It did not happen that way in the church, although at various times in history forces did come into play to bring about certain changes in the dress of some religious. For instance, in some countries restyling of religious dress became necessary as the countries secularized and enacted civil laws restricting the wearing of religious garb in public. Affected most immediately were priests, who tended in earlier days to move about more freely in public than religious women. Those who wore distinctive habits or the identifiable garb of a religious community had to change wardrobes. Long cassocks and flowing hooded robes by law had to be left in the rectory or behind monastery walls. Simpler, less conspicuous dress became the style—such as, for men, the black suit and Roman collar.

This attire—black suit and Roman collar—in time became the trademark of the priest, even in countries where they were legally free to wear whatever they pleased. A decorous public attire just seemed more proper for clerics in the pluralistic society and in countries where the Catholic population was small and scattered. The United States was no exception. The decree was subsequently eased, but in 1884 the Third Plenary Council of Baltimore directed religious-order priests to leave their habits at home and dress as did diocesan priests when they went out in public—in other words, in black suit and Roman collar.

It was not precisely the same with religious communities of women. By and large they tended to retain, year in, year out, the clothing styles of their origins, with the result that, like the vesting prayers of the priest, the garb of sisters and nuns too became archaic—although picturesquely so in some instances, as with that of the Sisters of

John Deedy

Charity, with their great white-linen winged caps, called "cornettes." That costume of the Sisters of Charity, incidentally, came about in manner similar to the costumes, or habits, of other religious orders. It duplicated dress of the day, in this instance that of peasant women of the neighborhoods of Paris of 1633. That was the period of the order's founding.

As years passed to decades and decades to centuries, many sisters' costumes virtually cried aloud for updating. Rome took note in time, and in the 1960s counseled a "prudent modification" of the garb of the sisterhoods, in keeping with what the *New Catholic Encyclopedia* called "the demands of reason, hygiene and well-ordered charity." There was also the auxiliary consideration of vocations. Instead of influencing respect for the religious state, the *Encyclopedia* explained in probable echo of Rome's logic, "outmoded garb serve[d] to alienate modern youth from entering religious life and provide[d] occasions of ridicule to the wearers."

Rome's instruction did indeed result in a modernization, tasteful and stylish, of the garb of religious women. But as happens so often in the process of change, there were accompanying developments producing effects of wholly unforeseen and unwanted kind, at least for some of the parties involved. For Rome, in this instance, it was the wholesale shedding of the religious habit, including veil, by sisters and nuns in favor of regular street dress, usually with only some small and generally unobtrusive object, like a lapel cross, being worn to identify them as members of a religious order.

RETROSPECT

Fashions and Statements

The shedding of the habit by many sisters and nuns has been decried by some church leaders and bewailed by many lay Catholics.

Whether their criticisms and laments are justified or not, this much seems certain: the putting aside of the veil and religious habit is not regarded as frivolous by those taking this step. On the contrary, in general they see the action as one breaking down barriers of communication and promoting greater apostolic cooperation. As one religious sister is on record:

"I was one of the first persons in my community to experiment with going without a veil. That was back in the late 1960s, early 1970s, right after we had changed from the traditional habit. At the time I was in a parish that was more progressive, more forward-looking than most in terms of being inserted into the secular life of the area. I was there, incidentally, as coordinator of religious education. I worked ecumenically, and I began to perceive the veil [and the formal habit] as a barrier to people, including people in the parish. It did not encourage the kind of lay independence and maturity which I felt we had to be encouraging in parish life."

What happened when she took the veil off and left the habit back in the convent? She and a colleague surveyed people and found that many related to them much more freely. "It seemed to foster a sense of us all working together, rather than my being the boss and everyone having to do what I said."

John Deedy

Undoubtedly something of the same rationale is behind the shedding of the Roman collar by many priests. Perhaps simple personal comfort enters into the decision with some priests, just as with some religious women personal comfort accounts for their preference of civilian dress over the religious habit. Even so, there are also those considerations of closeness and communication that the sister spoke of. For there are occasions when barriers can be broken down and distances more easily closed, when the circumstances are unencumbered by possibly complicating conventions of dress; a college chaplain, for instance, at times might more easily communicate with students when out of Roman collar rather than when in one.

At the same time, however, it must be allowed that a readily identifiable religious dress can also be a bridge to people, opening or keeping open doors of communication that might otherwise shut tight.

It is one reason why religious garb will unquestionably remain a part of Catholic religious life, for men as well as for women. Another reason is that religious garb is more than some kind of dress identifying a member of a particular profession, like an engineer's cap identifies a trainman or a helmet a football player. Religious garb will survive as long as religious life itself, as it is an external, visible sign of the commitment and union which exist between Christ and his church, Christ and those vowed to his service.

It is a delusion, however, to expect the wearing of religious garb to be so unconditional as stated in the terms of

RETROSPECT

Boniface VIII's *Ut periculosa*. The religious garb is an increasingly optional item now for those in vows, men and women, and it looks as though nothing is likely to change that. *Ut periculosa* will be more and more ignored, or more particularly will be interpreted differently. The element of surprise in all of this is that the process will be dictated not so much from outside, but rather by elements within the church. The reason why is easy enough to fathom. The charism of dress is not only lost on present generations of Catholics, but with many Catholics is alien to their religious sensibilities.

How changed the situation! Once upon a time, the large problem for the church's leadership with respect to the habit and religious garb was that of individuals continuing to wear the attire of religious life after being disciplined and dismissed from good standing as religious. The official codes were oblique on the topic, but common opinion held that the dismissed religious lost the "privilege" of wearing the habit. Today religious in good standing have almost to be begged to wear the habit.

The conveying of the habit on an individual is a privilege now as much as it ever was, but is so regarded in different ways. Another set of values is in force. Religious garb and the habit are proud symbols of a religious belief and a life commitment. Still, it is doubtful that the day will ever return when they will be donned and by that very act become as much a part of the person as one's baptism. We live in a different age.

10.

FEAST DAYS, HOLY DAYS:
Now, As Not in the Beginning

Earth, Sun, Stars, Moon

THE TWO great feasts in the liturgical calendar are Christmas and Easter, and it might be presumed that if any two dates on the Christian calendar were fixed from the start, it is those marking, respectively, the birth of Christ and his Resurrection—the more so since without either of these feasts there would be no such thing as a Christian religion. The presumption is wrong. Both feasts fall on evolved dates.

The observance of Christmas on December 25 goes back no further than the fourth century, when the feast spread from Rome through the Western church. No one knew then, nor knows now, the precise day that Christ was born. December 25 was decided upon by the church partly to co-opt the Roman civil holiday commemorating the birthday of Mithra, the Unconquered Sun, patron of the imperial army. Because the Roman feast was occasioned by the winter solstice, the observance of Christmas on December 25 may be said to have been governed more by the distance of the sun from the celestial equator than by any message from heralds singing from on high —more by the sun's entering the sign of Capricorn than a star's fixing itself above a stable in Bethlehem on one particular day. Or was that star really Halley's comet speeding by? Astrologers calculate that the comet would have been observable around the year 12 B.C.

As for Easter, its date was not set until the first of the church's ecumenical councils, the Council of Nicaea in 325. Initially the feast was timed to coincide with the Jewish Passover festival, the early Christian instinct being, of course, strong to parallel the religious observances of other groups with feasts of Christian contexts. For the better part of two centuries there was great controversy about the date of Easter, until finally the Council of Nicaea connected it with a Sunday (because ancient Christians believed Christ rose from the dead on the first day of the week) and the vernal equinox (the time in spring when the sun crosses the plane of the earth's equator, making night and day all over the world of equal length).

Easter, it was decreed, would be the first Sunday after the first full moon of spring—meaning that Easter can occur as early as March 22 and as late as April 25. One purpose in settling a date for Easter was in order to coincide observance of the feast worldwide. It was several centuries, however, before uniformity was achieved in the West, and to this day certain Eastern churches mark Easter on a different date, in accordance with calendar traditions of their own. Once again, as with Christmas so with Easter: no one has the foggiest notion about its actual date of occurrence. Easter's date in Roman Catholicism is credited not to revelation, but to the science of astronomy.

John Deedy

In any instance, with the dates of Christmas and Easter firmly agreed upon, the Roman or Latin Rite could now give definitive shape to a liturgical calendar of movable and immovable feasts—that is, feasts which occur each year on the same date (immovable feasts) and feasts which fall on variable dates, depending upon the date of Easter or the calendar date of a Sunday (movable feasts). Among the first steps was the firm emplacement of the Christmas-related feasts of the Circumcision (now observed under the more euphonious title of the Solemnity of Mary, the Mother of God) and Epiphany, and the Easter-related feasts of the Ascension (forty days after Easter) and Pentecost (seventh Sunday after Easter).

By the fourth century, all six of these feasts were well-established observances, and the foundation was laid for a liturgical calendar whose complexity, even with periodic revisions, would surely astonish the apostolic fathers. Their liturgical calendar had centered largely on Sunday, the Lord's Day. It was, as the encyclopedias tell us, the earliest feast in the Christian calendar. It commemorated the Resurrection, and was highlighted with the celebration of the Eucharist. Coincidentally, the Sunday observance became the Christian fulfillment of the mandate of the third commandment of the Old Law, to keep holy the Sabbath day (Exodus 20:8-9).

Months of Sundays

When the liturgical calendar began to expand, the results were nothing short of mind-boggling.

RETROSPECT

Popes declared feasts, but so also did bishops, who then had the ecclesiastical right to establish feasts for those under their jurisdiction. Some did so with such abandon that, between the thirteenth and eighteenth centuries, there were dioceses with one hundred and more major annual feasts, counting Sundays. The multiplication of feasts was hailed in Christian quarters as demonstration of religious growth and of the comparative freedoms existing within the Christian church as contrasted to the more fixed traditions of Judaism and various pagan systems.

Still, the multiplication of feasts (the more solemn additionally involving vigils of preparation and octaves of celebration) presented very real social and economic complications, since so much personal and civil accommodation was necessitated. Since many religious feasts were increasingly observed as solemn holy days, the faithful in the normal course were required not only to attend mass, but also to abstain from servile labor. Further, shortly after his conversion, Constantine decreed that there should be no suits or trials in law on Christian feast days. The courts were not allowed to sit; also, businesses closed; civil life came to a standstill. The problem was, how could the routine work of society and church get done, how could commerce be transacted, with so many church feasts to be observed? How awkward was the situation? The Decree of Gratian (c. 1150) provided for forty-one feasts, besides diocesan patronal observances. The Decretals of Gregory IX (c. 1235) were even more expansive. They listed forty-five public feasts and holy days, which meant that there were eighty-five days when no servile work could be done and ninety-five days when no court sessions could be scheduled. In some places, the entire Easter octave, all eight days, and several days following Pentecost were times of solemn, Sabbath-like observance.

Various pressures of state eventually brought about a radical scaling back in the number of church feasts. But even before states moved in deciding what days should be observed as holidays within their jurisdictions, the church had acted on its own to bring the number of observances of solemn feasts within reason. It abrogated some feasts, and for others established a category known as "half holy days"—feasts on which persons were bound to hear mass, but were also permitted to perform so-called servile work. Similarly, beginning in the thirteenth century feasts were grouped into dignities of importance (*festum simplex, semiduplex* and *duplex*), a system further refined in 1893, when the church established categories of primary feasts (those commemorating the principal mysteries of faith or celebrating the death of a saint) and secondary feasts (those connected with a particular feature of a mystery, such as an apparition). Within those general classes of primary and secondary feasts, those of Christ took precedence, followed by those of Mary, the Angels, John the Baptist (for centuries his was one of the church's more important festivals), Saint Joseph, the Apostles and Evangelists, and the other saints. Distinctions of ritual and the proper observance for each of these feasts were spelled out in great minuteness in the breviary rubrics.

One reason for the overcrowding of the liturgical calendar was the growing popularity in the Middle Ages of Mary as a saint to be venerated alongside the Apostles and the martyrs. Until the middle of the seventh century, the Western church knew but one major Marian feast, the commemoration of Mary as the Mother of God, a feast observed on various dates of the Christmastide— December 18 in Spain; January 18 in Gaul and much of Western Europe; January 1 in Rome. Between the reigns of Popes Theodore I (642-649) and Sergius I (687-701), however, four new Marian feasts were added to the liturgical calendar: the Purification, February 2; the Annunciation, March 25; the Assumption, August 15; the Nativity, September 8. A trend was in process.

The Mary Cult

Many more Marian feasts were to follow over the years, some of universal appeal, but others of strictly regional character and attraction.

Among others, Marian feasts included the Visitation, July 2; the Commemoration of Our Lady of Mount Carmel, July 16; the Immaculate Heart of Mary, August 22; the Holy Name of Mary, September 12; the Seven Sorrows of Mary, September 15; Our Lady of Mercy, September 24; Our Lady of the Most Holy Rosary, October 7; the Presentation of Mary, November 21; the

John Deedy

Apparition of Our Lady of Lourdes, February 11. There were so many Marian feasts, in fact, that they came to comprise a separate liturgical category, divided into three parts roughly corresponding to stages of Mary's life and her devotional cult—specifically, Mary's maternity, stages of her life, and her attributes or interventions.

Not all Marian feasts, it should be said, met with universal acceptance. Both Saint Bernard and Saint Thomas Aquinas, for instance, "energetically opposed" the Feast of the Immaculate Conception (December 8), a feast of twelfth-century English origin, objecting on grounds that the privilege conceded Mary (her being born free of original sin) was irreconcilable with the doctrine of universal redemption.

Many Marian feasts have been suppressed in the liturgical reforms resulting from Vatican II. The Feast of the Holy Name of Mary, which was introduced into the Roman calendar in 1684 to celebrate the deliverance of Vienna from the siege of the Turks the year before, was dropped because it was thought the feast duplicated that of the birth of Mary. But others have also made their appearance, at least on regional liturgical calendars. In 1987, as an example, the bishops of the United States incorporated the Feast of Our Lady of Guadalupe into the American liturgical calendar as part of an effort to broaden the appeal of the church in the U.S. to Hispanics. The feast is marked on December 12.

The Feast of Our Lady of Guadalupe, like so many others, involves no ecclesiastical mandate requiring attendance at mass or other form of reverential observance. Actually, the number of such feasts is sharply limited in terms of what used to be the case.

Into the Modern Age

The simplification of the liturgical calendar began in earnest in the eighteenth century.

In 1642, Pope Urban VIII (1623-1644) had curtailed the right of bishops to establish new holy days, but there still remained on the liturgical calendar thirty-six major feasts and eighty-five days free from labor. In 1727, Benedict XIII (1724-1730) allowed the Spanish church a liturgical revision reducing the major feasts (full holy days) to seventeen, while making the other nineteen abrogated or half holy days necessitating only the hearing of mass. Holy day reductions followed elsewhere, so that by 1806 in France only four holy-day feasts were formally retained (Christmas, the Ascension, the Assumption and All Saints), with the others being transferred to Sunday. The same held true for Belgium and German areas on the left bank of the Rhine.

In England, Catholics since 1777 had observed as major feasts Easter and Pentecost (two days each), Christmas, New Year's Day, Epiphany, Ascension, Corpus Christi, Annunciation, Assumption, Saints Peter and Paul, Saint George and All Saints—twelve feasts involving fourteen days of observance. With the restoration of the hierarchy in 1850, however, the Annunciation, Saint George and the Mondays after Easter and Pentecost were dropped from official observance.

Other countries followed suit, though generally retaining feasts of national patronal significance—in contrast to England, where the patronal feast of Saint George was dropped out of a combination of ecumenical and diplomatic considerations. Scotland, for instance, kept the feast of Saint Andrew as a holy day, and Ireland kept that of Saint Patrick.

The church in the United States did not agree on a uniform schedule of holy-day feasts until the Third Plenary Council of Baltimore in 1884. Until then the holy-day observances had varied from diocese to diocese, region to region. In point of fact, the American church at one time observed fewer solemn feasts than Rome preferred, and the First Plenary Council of Baltimore (1852) was disposed to limit the number of holy days to four. Rome, however, in approving the Council's decrees exhorted the American bishops to consider adding the feasts of the Circumcision and the Immaculate Conception. The recommendation became American church law thirty-two years later when the Fathers of the Third Plenary Council of Baltimore decided that there would be six holy days of obligation in the American church: Christmas, December 25; the Circumcision, now the Solemnity of Mary, January 1; Ascension, to be observed on the sixth Thursday or forty days after Easter; Assumption, August 15; All Saints, November 1; Immaculate Conception, December 8.

The number could actually have been larger, as Rome at the time marked more than a dozen dates as feasts of "double precept"—feasts, that is, on which the hearing

166

of mass and abstention from work were expected. Even today the Western church carries on the official books four holy days of obligation which are not formally observed in the United States: the feasts of Epiphany, Corpus Christi, Saint Joseph and Saints Peter and Paul. The practice of the American church is to reschedule the feasts of Epiphany and Corpus Christi, when necessary, to coincide with a Sunday; the feasts of Saint Joseph and Saints Peter and Paul are observed on their respective dates (March 19 and June 29), but with no mass or other disciplinary obligation of a religious kind applicable to American Catholics.

Of course, Sundays technically may also be considered to be holy days, as they carry the obligation of attendance at mass and a reverential observance of the rest of the day.

In recent years, there has been considerable speculation that the number of holy days would be reduced once again. The American bishops at least twice entertained thoughts of trimming the number to three—either Christmas, the Solemnity of Mary and the Ascension; or Christmas, All Saints and the Immaculate Conception. Each time they were dissuaded by popular reaction, much of it generated by diocesan newspapers, which submitted the proposals to unscientific coupon-polls of their readership and predictably found opinion strongly against the move. (One observer said it was a little like taking a capital punishment poll among occupants of death row.)

The draft of the new 1983 Code of Canon Law would have reduced the number of holy days of obligation to two—Christmas and a Marian feast to be determined by individual national hierarchies. The proposal survived, in fact, to the document that went to the desk of Pope John Paul II for his signature of ratification. The pope's signature was considered so *pro forma* that discussion had passed in some places to what Marian feast was preferred as the holy day to be observed. John Paul II had other thoughts, however. He quietly struck the proposal from the document, and thus retained the number of holy days at the current figure: ten. Not everything is resolved, though.

From Sin to Circumstance

Considerable confusion occurs when a holy day of obligation falls on a Saturday and accordingly is back-to-back with the mandated Sunday observance.

New liturgical law allows one to fulfill one's Sunday obligation by attending a so-called mass of anticipation on Saturday. Does it follow that when Saturday is a holy day, one can fulfill both the holy day and Sunday obligations by attendance at one Saturday mass? The textbook answer is no, that two Saturday mass attendances would be necessary—one in the earlier hours marking the holy-day feast and one in the evening hours anticipating the Sunday obligation.

In some dioceses (in Ohio, Michigan and Hawaii), bishops have dispensed Catholics from attendance at a holy-day mass, not just when the feast falls on a Saturday, but on a Monday as well. The considerations are not alone the convenience of the faithful, but the pastoral problems of priests—some of whom may be in delicate health; others of whom must minister to more than one community, sometimes miles removed from one another. But whatever the individual priest's situation, a holy day's abutting a Sunday on the calendar can inject problems of endurance and other difficulties into the ordinary exercise of ministry.

How seriously was the holy-day obligation taken?

As late as 1961, the silver jubilee edition of Bishop Morrow's book *My Catholic Faith* (an edition carrying a ringing endorsement by Pope John XXIII's Secretary of State, Cardinal Tardini) was providing the following opening question and answer in Chapter 120, "First Commandment of the Church":

What sin does a Catholic commit who through his own fault misses mass on a Sunday or holy day of obligation?

A Catholic who through his own fault misses mass on a Sunday or holy day of obligation commits a mortal sin.

The church does not talk these days in such apocalyptic-like terms, nor does it go about providing strained qualifiers, like those of the Morrow book relating to the question above: "The precept is not binding on one who must care for the sick, or lives rather far from a church, or who has urgent work, or is ill." The church is today realistic enough to admit that it cannot precommit Almighty God and his judgment on anything so non-consequential as a disciplinary regulation pertaining to attendance at mass. The church contents itself with less harsh and more vague terminology, declaring that Catholics are "seriously obliged" to assist at mass on Sundays and on holy days. The church today, in sum, is restrained on the point rather than dogmatically presumptive and prejudgmental.

Furthermore, the church appears less anxious to multiply external acts of worship and devotion on the part of the faithful than it is to foster a truer, more solid appreciation of what the individual feasts and holy days represent. In this spirit, the Fathers of Vatican II urged "all concerned to work hard to prevent or correct any abuses, excesses, or defects which may have crept in here or there, and to restore all things to a more ample praise of Christ and of God" (*Dogmatic Constitution on the Church,* 51).

In due course Pope Paul VI issued his apostolic letter of February 14, 1969, *Mysterii paschalis celebrationem,* ordering a revision of the church's feast days and its calendar. Four broad principles were to be implemented: (1) histories of the lives of saints then mentioned in the liturgical calendar were to be subjected to critical study; (2) the number of devotional feasts was to be lessened; (3) only saints of universal significance were to be selected for inclusion on the universal calendar; (4) saints on the universal calendar were to be chosen from every race and period of history. Paul VI's direction was directly derivative of Vatican II's instruction that feasts of saints were not to take precedence over feasts which commemorated the mysteries of salvation.

Everyone knows what happened. Many saints dropped from sight, and from the public prayers of the church—

some because their authenticity came into doubt; others because their feasts were redundant on an already crowded liturgical calendar. Passing into obscurity, therefore, were such presumed heroes of Christian history as Canute, Philomena, Valentine, Alexius, Christopher and Eustace, though for convenience' sake their names and the names of others associated with churches, religious orders and popular devotional practices were allowed to remain on the books.

Keeping a Proper Perspective

Although enthusiasms produced saints that never were and feasts of no lasting significance, the rationale for honoring the heroes of Christian history with days and liturgies dedicated to them is as valid as ever.

Aside from the theological question of whether saints should be regarded as actual intercessors before the throne of God, individuals revered as saints almost invariably qualify as role models of one kind or another for those anxious for the preservation and continuum of particular saintly and heroic virtues. There can be problems, though, in particular instances, as the case of Saint Maria Goretti demonstrated. Her heroic virginity apparently was not so uncompromised as thought when the argument was being made for her canonization in the 1940s; she did yield on occasion in order "to save her life," according to a 1985 book, *Poor Saint, Poor Assassin: The Story of Maria Goretti,* by Giordano Bruno Guerri.

The book's revelations—presuming their accuracy—do not undermine the church's fundamental theology of sanctity. Nonetheless, it is hard to conceive of the church pushing ahead with her canonization if the allegations had surfaced at the time her cause was being processed. But then again, who knows? The church hesitated in the case of Father Junipero Serra, the eighteenth-century California missionary, then went ahead with his beatification, despite allegations that he herded Indians into forced labor at his missions and flogged them if they disputed church teachings. Originally it was thought that Junipero Serra would be beatified during Pope John Paul II's 1987 visit to the United States; the ceremony finally took place in Rome on September 25, 1988, church authorities in the meantime deciding that rather than oppressing Indians, Father Serra had protected them from exploitation by Spanish troops.

The Serra case, like the Goretti one, is something of an embarrassment; saints are supposed to be above suspicion as well as reproach. Philomena, Christopher and the others are embarrassments too, but nothing more than that. The misconceptions and pious misjudgments connected with them do not touch the core of faith, neither singularly nor in sum. Nor do they vitiate the legitimacy of feast days and of holy days. The church itself obviously understands this. Thus during the very postconciliar period that it was acting to correct abuses and defects in the liturgical calendar, it was also adding feast days which, though having the effect of making the calendar less Western—specifically less Western European—made it more authentically universal. This was achieved by such additions to the calendar as the feasts of Saint Charles Lwanga and Companions, the Ugandan martyrs (June 3), Saint Turibius of Mogrovejo (March 23), and Saint Paul Miki and Companions (February 6).

Is the church's calendar of feasts and holy days at last beyond revision and critique? Probably not. The only thing certain is that it is a better calendar of feasts and festivals than some reformers would bequeath us. At the time of the French Revolution and the Robespierre ascendency, for instance, it was proposed that the Christian calendar of feasts be scuttled in favor of one that replaced Sunday with a tenth day of rest (*Decadi*) and introduced feasts of "the Supreme Being and of Nature, of the Human Race, of the French People, of the Benefactors of Mankind, of Freedom and Equality, of the Martyrs of Freedom, of the Republic, of the Freedom of the World, of Patriotism, of Hatred of Tyrants and Traitors, of Truth, of Justice, of Modesty, of Fame and Immortality, of Friendship, of Temperance, of Heroism, of Fidelity, of Unselfishness, of Stoicism, of Love, of Conjugal Fidelity, of Filial Affection, of Childhood, of Youth, of Manhood, of Old Age, of Misfortune, of Agriculture, of Industry, of our Forefathers, of Posterity and Fidelity." Better a festival system which in its pious zeal raises up non-existent "saints" or non-qualifying "virgins and martyrs" than nonsense of that sort.

11.

DEVOTIONAL EXERCISES:
The Popular Encounters a Measure
of Unpopularity

Barometers of Change

IN THE language of ascetical writers of yesterday's church, devotion denotes an ardor of affection for the things of God.

Such at least is the definition provided by the old *Catholic Encyclopedia* (New York, 1913). This "ardor of affection" has traditionally expressed itself in exercises such as the rosary, novenas, stations of the cross, Benediction of the Blessed Sacrament, the wearing of scapulars, the bedecking of oneself with medals. Over centuries, devotions such as these developed as external practices of piety, the vehicles through which that ardor of affection for the things of God found life and achieved expression. No organized religion has developed a greater variety of devotions and devotional exercises than Roman Catholicism. The surprise for many is that the popular has suddenly become unpopular. Devotional exercises in Catholicism are on the wane. Or are they merely just momentarily out of fashion?

The best answer to that question is probably found in church history itself. Popular devotions have been forever coming and going. The devotion of the Nine First Fridays, for instance, hangs on, albeit somewhat tenuously. But does anyone remember the Six Sundays of Saint Aloysius, the Five Sundays of Saint Francis' Stigmata, the Seven Sundays of the Immaculate Conception, the Seven Sundays of Saint Joseph, the Ten Sundays of Saint Francis Xavier, the Ten Sundays of Saint Ignatius Loyola? Once upon a time each of these devotions enjoyed ecclesiastical authorization and a following to one degree of popularity or another, as each had a claim on the devotion of the faithful. Yet today they are as dead as the Latin language and the Latin mass. Long dead, in fact.

What Catholic history seems to be saying, in a few words, is that devotional exercises are subject to the swings of the devotional moods of the faithful. Thus, what is popular with Catholics of one generation will not necessarily be popular with Catholics of the next. The appeal of individual religious devotions, in short, is cyclical, and has ever been such.

The difference between past and present, however, is that it is not a particular devotional exercise or two that are passing from favor, or indeed several of them, but devotional exercises in general. Further, the phenomenon is occurring despite the counsel of the Council. Though the tone was cautionary, the Fathers of Vatican II supported devotional piety in the Constitution on the Sacred Liturgy, declaring: "Popular devotions of the Christian people are warmly commended, provided they accord with the laws and norms of the church, above all when they are called for by the Apostolic See. Devotions proper to individual churches also have a special dignity, if they are undertaken by the mandate of the bishops according to customs or books lawfully approved. But these devotions should be so drawn up that they harmonize with the liturgical seasons, accord with the sacred liturgy, are in some fashion derived from it, and lead the people to it, since the liturgy by its very nature far surpasses any of them"(13).

The cautionary note is understandable, for an historical paradox is connected to popular devotions. There's no secret involved here. Quite simply, popular devotions at times have severely distorted liturgical life in the church by diverting the piety of the faithful from more essential forms of worship, including even the mass. Nor were the Fathers of Vatican II the first to express concern in this regard. In the nineteenth century the Fathers of Vatican I voiced alarms about "comforting extravagances" of devotional life that official voices were lax in rebuking. Even pre-Vatican II catechetical primers, like Louis LaRavoire Morrow's *My Catholic Faith,* were warning as late as 1961 against devotional "exaggerations" that would make "piety ridiculous and subject it to contempt."

A Tradition of Excess

The problem of exaggerated popular devotions was not one merely of recent centuries—the problem went way, way back, with the exaggerations often taking on strange, exotic forms.

In the Middle Ages, for instance, devotion to the host reached such a peak of extravagance that persons would rush from church to church, mass to mass, not to assist at the ceremony itself, but to be present for the elevation of the host at the consecration. It was all a matter of timing. To view the elevated host was considered by many then to be the most vital element in attendance at mass. The belief was not only not discouraged; it was indulged. Indeed, some churches even went so far as to hang backdrops, like black velvet screens, in order to sharpen the outline of the host for viewers in the congregation. So intense, in fact, was devotion to the host that dying persons physically unable to receive a final communion—because of, say, vomiting or a swallowing impediment—were brought the host simply to gaze upon. It was a practice subsequently proscribed, along with a number of other devotional extravagances.

Yet devotion to the sacred host gave birth to many legitimate devotions, some of which are still a part of the church's liturgical life, however tangentially in more than one instance. Most notably there is Benediction of the Blessed Sacrament, a ceremony first recorded at Hildesheim, Germany, in the fifteenth century. With the church's eventual approving of Benediction of the Blessed Sacrament, a formal ritual of adoration existed for the sacred host. However, though this ritual satisfied the devotional needs of many persons, it also produced excesses of new kinds, so that eventually warnings had to be sounded against people's substituting Benediction for the mass and priests' giving Benediction greater solemnity than that accorded the mass.

Actually, all sorts of excesses were taking place. In 1947 the church canonized Louis-Marie Grignion de Montfort (1673-1716), the French preacher and missionary who founded two religious orders and wrote the famous tract *True Devotion to the Blessed Virgin.* The church approved Louis de Montfort's Act of Consecration, which was based on Mary's part in her son's word of redemption. However, the use of slave-chains as a symbol of Marian devotion had to be expressly forbidden, two popes speaking out on the matter.

Coincidentally, the same year that Louis de Montfort was canonized, Pius XII was issuing *Mediator Dei,* the encyclical which proclaimed that the liturgy must evolve with society. It was one of Pius XII's more important encyclicals, for it laid the groundwork for many liturgical innovations to occur later in his pontificate, such as evening masses for the convenience of the faithful, modifications in the eucharistic fast, and revisions in the Easter liturgies. Pius XII also addressed the topic of popular devotions in *Mediator Dei,* saying that instead of opposition between liturgy and personal piety, a union of the two should prevail—although, he cautioned, both archaeologism and novelty were to be reproved.

To be sure, archaeologism and novelty were twin contributors to devotional excesses. But other forces were also at work to channel the piety of the faithful in problem directions. Shut out from meaningful participation in the mass, for instance, many of the faithful cast about for alternative outlets for the expression of piety. One attractive devotional alternative turned out to be the novena.

Petitions and Favors

By the nineteenth century, the novena was a favorite devotional practice for millions worldwide.

To be sure, novenas spoke to the heart, and this accounted for a large measure of their popularity. But, as the liturgist Father H.A. Reinhold once pointed out, novenas also gave the congregation something that the mass which evolved out of the Middle Ages did not. It gave them a role to play. Novenas were full of action and response. They engaged the faithful as active participants. The faithful could understand the prayers. They were encouraged to raise their voices in song. They prayed aloud with the celebrant. In a word, they were involved in direct ways as the novena's action crossed and recrossed altar rails in a lively interchange of sound and thought. However unconsciously intended, it is the mood of those novenas of yesterday which the new mass attempts to recreate.

The novena is a popular Catholic devotion with a particularly fascinating evolutionary history. The devotion draws its name from the Latin word for nine, *novem,* and is basically a period of prayer extending over nine days or, alternatively, over a period of nine weeks. The novena practice is said to have originated with the Apostles and disciples as, along with Mary presumably, they awaited the coming of the Holy Ghost (Pentecost) after the Ascension. In any instance, the novena was to take many forms. In the Middle Ages, for instance, princes and the rich would provide in their wills for a novena of masses to be said on the nine days after their deaths. Later, the novena of preparation came into being as prelude to major feast days. This type of novena originated in France and Spain in connection with the observance of the Feast of Christmas, the nine novena days representing the nine months that Jesus spent in Mary's womb. Developing alongside that novena was the novena of prayer, a devotion that could be either public or private. Essentially this was a novena of petition, for the focus was on favors—personal favors, such as recovery of health. These novenas tended to become very specialized. For instance, one made a novena to Saint Hubert for cures against madness resulting from the bite of a mad dog or wolf, and to Saint Marcolf for recovery from scrofula, the disorder characterized by swelling and degeneration of the lymphatic glands. Finally came the indulgenced novena so popular with Catholics until very recently.

The indulgenced novena is really a nineteenth-century development. In the seventeenth century, Alexander VII (1655-1667) attached indulgences to a novena in honor of Saint Francis Xavier made in Lisbon, and in the eighteenth century Clement XI (1700-1721) indulgenced a novena in preparation for the Feast of Saint Joseph made in Rome's Church of Saint Ignatius. Other novenas were also approved, but as with the novenas cited, they were approved on a local basis. It was actually not until the beginning of the nineteenth century that novenas were universalized and one could gain a novena's indulgence by making it anywhere in the church. Indulgenced novenas rapidly multiplied in number and dedication. There were novenas in honor of the Archangels Michael, Gabriel and Raphael, the Infant Jesus, the Guardian Angel, Saint Stanislaus Kotska, Saint Vincent de Paul. Not forgotten either was Saint Joseph, the foster-father of Jesus. He was honored with two novenas, one memorializing his "seven sorrows" and the other his "seven joys." But the leader was the Blessed Mary, who entering the twentieth century had no less than eleven novenas going in her honor: those of the Immaculate Conception, Nativity of Mary, her Presentation in the Temple, the Annunciation, Visitation, Maternity of Mary, her Purification, her Seven Dolors, the Assumption, the Holy Heart of Mary, and the Holy Rosary.

But popular as novenas were to become, they were never the preeminent Catholic popular devotion. That distinction belongs to the rosary.

The Importance of Numbers

Catholic calendar art depicts the rosary as a devotion resulting from an apparition of Mary to Saint Dominic (1170-1221), founder of the Dominican Order.

The reality is that, rather than the rosary's being

handed ready-made to Dominic with a neat set of instructions for a formula of prayer, it went through a long period of evolutionary development, and was itself derivative of other devotions.

From time immemorial the devout employed a system to keep count of their prayers. They had to, as great importance was attached to saying a precise number of prayers. The fourth-century hermit Paul kept count with pebbles, casting one away as a prayer was finished, until at last there were none. (Paul had a regimen of three hundred prayers a day.) Moslems and Buddhists strung beads on strings to keep count of their prayers. So did Catholics of the early Middle Ages. But they didn't call their beaded strings "rosaries." Rather they called them "Paternosters," for on them the devout counted *Pater Nosters,* recitations of the Our Father. Keeping count was important, because particular circumstances dictated the saying of precise numbers of prayers. The "Ancient Customs of Cluny" (1096) required priests to offer mass and non-priests to say fifty psalms or fifty Our Fathers on the death of a colleague; Knights Templars who could not attend choir were required to say the Our Father fifty-seven times. Counters protected against confusion. What if a Knight Templar lost count and only said fifty-six of the prayers? Incidentally, the Hail Mary didn't figure early on as a common prayer of devotion, as it was not actually shaped into a prayer until the mid-1100s.

Returning to Saint Dominic: in his celebrated campaign against the Albigensian heresy, Dominic to be sure preached devotion to the rosary as an antidote to the distortions of good and evil that threatened religious and social fabrics of the time. However, the rosary did not originate with or through him. The practice of reciting fifty or one hundred and fifty *Ave Marias* or Hail Marys was familiar well before Dominic took on the Albigensians. The Marian rosary was at first a 150-prayer devotion, and it was not until some two centuries after Dominic's death that the rosary was subdivided for meditative purposes into three sections or sets of mysteries, each comprising fifty Hail Marys. The mysteries, of course, were the joyful, sorrowful and glorious, and today meditation on them is regarded as the essence of the rosary devotions itself.

The rosary was given great impulse into this century by Leo XIII, who devoted no less than fifteen encyclicals to the subject. One—*Octobri Mense* of September 22, 1891 —designated October as the month dedicated to the rosary. Bumped were the Guardian Angels. Subsequent popes have added their endorsements of the rosary devotion. And although the popularity of the rosary has waned in recent years, it is still common for Catholics to exit this world with a rosary entwined between their fingers, for that's the way most deceased Catholics are laid out in their caskets.

Stations and Hours

As with the rosary, so other popular devotions evolved, usually out of some other devotion, for the obvious reason that devotions have tended historically to spawn imitations.

The devotion of the Stations of the Cross, for instance, evolved out of the early Catholic emphasis on pilgrimages as both a religious exercise and a purifying activity. By making a pilgrimage one could free oneself from canonical penalties or, being free of sanction, one could gain graces to be applied to one's spiritual life. The Holy Land was the most revered of pilgrimage objectives, for there one could quite literally walk in the footsteps of Christ. In the early church the Holy Land was the primary objective of Christian pilgrims. But as Christianity spread westward across the Mediterranean world, the Holy Land grew further and further distant, becoming for millions an almost impossible objective. For it was travel by horse and foot then, not jet plane. Thus in the fifth century the Stations of the Cross came into use as a substitute, miniature pilgrimage, stations being sculpted, carved or painted on canvas to represent the holiest places of Jerusalem—those associated with Christ's passion and death. The number of stations varied greatly before being fixed at fourteen. The Stations of the Cross devotion received great impetus in the twelfth and thirteenth centuries thanks to popular piety focused on the passion. Still, it was not until the sixteenth century that Clement XII (1730-1740) codified the devotion, giving it pretty much the form known today, and not until the end of the seventeenth century that the stations were to be commonly found in parish churches.

RETROSPECT

By contrast, the Forty Hours devotion evolved out of what has been described as a "novelty" originating in Milan. There in the 1530s the custom was introduced of churches displaying the Blessed Sacrament in serial sequences of forty hours before relays of worshippers. The number forty was arrived at on the pious calculation that forty hours was the length of time Christ's body was in the tomb after the crucifixion. Forty hours also happened to be the length of time that the Blessed Sacrament was left in the Easter sepulchre in the Middle Ages.

Whatever the numerology, the idea of uninterrupted prayer before the exposed Blessed Sacrament quickly commended itself to officials in Rome, who saw it as an instrument for the preservation of peace in their time. The big threat was from the Turks to the east. Accordingly, Paul III (1534-1549) directed that the prayers of the Forty Hours devotion be offered in order to bring "to nought the efforts and machinations of the Turks who are pressing forward to the destruction of Christendom." Harboring the same worry, Clement VIII (1592-1605) called for "prayer . . . without intermission" in excoriating the "dreaded Turks, who in the heat of their presumptuous fury threaten slavery and devastation to all Christendom." In the United States, the father of the devotion was St. John Nepomucene Neumann. He introduced the Forty Hours on a diocesan-wide scale after becoming bishop of Philadelphia in 1852, and from there the devotion spread across the country until eventually almost every American parish had its annual observance.

Like other devotions, the Forty Hours has waned of late in popularity. Where it survives it is via truncated and greatly simplified observance.

Christ, His Wound

Another once extremely popular devotion was that of the Sacred Heart.

This devotion grew out of a fascination which hardly exists anymore—that with the twin natures of Christ, the human and the divine. However, unlike some devotions, which sprung to popularity overnight, devotion to the Sacred Heart evolved quite slowly and over long centuries. Its roots are actually back in patristic times, when early theological theory held the wound of Christ's side and the blood flowing therefrom to be a source or stream of divine and unending grace. Essentially, the devotion celebrated God's redemptive love through the humanity of Jesus, and by medieval times had seized on the heart as the human organ through which the devotion could be best expressed. In theory, the devotion could have glorified any part of Christ's body, but the heart commended itself, since as the battery of life it logically was the physiological link in the hypostatic union of Christ's human and divine natures. In addition, the heart was the symbol of Christ's redemptive love.

Devotion to the Sacred Heart enjoyed enormous popularity in the thirteenth and fourteenth centuries, went into a period of decline, then rejuvenated in the seventeenth century as word spread of apparitions to a Visitantine nun, Saint Margaret Mary Alacoque, and of divine messages to her to spread the devotion. According to devotional history, Saint Margaret Mary Alacoque was commissioned by Our Lord to campaign for a feast day honoring the Sacred Heart and to promote specific devotional exercises, such as holy hours and communions of reparation for outrages committed against divine love. It was this sister and those messages which shaped devotion to the Sacred Heart into the twentieth century.

Devotion to the Sacred Heart came under fire not infrequently for being sentimental and macabre, many worshippers being turned off by artistic representations which they found grisly—specifically, the fleshy heart girdled by thorns, dripping blood, shooting flames, and crowned with a cross. It was a bit graphic. Nonetheless, a feast day of the Sacred Heart was declared and extended to the universal church. Popes wrote encyclicals celebrating devotion to the Sacred Heart. Communities, states, nations consecrated themselves to the Sacred Heart. Then Leo XIII went them all one better—he consecrated the whole world to the Sacred Heart in 1899. The Confraternity of the Sacred Heart came into being under the aegis of the Jesuits, and devotion to the Sacred Heart spread near and far through the organization known as the Apostleship of Prayer. Finally, by the tens of thousands, families "enthroned" the Sacred Heart in their houses, giving places of honor in the process to statues and pictures featuring bleeding hearts bared on chest and held in hands.

John Deedy

Into the Secular Age

It is impossible to itemize here—or perhaps anywhere —all popular devotions found within Catholicism.

They number in the thousands, and exist in all forms— the wearing of scapulars and medals, recitation of litanies, pilgrimages, prayers, first Fridays, first Saturdays (as said, devotions tend to multiply imitations), triduums, holy years, Bible vigils, parish missions, days of recollection, weekend retreats, eucharistic congresses, and on and on.

Some of these devotions are of relatively recent origin. Many more, however, have their origins back in the Middle Ages, the so-called ages of faith, when the whole of life centered about the church and no one doubted that it was religion which gave life its meaning. The paradox is that these ages of faith were also ages of distorted subjective piety. Fueling the problem was the priest at mass, hunched over the altar, his back to the congregation. This public and most solemn act of worship had pretty much become the private devotion of the celebrant; the people were left to their own devices. Some followed the mass as best they could with Latin/English missals; some sat like telephone poles; other went about their devotions —fingering beads, praying novenas, or even, again as mentioned earlier, moving up and down the church's side aisles "doing" Stations of the Cross. Private devotions, not the mass, had become central to the spiritual lives of disproportionate numbers of Catholics.

Devotional Catholicism of this sort is in eclipse at the

moment, and there are those who anguish over the fact, particularly since the decline in devotional piety, which of course is extra-liturgical, has not been compensated by greater interest or wider participation in the purified liturgy.

In his book *Christianity in the Twentieth Century* (New York, 1971), Jesuit Father John A. Hardon attributes the decline in popular devotions to three causes: cultural pressure (rejection of the old Baroque and Romantic notions of worship); the ecumenical movement (anxiety not to burden the hope of unity with devotional practices foreign to Protestants); and the gradual acculturation of Catholicism to the environment ("As expressions of religious faith waned among the people in general, Catholics soon fitted into the same pattern").

There is substance to what Hardon says.

Still the fact remains that the popularity of extra-liturgical devotions came at the direct expense of the mass, the act of worship which is the core of the church's very existence. That problem existed in our very lifetimes. A correction was overdue. The question is whether the correction has been too drastic. There are those who say yes, and maybe they have a point. If nothing more, popular devotions were signs of the church's vitality and of the Catholic imagination. But if history is still a teacher, one day popular devotions will again enjoy favor. Christian history, after all, can be as cyclical as any other.

12.

SACRAMENTALS:
The Way We Were Isn't the Way We Are Now

Pious Accents

The old *Catholic Encyclopedia* (1913) details what Catholics of a certain age knew virtually from the time they learned the Hail Mary, that "one of the most remarkable effects of sacramentals is the virtue to drive away evil spirits whose mysterious and baleful operations sometimes affect the physical activity of man"—and presumably also of woman.

No problem about crediting that. I remember summer thunder and lightning storms of my growing-up years, the impression engraved in memory not for nature's wondrous flexing of muscles, but because downstairs, two flats below, serious thunderstorms touched off a great flurry of activity on my grandmother's part. The blessed candle was lighted; holy water was sprinkled about the house; the foreheads of young children were signed, then the sign of the cross would be administered to self—and presumably with notable efficaciousness, for the worst that ever happened to that turn-of-the-century three-decker was the loss of some roof shingles during a hurricane one September.

RETROSPECT

What were these, the lighted blessed candle, the holy water sprinkled everywhere, the sign of the cross hurriedly made? They were sacramentals of the kind referred to by the *Catholic Encyclopedia*—activities, displays and items of faith that a generation or two ago were part and parcel of the faith. Sacramentals once defined the Catholic almost fully as much as did the sacraments—from which, incidentally, sacramentals took their name. And why not? Sacramentals accented sacraments. It was their very reason for being. They were sacred signs instituted by the church to prepare for and prolong the sanctifying effects of the sacraments instituted by Christ.

In some ways sacramentals retained the characteristics of sacraments. For one thing, sacramentals, too, were "visible signs" of God's benediction invoked on persons, places and things. Today it would be hard to find a young Catholic who would know off the top of his or her head what a sacramental was, never mind its visible sign. But once upon a time every Catholic knew: sacramentals were holy objects or actions instituted by the church for the promotion of devotion among the faithful.

Sacramentals are not necessary for salvation, never were. Even Trent, the council of reaction, conceded that (Sess. XXII, 15). Sacramentals, said the Fathers of that Council, enhanced the dignity of the Holy Sacrifice, the mass, and aroused the piety of the faithful.

In less sensitive ecumenical times, Catholics were habitually told that sacramentals also helped distinguish them as believers from "heretics," a not so oblique gibe at Protestant and Anglican reformers, who formally did away with sacramentals or, as the old *Catholic Encyclopedia* said with bluntness, "use[d] them arbitrarily and with little intelligence." Catholics don't write that way anymore, at least not usually, which is just as well.

Looking Back

The church's understanding of sacramentals was broad almost from the very beginning.

It would seemingly have to have been, since almost any well-intentioned article or action could be caught within the terms of definition. Sacramentals could be lights, incense, holy water, palms, roods; they could be blessings, medals, scapulars, rosaries, statues, icons; they could be candles, ashes, holy oils, bells and carillons. They were the actions of the priest in his ceremonial rituals—bowing, genuflecting, chanting, prostrating himself on the sanctuary floor. They were prayers. They were the bestowing of alms in the name of God and his church, as distinct from the giving of alms as a private deed. Finally, they were blessings, such as those extended to a mother after childbirth (to return her to a state of purity), or pronounced over buildings, houses, businesses, fields and crops, pets and beasts of burden, work animals, as well as over objects, like medals, cars, motorcycles. In point of fact, blessings were the first sacramentals, and to this day they remain the largest and most common class of sacramentals.

The word "sacramental," so close to sacrament, came into use with the refinement of the term sacrament by scholastic theologians of the twelfth and thirteenth centuries. Sacramentals complemented sacraments. An early theological question was whether, like sacraments, sacramentals worked *ex opere operanto*—that is, whether they effected grace by virtue of their administration, and not solely through the faith in divine promises. This was a knotty theological problem in its day, with some holding that sacramentals worked *ex operere operantis;* that is, through the merit and disposition of the user. It was at last decided that sacramentals communicated grace *quasi ex opere operanto;* that is, in a way resembling the sacraments, but not automatically—like the sacraments themselves—by virtue of the rite or substance employed. To this day this understanding constitutes the essential difference between sacramentals and sacraments. The effect of sacramentals depends on the pious dispositions of the persons using them.

Besides grace, sacramentals were piously said to convey other favors from God, among them forgiveness of minor sins, remission of temporal punishments due to sins, health of body, material blessings and protection from evil spirits.

Still, as said earlier, sacramentals complement sacraments. It is, in the church's understanding, their reason for being. For instance, the blessing of holy water is a sacramental connected to the sacrament of baptism; the blessing and distribution of ashes on Ash Wednesday accent the sacrament of penance or reconciliation; the blessing of the home and the various blessings of women relate to the sacrament of matrimony; the blessing of persons at various stages of sickness, the commendation of souls of the departed and the burial rites themselves are sacramentals of the old sacrament of extreme unction, now called the anointing of the sick. The late Monsignor Martin Hellriegel, a pioneer in the liturgical reform movement in the United States, called sacramentals such as these "little sacraments" by virtue of their being extensions of the central work of the church in the sanctification of souls.

In time, objects blessed—candles, holy water, ashes, icons, medals, statues, whatever—came themselves to be regarded as sacramentals, and were officially admitted by the church under that heading. The rationale was elementary. The object blessed acquired a special holiness merely by the fact of its being blessed. The logic was uncontestable, but doors thus were opened for the blessing of anything that anyone might conceive of as helping to elevate religious piety and devotion.

Most everything qualified for blessing—para-sacramentalization, as it were—that could be conceived of as being "in the service of the sacraments," including some things whose qualifications might be questioned, at least in terms of intention. For instance, a ninth-century codex of Heribert, Archbishop of Milan, provided the following blessing for an oil:

"Be thou graciously pleased by the infusion of the Holy Spirit to strengthen and enhance the substance, of old approved by thee, of this oil here before thee; to the end that whatever in the human kind hath been touched therewith may speedily pass to a higher nature, and that the ancient Enemy may not, after anointing with the same, claim aught for himself, but that he may grieve for that he is exposed to the shafts of this blessed engine of defence, and groan because by the oil of peace the swellings of his antique fury are kept down and repressed: through Our Lord Jesus Christ, who lives and reigns, world without end."

Most blessings, however, were both meritorious of intent and purpose, such as that connected with the water for baptism found in the Ethiopic Statues of the Apostles: "God, my Lord almighty, who madest heaven and earth, . . . who mingledst and unitedst the immortal with the mortal, who madest living man a combination of the two, and gavest to that which was made a body a soul also, which thou causest to dwell within: stir this water and fill it up with thy Holy Spirit, that it may become water and Spirit for regeneration of those who are to be baptized: work a holy work and make them to become sons and daughters of thy holy name."

Popular Piety

Blessings such as those above were common from the very early days of Christianity, and helped seed the idea that a divine virtue or supernatural spirit could be twinned to a material object, thus making it holy and capable of producing certain spiritual effects of a temporal nature.

Not every Christian subscribed initially to this idea, contending that prayers and incantations directed toward and into inanimate objects played the devil's game and implied that the world was incapable of harboring a pure spirit. Thus it was that Manicheans rejected entirely the notion of relics, and that some even dissented from the use of water in the administration of baptism, maintaining instead that a laying on of hands was sufficient for the efficacy of the sacrament. Objections such as these were overridden, however, and sacramentals took their place as an integral part of the Christian religion.

Indeed, sacramentals became so much a part of the Catholic religious experience as to sum in time to a style of life as well as one of faith. Every Catholic home had its blessed candle, carefully tucked away for emergencies. Catholics wore scapulars or Marian medals around their necks. Catholic men tipped their hats on passing a Catholic church. Catholics, male and female, genuflected on entering and leaving church. They signed themselves with holy water, and made sure their rosaries were in proper spiritual working order by having them blessed. Chaplains sent armies off to battle with blessings. Catholic baseball players drew crosses in batter boxes before standing to the plate. Spiritual counselors blessed athletic teams before coaches sent them on the field to play. One of the quaintest memories from the Jerry Faust coaching era at Notre Dame, one captured on TV, is of Faust barking the signal to football players along the sidelines during a particularly tense game situation, "Say a Hail Mary."

RETROSPECT

By and large, that's a style of faith that is pretty much gone. Sacramentals remain a part of Catholic life, however. Priests still use incense at certain liturgies. Rosaries are fingered in prayer, and blessings are still dispensed at dedications of buildings intended for devotional or religious purposes, such as churches, chapels and centers of religious education.

Some sacramental liturgies have even spilled over to the general community, where they remain securely in place. For instance, in seaport communities such as Provincetown and Gloucester one still finds the annual ceremony of the blessing of the fleet, an especially colorful sacramental liturgy, although one sometimes suspects that those blessings are today civic as much as religious occasions—galas whose elimination would probably be protested more energetically by the local Chamber of Commerce and tourist boards than by Catholic parishioners of the communities acting out of purely devotional instincts.

Born-again Christians in Protestant fundamentalism have adopted many of the signs and practices associated with or thought of as Catholic sacramentals. They wear religious objects, like a cross, and bless one another. Born-again Christian athletes may kneel publicly in prayerful thanksgiving during moments of triumph. A person delivered from a harrowing experience may attribute the good fortune to some accident of faith, like a Bible, a cross, a holy object—sacramentals in the Catholic idea of things. But at the same time that this development is occurring within a branch of Protestantism, within Catholicism itself sacramentals are becoming less than what they used to be.

Modern Revisions

Historically, in the Catholic tradition, the chief benefits of sacramentals were said to be acquisition of actual graces, forgiveness from venial sins, remission of temporal punishments due to sin, protection from evil spirits, health of body, and material blessings.

For instance, the person who wore the Carmelite brown scapular in holy fidelity was assured that he or she would be safeguarded from dangers and would escape eternal damnation. The person who had his new car blessed by a priest could believe that he was now safer on the road. So was the woman who installed a plastic Saint Christopher statue on her dashboard. But those assurances, whether formally encouraged or not, belong to a Catholic yesterday, and it's understandable in a way. A scapular could never be an Annie Oakley to heaven, and speed limits and mandatory car-inspection laws do more for traveler and road safety than a Saint Christopher statue ever could, presuming Saint Christopher had existed which, it seems now, he didn't.

Actually, the de-emphasis that has come to sacramentals within Catholic life might have been expected. Obviously, matters were out of control when, for example, blessings were being dispensed on cats and dogs—and of all things on such objects as snowmobiles, which then would tear about the countryside terrorizing animals and wreaking ecological havoc generally. The tailoring of sacramentals has had the effect of eliminating abuses while at the same time returning sacramentals to their original purposes, or closer thereto.

Church leaders themselves were aware that abuses existed, and conceded so at Vatican II in the Constitution on the Sacred Liturgy with the observation: "With the passage of time . . . there have crept into the rites of . . . sacramentals certain features that have rendered their nature and purpose far from clear to the people of today; hence some changes have become necessary to adapt them to the needs of our times"(62). The Council Fathers were not distancing themselves from sacramentals; quite the opposite. "Holy Mother Church has . . . instituted sacramentals," they declared. "These are sacred signs which bear a resemblance to the sacraments; they signify effects, particularly of a spiritual kind, which are obtained through the church's intercession. By them men are disposed to receive the chief effects of the sacraments, and various occasions of life are rendered holy"(60). But, they added, "the sacramentals are to undergo a revision which takes into account the primary principle of enabling the faithful to participate intelligently, actively, and easily"(79).

This has been accomplished largely through the revision of the church's liturgies and rituals, a step carried out in the context of theological opinion holding that the rituals involved in the administration of a sacrament are in fact the primary sacramentals—as, for instance, the exorcisms, the signs of the cross, anointings, impositions of hands, and the symbolic presentation of the white garment and candle in the ceremonies of baptism and the restored catechumenate.

In the same process of revision, items traditionally thought of as sacramentals, such as the blessed images of Christ, Mary and the saints that were venerated in all churches, were to be placed, resituated if necessary, so as not to distract the faithful in their participation in the sacred liturgy of the mass, the principle ceremony taking place in a church. The rearrangement had the effect, however subtle, of emphasizing that sacramentals are in the service of the sacraments and relate ultimately to the Eucharist and the sacrament of the mass.

A Disappearing Market

Revisions and rearrangements have undoubtedly brought a greater liturgical purity to the use of sacramentals in the church's rituals.

But so far as many people in the pews are concerned, there's an esoteric quality to it all. For many still think of sacramentals largely in terms of blessed objects of devotion—medals, candles, scapulars and the like. Different attitudes exist, however, in their regard. Maybe there are some who still regard a particular blessed object, a sacramental of their understanding, such as an amulet, as a kind of holy charm capable of warding off evil and bringing good luck. This was a common enough group in the past. Even in very recent times, sacramentals were so revered that people actually troubled over what to do with last year's palms (could one just throw them out with the trash, or did one have to burn them?) and such things as the rosaries that arrived unsolicited in the mail from, say, Indian missionaries out West (was one morally obliged to send an offering in return? Also, what was one to do with rosaries one didn't need, or wouldn't want to be caught dead with, so cheap was their composition? How was one to dispose of them, particularly those that arrived already blessed?).

Nowadays most Catholics don't waste much time over questions such as these. They mark the envelope "return to sender," or just pitch the objects out. Sacramentals are not necessary for salvation, and sacramental objects do not exert automatic claims on one's reverence, especially those mass-produced plastic items costing no more than a few cents to make.

It is not that sacramental objects are uniformly despised and rejected by the new generation of Catholics. It is rather that today's Catholic tends to look upon sacramental objects, if not suspiciously or, alas, laughably then, as minor devotional tools to be accepted by them or not. The last things they are regarded as are magical instruments guaranteeing anything—health, safety, happy death, divine deliverance, whatever.

The attitude might seem cynical, and maybe with some it is. To the extent that it is, it is probable that the blame-worthy party is not the one spurning the sacramental, but the party foisting it on the public—like the religious order whose 1988 Valentine mailing, featuring a shocking-pink envelope festooned with lovers' hearts, promised remembrances at masses honoring Saint Valentine (Valentine's consignment by Rome to the ranks of the fictitious notwithstanding) and, in return for seven dollars or more, a "blessed golden braided rope bracelet" recalling "the belt of the Poor Man of Assisi," St. Francis. The mailing might seem harmless enough to some, except that it is exploitative; it evokes old rejected conceptions of salvation by popular mechanics, conceptions which centuries ago helped fuel the fires of reformers.

Nothing so dramatic or institutionally cataclysmic is apt to be repeated in our time in protest over sacramental excesses. Today such excesses are more likely to provoke mockery rather than militancy—a different kind of problem, to be sure, though not necessarily less dangerous to the integrity of the faith, since mockery can be a devastating enfeebler of the faith in individuals.

Retaining the Essence

Consciously or not, sacramentals remain a distinct element of faith in today's church.

The blessing of throats on the Feast of Saint Blaise may not be as much of a draw as it used to be, but the reception of ashes on Ash Wednesday is, even among those Catholics generally careless about the Sunday mass obligation. The blessed ashes are a sacramental, of course.

Catholics receive blessings. They pray and give alms. They revere or respect objects of a holy character—there is a crucifix on the wall of most Catholic homes, for instance. Whether realized or not, all those gestures and articles are sacramentals.

Some sacramentals have fallen into disuse, sadly, through dissolution of certain ethnic customs—the blessing of the Easter breads, for instance. But the drawing of the line on sacramentals by the new generations of Catholics has been mainly on the schlock that came to pass for sacramentals—the tawdry gadgets like the dashboard Saint Christophers and the crosses that glow in the dark which are supposed to arouse instincts of piety and devotion. Of course they don't, at least not with the new generations, and that development is new to the history of sacramentals, at least its modern chapter.

The rejection of the schlock does not amount, however, to the wholesale rejection of sacramentals. The new generations of Catholics seem to realize more clearly than their forebears that sacramentals are less than sacraments. Certainly they do not tend, as did Catholics of another age, to exaggerate sacramentals at the expense of sacraments. This sums inevitably to a change in religious lifestyles. But sacramentals continue as an integral part of the Catholic religious experience. The mobs that line up for the blessed ashes on the first day of Lent would seem proof positive of that.

It would also seem to indicate that today's Catholics have absorbed the message that the church has traditionally sought to convey with respect to sacramentals. Along with the teaching church, today's Catholics believe that though sacramentals might be less than sacraments, they are more powerful than purely private prayer.

There has been no evolution in the church's thinking on that point, only a natural evolution in the way Catholics have applied the teaching in their practical, worshiping lives.

13.

SPIRITS, PURE AND OTHERWISE:
Of Angels and Devils and Such Things

The Scriptural Evidence

An enduring, if now seemingly quaint instruction, which Catholics of a certain age remember from parochial school religion class, is that pertaining to the guardian angel.

We were taught that we all had one, the teaching being reinforced in my school by a large framed color-print of an angel guiding a little boy and girl across a rickety footbridge over angry waters. Thinking back, that guardian angel was doing double duty, but at least the angel had an assignment. It is not certain how many are on duty today. Believers are not conscious of angels the way they used to be.

That's a change, for angels were not only a large part of Catholic consciousness, they were also a large part of biblical history—as messengers of the Lord, as instruments through whom the will of God was conveyed to people, as attendants upon the throne of God, even as intercessors on the part of persons. As for guardian angels, it was Saint Jerome who proposed the idea that everyone has his or her own. "The dignity of a soul is so great," he

said, "that each has a guardian angel from its birth."
Peter Lombard, though, felt a mite different. He inclined
to the theory that one angel had charge of several individuals—which, come to think of it, could make the representation of that old color print authentic after all. The
point is that once upon a time angels were taken with
great seriousness, not only in the Christian religious nar-
rative, but in the Judaic one as well.

The Old Testament, in fact, is replete with stories involving angels.

It was an angel, for instance, who by a spring in the
wilderness found Hagar, the Egyptian maidservant made
pregnant by Abram, after she had fled to escape the
abuse of Abram's wife Sarai, and consoled her in her
distress. Hagar returned, of course, and bore Abram's
son Ishmael (Genesis 16).

There were two angels in the appearance of men who
came to Sodom one evening, feasted at Lot's house, then
were subjected to the overtures of the Sodomites, who
found the angels disguised as men more enticing sexually
than Lot's two daughters. Fire and brimstone rained
down in the morning on Sodom and the neighboring
community of Gomorrah but, led by the angels, Lot and
the daughters escaped. Not Lot's wife; she looked back,
it will be remembered, and was turned to a pillar of salt
(Genesis 19:1-26).

It was an angel who announced to Gideon that he was
to save his people (Judges 6:11-18); an angel who instructed Daniel on the vision of the ram and the goat
(Daniel 8:15-27); an angel who foretold to Manoah's bar-

ren (and nameless) wife the birth of a son who would begin to deliver Israel from the Philistines, the son they called Samson (Judges 13:3-24). It was an angel who was promised to God's people (Exodus 23:20 and 33:2), and an angel who led the people of Israel out of Egypt (Numbers 20:16). The citations go on and on.

The references to angels are equally multiple in the New Testament.

An angel, Gabriel to be specific, appeared to Mary to announce that she would bear a son named Jesus (Luke 1:26-38), to which she replied, of course, "Let it be done according to thy word." It was an angel who reassured Joseph about Mary's pregnancy (Matthew 1:20-21) and who, after Jesus' birth, instructed Joseph to flee with his family to Egypt in order to be safe from Herod's savagery (Matthew 2:13-20).

An angel appeared to Jesus to strengthen him during his agony in the Garden of Gethsemane the night before he died (Luke 22:43), and an angel announced the Resurrection to Mary Magdalene and the other Mary on the first Easter Sunday morning (Matthew 28:2-7).

Angels continued to be active as Christianity struggled to secure roots. An angel appeared to Saint Paul during his stormy trip across the Ionian Sea from Myra to Crete (Acts 27:23), and an angel conveyed to John the Apocalypse, the book of prophecy or revelation of things that were, are and will be (Revelation 1:1-ff). There were many more appearances of angels in the New Testament.

With a biblical pedigree such as that it was inevitable that a complex theology would evolve, and indeed one did. Angelology offered the names of only a handful of angels—Michael, Raphael, Gabriel, Uriel, Chamuel, Jophiel and Zadkiel. Michael, Gabriel and Raphael were the only ones actually mentioned in the Scriptures. But lack of a long roster of names did not daunt believers. Pope Gregory the Great (590-604) joined references to angels in the Scriptures and gave his blessing to the proposition that there were nine orders or choirs of angels in heaven, divided, according to the gifts given them and the tasks assigned, into three hierarchies of three choirs each. In the first circle were Seraphim, Cherubim and Thrones; in the second, Virtues, Powers and Dominations; in the third, Principalities, Archangels and Angels. Still, Gregory's was not the first such listing of a celestial hierarchy. The initial development of an organized hierarchy of angels actually belonged to Jewish literature of the period between 200 B.C. and 100 A.D.

Winged History

Catholic understanding with respect to angels did not differ substantially from that of other monotheistic religions, including Judaism and Mohammedanism.

Angels were subordinate superhuman beings, pure spirits (though they were recorded as eating and drinking) and, if possessing gender, male; at least angels are constantly referred to in Scripture as "men." They were said to be infinitely numerous and able to exercise miraculous power, even being able to fly—though except for the Cherubim and Seraphim, who purportedly hovered about the throne of God, angels were not spoken of in the Scriptures as having wings.

In fact, winged angels may well be an admixture of Christian artists, and further a representation that came later in the Christian story.

The reality is that angels did not figure in earliest examples of Christian art—partly, it is thought, because in a period when polytheism was still common, the depiction of angels might have obfuscated the unity attributed to the God of monotheism; partly, too, because winged figures were favorite subjects in secular classical art, as to represent victory in battle, and an idolatrous connection might have been made between the sacred and the profane. In any instance, it was not until the fourth century, when Christianity's place was secured under Constantine and there was less possibility of angels being misunderstood for anything other than what they were, creatures of God, that they began to put in appearances in Christian art. By the fifth century, angels were favorite subjects of the Christian artist, and not merely as decorative items in a larger tableau, but as figures whose presence was demanded in order to complete a theological story, such as angels being messengers to Mary or attendants on the Lord.

As with art, so with theology: a tradition took form, and by the time the church moved into the new millennium, there were numerous questions to sort out and settle. Thomas Aquinas took on the task squarely in the thirteenth century, devoting some one hundred and twenty-six pages of the *Summa Theologica* (Random

House, 1945 edition) to the subject of angels—and not to such esoterica as how many angels can dance on the head of a pin, a caricature of his concerns, though to be sure he did ponder whether several angels can be in the same place at the same time. (He concluded that there can be but one angel in one place.) Aquinas's focuses were on such issues as the mode of angelic knowledge, whether angels had free will, the perfection of angels in the order of grace and glory, the love or predilection of angels, and the like.

Theologians do not spend much time on topics of that sort nowadays, but they mattered greatly during the centuries that the church was defining the doctrines and tenets of faith. What the church decided—"defined as dogma," according to the *New Catholic Encyclopedia*—was that before the creation of the world, God actually created a kingdom of invisible spirits, called angels, and that the angels were to be regarded as personal beings and not as mere powers or the like. Dogmatic definitions stopped short, however, of including specifics about orders or choirs of angels. It was Lateran Council IV of 1215 that pronounced on angels, declaring that before God created the world he created a kingdom of invisible spirits, called angels, who were good by nature, though some fell later into badness. (Vatican II's references to angels were in passing, and the contexts largely neutral.)

It may appear wondrous to the modern Catholic mind, but the concept of angels came to claim a strong grip on Catholic consciousness and the Catholic imagination of yesterday. By 1630, the cult of the angels was widespread throughout Christendom, and a variety of liturgical and non-liturgical rites and practices became associated with them. It became common, for instance, to dedicate churches to angels, singularly or as a body. Angels were invoked in prayers and novenas, and included in litanies among the heavenly company of the petitioned. Pope Clement X (1670-1676) was an enthusiast, and gave impetus to devotion to guardian angels by establishing October 2 throughout the Western church as a feast in their honor—a feast subsequently displaced.

Sources of the Demonic

One reason helping to explain theological preoccupation with the subject of angels was the urge, indeed the necessity, to account for the existence of evil in the world.

How, for example, did one explain the reality of evil when, at least theoretically, all that existed came from a God who was infinitely good? If one thanked God for the good that touched his or her life, did one then blame God for any evil that came upon the person? Today the church differentiates between various kinds of evil. There is physical or natural evil—evils of nature essentially, like the drought that ruins the harvest or the windstorm that tears the roofs off homes; there is moral evil or sin—a disorder of the human will by and large, evidenced in such incidents as small as a petty meanness and as major as mass murders; and then there is metaphysical evil, evil that might be attributed to some transcendent force.

Once upon a time, the common impulse was to attribute all evils to a transcendent force, even on occasion to God acting out of some spirit of vengeance, meting out evil as punishment due to sin. This impulse became less instinctive, however, as the sciences unlocked secrets of nature and of personality that lay behind certain evil. Also, God got off the hook as understanding grew that one who was infinitely good could not be the cause of evil. But that still left large, seemingly unaccountable evils—evils so monstrous as to appear for all practical purposes to be beyond the capacities of individuals, or so enormous as to defy any talk about coincidences resulting from natural forces coming together in strange and unfortunate circumstances.

The Holocaust might seem a case in point. The source of that evil is clear enough on one level. Still there are some who believe that the evil of Hitler is not to be explained solely in terms of pathology, whether with respect to Hitler as an individual or the party of people he rallied under the name of Naziism. In other words, there are those who hold that out there floating about in the world is an actual presence, an evil spirit, ever ready to ply on human weaknesses and work an assortment of mischiefs and horrors.

Actually this is traditional Catholic thinking, has been from the beginning, and that evil spirit goes under the name of Satan or the Devil, though he is known also as

RETROSPECT

Lucifer, the Demon, the Evil One, the Adversary, among other designations. Like the angels, Satan, the Devil or whatever is a pure spirit—spirits actually, in the plural, since the name is a collective for those angels who went bad, the group biblical history knows as the "fallen angels." According to traditional teaching, they too were created by God, at the same time ostensibly as the good angels. But at some point they revolted—no one knows exactly why, though pious theory has their revolt bound up with arrogance and pride and envy of God's creation. In any instance, the bad angels were routed by the good angels, led by the Archangel Michael, and were banished from heaven. It all happened long ago, before Adam and Eve were even around.

Gradually, there developed the notion of two spiritual kingdoms—the one existing in glory on high; the other in some dark nether world, from which all kinds of troubles were originated by the "multitudes" of bad angels (the number had grown to that open-ended noun) who were drawn by Satan in his train.

The Devil in the World

Satan was busy in the Old Testament, where he was even said to function through women known as sorceresses or witches, such as the Witch of Endor in 1 Samuel 28:8-25.

But Satan's job was virtually a full-time one in the New Testament. Satan tempted the Lord during his fast of forty days and forty nights in the desert (Matthew

213

4:1-11). Satan possessed the bandits who plied the road near Gadara until being expelled into the swine that rushed into the sea and drowned (Matthew 8:28-32). He was the figure in the parable of the sower and the seed who took the word out of people's hearts (Luke 8:12). He was the evil power who disguised himself as the angel of light in order to deceive people of good faith (2 Corinthians 11:14). Satan was, in sum, the father of all that was wicked, the prince of the world who, like a roaring lion, went about looking for someone to devour (1 Peter 5:8).

The biblical assurances that Satan had been overcome were equally numerous. The Lord himself had said that he had "watched Satan fall from the sky like lightning" (Luke 10:18), and the disciples rejoiced that "even the demons were subject" to them in God's name (Luke 10:17).

Nonetheless, belief in an operating Devil was a persistent one. By the Middle Ages, the concept of a demonic force was so great that many saints thought themselves and others to be in constant conflict with the powers of evil. Saint Anthony and Saint Teresa were but two among many who believed they suffered temptations and evil ministrations from Satan. It was between the thirteenth and fifteenth centuries, however, that feelings were strongest about the sinister presence of an evil one, and these feelings were to carry into Protestantism. Luther, for instance, was convinced that Satan hovered near, ever the Great Tempter. "As I found he was about to begin again," Luther wrote on one occasion, "I gathered together my books, and got into bed. Another time in the night I heard him above my cell walking on the cloister, but as I knew it was the Devil I paid no attention to him and went to sleep.''

Indeed, the spell of a devil passed from immediate religious experiences and seized the popular imaginations of artists, writers and makers of music. In art, the Devil began to appear as prince of the world in scary representations, as with forked tongue, cloven hoofs, horns, tail —concepts, incidentally, that owed perhaps more to Greek and Roman mythology than to speculative Christian theologizing.

In other artistic fields, Milton in his *Paradise Lost,* published in 1667, depicted a Satan rousing fallen angels with rumors of a new world about to be created and, after a series of adventures in which he was variously disguised as a good angel and as a cormorant, emerging triumphant with the fall of Adam and Eve; "Better to reign in hell than serve in heaven,'' says this Satan (Book 1, line 263).

In Goethe's *Faust* and Gounod's opera of the same name, Satan became the evil spirit, the Devil, who operated under the name Mephistopheles (possibly from the Greek for "not loving the light"). He was the devil on two sticks in Le Sage's 1709 satirical romance *Le Diable boiteux* and, closer to our own time, the one who sought to persuade the New England farmer Jabez Stone to sell his soul in return for material prosperity in Stephen Vincent Benet's widely anthologized *Saturday Evening Post* short story "The Devil and Daniel Webster''—an effort, it will be recalled, which was foiled by Webster's oratorical eloquence worked on a demonic jury.

Much as it might be denied, the Christian preoccupation with good spirits and evil spirits, angels and devils, was a reflection in some ways of the idea, seemingly diffused among humans going as far back as research carries, of a duality of good and evil in the scheme of things. It is an idea expressed by ancient Semitic belief in genii and spirits, which cause good or evil—traces of which may be found in the Bible; similarly, it is the idea expressed in the Ormazd and Ahriman of the Persians and of Zoroastrianism, Ormazd being the god of goodness and light in perpetual conflict with Ahriman, the spirit or principle of evil.

Emphasizing Evil

Catholic theologians believe as strongly today as ever that it is important to keep focus on the possibility of an evil presence in the world, partly because so much that is evil—again, the Holocaust—is beyond human comprehension; also because, as Passionist Father Carroll Stuhlmueller has observed, the degree of evil in the world manifests the limits of theology.

The paradox is that, as the church and its theologians insist on the possibility of this evil presence—call it Satan, the Devil, whatever—they say little about those who are historically represented as their opposite; namely, angels good and guardian. As a consequence, while the Devil's stock has gone up, so to speak, that of angels has gone down, and more and more angels are regarded as tenuous inventions that belong more to legend, fairy tales and childhood imaginations than to religion per se.

There is an apparent inevitability about all this. A more sophisticated believer looks for natural explanations for happenings that once might have been attributed to angels—and generally finds them without great difficulty. To be sure, one can also find natural explanations for much of the evil that occurs in the world without casting about for some supernatural cause. The difference is that a good is usually accepted without wonder as to reason why, whereas evil seems so unnatural as to demand a cause beyond the cause, a source beyond the source. Proximate causes and sources are not enough. A person can thrill at some great stroke of good fortune or luck, and accept it at face value; a stroke of bad luck, on the other hand, will prompt many people to wonder if they are under some evil hex.

The sum of it all is that in much of today's world the Devil is in; angels are out—culturally as well as theologically. We have movies, for instance, that explore devil worship and the diabolic possession—"The Exorcist," "Friday the 13th," "Poltergeist," and the like. Anyone who put an angel of heaven into a movie would be mocked into bankruptcy. Angels belong to symbolic imagery; they are illusions for the poet to invoke, not the realist.

Perhaps the state of the world helps account for the phenomenon that a Satan can be logically possible, but an angel totally impossible. Evil is blatant, far more easily recognizable much of the time than a transcendent reality representing good. Besides, as suggested, good is presumed, and often accepted as nothing more than one's due; evil, also as suggested, is forever so unacceptable that the impulse is to reach beyond the explainable for reasons accounting for its intrusion into one's life.

Thus the final irony: the church, whose tradition holds that there is an order of spiritual beings between God and human beings . . . the church, which saw undue emphasis on the cult of angels grow to such proportions that it was actually compelled to sound alarms (one of the first originated with Paul, who cautioned on the cult in Colossians 2:18) . . . the church where none other than John the Evangelist was once rebuked for offering worship to an angel (Revelation 22:8-9) . . . that church where belief in angels was once so terribly strong, that church (more accurately, the elements of it that care) is now virtually reduced to pleading just in order to keep the concept of angels alive.

A case in point would be the entry on angels in the *New Catholic Encyclopedia.* Two "extremes" are to be avoided in evaluating accounts taken from the Bible and Christian tradition, says the entry: "On the one hand, not everything that is therein contained can be taken as fact, because much of it belongs simply to the philosophy of life in antiquity and must be discarded; so, too, the existence and efficacy of angels cannot be denied out of hand simply because it is possible today, because of more accurate knowledge, to explain by natural causes what was once attributed to angels." That's a rationale with the ring of theological plea bargaining—though in fairness to the writer of the entry, he did eventually allow that "the Christian can no longer postulate angelic activity where he (sic) knows that impersonal forces are at work."

Essentially what the writer was reduced to was the invocation of tradition: "The believing Christian . . . will even today maintain that there are angels because the Bible and the church teach it." It is a statement that catches the echo of Saint Augustine: One knows the angels exist through faith, *esse angelos novimus ex fide.*

And indeed once upon a time faith and teaching would have been enough to settle the matter, but not today. Angels have but the faintest hold at the moment on Christian consciousness. Devils, on the other hand . . . well, for many persons they are as real as ever. There's an obvious dichotomy in the situation, but then so much of religion is a dichotomy, a tension between faith and reason, the logical and the illogical, the known and the unknowable. If at one time one element is stronger than the other, no one should be surprised. The church's pendulum swings too. Always has.

14.

THE BIBLE:
A Holy Book with a Sometimes
Unholy History

Accurate and Authentic

IT WAS back in the early 1950s. Catholic diocesan newspapers, including the one of which I was editor, were closing their special Christmas editions, many of them planning to banner across the top of page one a decorative two-color plate furnished by a national Catholic news agency.

Suddenly there arrived in editors' offices an urgent telegram ordering the plate killed, and information that a replacement was en route, posthaste. The problem? It seemed that somehow the news agency's graphic artist had used a Protestant rather than a Catholic-approved version of the Bible in quoting, as memory has it, the cry of the multitude of the heavenly host cited in Luke 2:14, "Glory to God in the highest, and on earth peace among men of good will."

It is hard to imagine any Catholic agency or individual today getting worked into a panic and causing consternation in editors' offices across the country over the use of a scriptural quote from a Protestant rather than a Catholic source. But yesterday was different. Catholics took their Bible translations seriously, for it had been drilled into them for centuries that the Catholic Bible was theologically precise, while the others—well, likely they were inaccurate, if not also heretical. Today, because of Catholic, Protestant and Jewish scholarly cooperation, Catholics use common or interconfessional Bibles—Bibles that are interchangeable with those of people of other faiths. That's a remarkable ecumenical advance from the recent past, when Catholics believed not only that theirs was the only theologically accurate Bible, but also that the Catholic Church was solely and unilaterally the Bible's only authentic interpreter.

In fairness, it is easy to understand the insistence on accuracy. The Bible is the fundamental source of dogma and is central to thought and teaching, not only of Catholic Christians, but also of Protestant and Anglican Christians, Eastern Orthodox, and Jews. Divided into two testaments of seventy-three books, forty-six in the Old and twenty-seven in the New, the Bible is concerned primarily with the acts of God for the salvation of his people—wrought in the Old Testament through God's covenant with Israel and the mediatorship of Moses, whereby the salvation of Israel is assured, and in the New Testament through God's covenant with his son, through whose mediatorship salvation is assured for the new people of God, the Christian church.

The Bible is regarded as the inspired Word of God, but it did not arrive among believers full-blown and air-tight, written by the finger of God and carved in stone like the ten commandments that Moses received on Mount Sinai.

John Deedy

The Bible was written in separate fragments and over several centuries before being drawn together into the one book.

Collecting the Canon

The Old Testament, the heftier by far of the Bible's two testaments, was at least four hundred years in the writing, its composition ranging from the third century or earlier before Christ to the early second century after Christ.

The Old Testament is thus, strictly speaking, not entirely a pre-Christian-era document, though to be sure most of its writing preceded Christ's time on earth. As it was to be with the New Testament in its time, the Old Testament was originally a loose collection of writings. The writings came to be drawn together with the recognition that a fundamental theme ran through them, a theme sacred in that it contained the Word of God. To this cultic value was added that of ethos. The Old Testament writings defined a people, quickening impetus to draw the writing into a single canon.

Also at work was a variety of pressures on Jewish cohesiveness, among them the rise and spread of apocalpytic literature, and the growing rivalry between the Greek and Jewish cultures. These developments were seen as threats both to Jewish faith and culture. Marshalled as a convenient bulwark against them was that large reservoir of Jewish writings held to be both sacred and authoritative, what is known now as the Old Testament. Forty-six books were gathered into a canon with four divisions: the Torah, or Law (these are the first five books of the Old Testament, called the Pentateuch), the Historical Books, the Books of Wisdom and the Prophetic Books.

The New Testament, by contrast to the Old, was a much shorter time in the writing, the Gospels and twenty-three other books comprising it being set down by persons belonging chronologically to the one apostolic era. Still, the authors of the New Testament did not rush into print, as it were. It was probably two decades after the death of Christ before specifically Christian writings began to make their appearance. Biblical scholars theorize that the first generation of Christians felt no great compulsion to set pen to scroll. They lived in the daily expectation of the Second Coming of Christ, a conviction so strong as to negate impulses to establish a permanent record. A permanent record, it seemed, hardly was necessary with the kingdom so close at hand. In a real sense, the first Christians dealt with day-to-day, not long-term Christianity. When it became apparent that the Second Coming was not exactly imminent, the urgency grew to get the historical details on paper. The record filled in fairly quickly; the New Testament came into being.

One looks at the result, and obviously the four Gospels —the narratives of Matthew, Mark, Luke and John— form the backbone of the New Testament. The paradox is that the writings of Paul were collected and in circulation well before the four Gospels. In fact, the four Gospels, which initially had come into being to serve Christians of separate geographical areas, did not acquire the status and canonical authority of the Old Testament until around the middle of the second century. A similar delay attended acceptance of the other books of the New Testament. Thus, it was not until the fifth century that a New Testament canon was stabilized, and it was not until the Council of Trent in the sixteenth century that this canon received its dogmatic definition. The Bible might have been the inspired Word of God, but experts and exegetes had trouble hearing it in concert and agreeing on all the notes.

An early difficulty was born of language. Parts of the Old Testament were written originally in Aramaic and Greek, but most of it was composed in Hebrew. The Old Testament being essentially a Jewish document, and Hebrew being the language of the Jewish people, problems of language tended from the beginning to be minimal. It was not so with the New Testament. All of the New Testament was composed in Greek. This was no language problem when Greek was the language common to Christian areas. But language did become a problem when Christianity began to spread among people with little or no grasp of Greek. If the Bible was to be the sacred book of these people, it became necessary to translate it into a variety of languages. First, accordingly, came a Latin Bible, for Christians of the West; then a Syrian Bible for Christians of the East; then a flood of others— Coptic, Ethiopic, Armenian, Slavic, German, Dutch-Flemish, French, Spanish, etc.

RETROSPECT

Tracking the Vernacular

Curiously, one of the last languages to acquire a Bible of its own—certainly the last of the important European languages—was English.

There was not a printed Bible in English before the Reformation, earlier Bibles of England being combinations of Norman-French and Anglo-Saxon, and incomplete at that. With the rooting of the English language, various private translations began to appear. Finally, in 1530 King Henry VIII commissioned a study into the expediency and necessity of there being "in the English tongue both the New Testament and the Old"—the result of which was the Great Bible of 1539. The famed King James Bible, named for its commissioner, King James I, appeared in 1611 as a revision of the Bishops' Bible of 1568.

The first Catholic-authorized Bible in English was the Douay-Rheims version, so called from the French communities where it was prepared and printed by so-called "Romanist refugees" from the persecutions in England. The New Testament was first published at Rheims in 1582, and the Old Testament at Douay in 1609, with both testaments subsequently revised by Bishop Richard Challoner in 1749 and 1750.

Once English Bibles gained circulation, Catholic and Protestant versions were in their separate orbits until the ecumenical rapprochements of the mid-twentieth century.

The multiplication of Bible translations served the

great purpose of keeping the Bible in circulation among Christians of new tongues. But this proved something of a mixed blessing for a church which tended to become more and more authoritative. For with the new translations came new interpretations, as translators departed from strictly literal renderings of the texts and introduced flourishes that had theological as well as literary implications.

This was not exactly a new problem for the Catholic Church. Variations in the Latin texts were common before the invention of the printing press, when reproduction depended on the copying of manuscripts by hand. Inevitably there would be errors, omissions, inconsistencies, innovations. It was a state that early on had prompted Pope Damasus (366–384) to commission the drawing up of a single authorized biblical text in Latin from the original languages. The task was undertaken by St. Jerome, of course, and completed around 404. It was Jerome who produced the text known as the Vulgate, the name deriving from *Vulgata,* meaning ''common'' or ''popular'' in the Latin. Jerome's text would stand as the standard Latin text for centuries—in fact, until a critical revision was completed in 1977. But, as the history of the English Bibles makes clear, it did not bring the issue of variant translations totally under church control. Any number of vernacular Bibles rolled from presses of which the Catholic Church would be disapproving—vehemently so, as we shall see.

There were problems, however, in the meantime, notably connected with the canon of the New Testament.

RETROSPECT

During the third and fourth centuries, doubts cropped up over the canonical authenticity of several New Testament books—namely, the Epistle to the Hebrews, the Apocalypse, 2 Peter, 2 John, 3 John, James and Jude. The last five, especially, had a troublesome period of acceptance. The synods of Hippo (393) and Carthage (397), for instance, regarded the Epistle to the Hebrews as canonical, but did not credit it as being Pauline. In 405, Pope Innocent I (401-417) listed all twenty-seven books of the New Testament as official in a letter to Exuperius, but exegetes were inclined nonetheless to make a distinction between "protocanonical" and "deuterocanonical" books —in other words, those belonging to a first list that were universally accepted, and those of a second that had doubt associated with them. Still, debate over the books was largely academic until the Reformation. It was only when reformers began to challenge the canon, and Protestant editions of the Bible started to footnote the deuterocanonical books or omit some of them entirely, that Catholic authorities felt impelled to make an authoritative statement on the matter.

The initiative came with the Council of Trent. The Council of Florence in 1442 had formally specified the canon of the Bible, but Trent was unqualifiedly blunt in the document *Sacrosancta* of April 8, 1563: "If anyone . . . does not accept, as sacred and canonical, the same books entire with all their parts, as they are accustomed to be read in the Catholic Church and as they are contained in the old Vulgate Latin edition . . . let him be anathema." *Sacrosancta* thus settled for Catholic Chris-

tians not only the issue of the canonicity of the deutero-
canonical books of the New Testament, but also of the
Old, such as the deuterocanonical sections of Esther and
Daniel.

A Bane and a Blessing

But now another problem was spawned for Rome, one
much greater than that relating to the canon.

It was a problem born of the extraordinary interest in
the Bible created by the Reformation and the Reformation's favoring of private interpretation of the Bible,
a notion anathema to Roman ears. Ultimately it was a
problem that would put the Catholic Church at odds with
itself, for the reason that at the same time the church was
urging Catholics to read the Bible, it was also warning
against reading it. A strange dichotomy, indeed, had
been set in place.

With the Reformation, the Bible found itself established within much of Protestantism both as an instrument of proselytism and an indispensable tool of salvation. Bible societies mushroomed, which not only
brought together skillful translators for rendering the
Bible into the most obscure of tongues, but also sent
forth assiduous missionaries for the distribution of
Bibles by the hundreds of thousands among rank and file
Christians in a number of countries. The largest and
most effective of these groups, the British and Foreign
Bible Society, founded in 1804, was disposing annually

of as many as 5,190,000 copies of the Scriptures—whole Bibles, New Testaments, and portions.

Upsetting Rome was the double-edged vexation that these Bibles were being circulated (1) without note or comment, or (2) with such notes and commentary of which Rome could hardly be expected to approve as the sole "divinely appointed custodian and interpreter of Holy Writ." Predictably came warnings and condemnations, one of the sternest from Pope Leo XII (1823-1829) in the encyclical *Ubi primum,* addressed to the bishops of the world: "You are aware, venerable brothers, that a certain bible society is impudently spreading throughout the world, which, despising the tradition of the holy Fathers and the decree of the Council of Trent, is endeavoring to translate, or rather to pervert the Scriptures into the vernacular of all nations. . . . It is to be feared that by false interpretation, the Gospel of Christ will become the gospel of men, or still worse, the gospel of evil." Leo XII then urged the bishops to admonish their flocks that, owing to human temerity, more harm than good may come from indiscriminate reading of the Bible.

Pius IX (1846-1878) echoed the admonition in the encyclical *Qui pluribus* of 1846, saying: "These crafty bible societies, which renew the ancient guile of heretics, cease not to thrust their bibles upon all men, even the unlearned —their bibles, which have been translated against the laws of the church, and often contain false explanations of the text. Thus, the divine traditions, the teaching of the fathers, and the authority of the Catholic Church are rejected, and everyone in his own way interprets the words of the Lord, and distorts their meaning, thereby falling into miserable error.''

The din was insistent. Pius VIII (1829-1830) and Gregory XVI (1831-1846) also sounded warnings—in 1829 and 1844, respectively.

The cumulative result was the inculcation of an impression among Catholics that somehow Bible reading was not a fully approved practice. In Catholic families, the Bible suffered a strange neglect. The lessons of the mass were drawn from the Bible, Catholic doctrine derived from it, and Catholic behavioral codes were based upon it. Yet, the Bible collected dust in most Catholic homes, and accordingly there never developed, as there had in much of Protestantism over the centuries following the Reformation, that aspect of devotional life known as biblical spirituality.

The Bible might have been in most every Catholic home, but there it was the great unread book. Certainly it was not read by Catholics on any regular or systematic basis, as was the case with many more Protestants.

Toward Bible Literacy

A succession of popes of the late nineteenth and early twentieth centuries sought to turn this situation around by granting indulgences for the reading of the Bible, and by celebrating in an assortment of papal messages the love in which it was held and the acclaim which the Bible historically enjoyed among the devout, from the first Christians, to Jerome, to Dante.

But the results were mixed, as was virtually conceded by Vatican II, which lavished praise on the "love, veneration, and near cult of the sacred Scriptures" which existed in the separated Christian churches, in unremarked but obvious contrast to the condition that was to be found in Catholic ranks.

Vatican II was emphatic in its endorsement of a Bible-oriented spirituality, encouraging Bible services, for instance, and directing that there be a much wider cycle of Bible readings in the mass and other church liturgies than had previously been the case. All that helped. But in reality Vatican II was only building on one of the great encyclicals of Pius XII (1939-1958). For if anything helped correct ingrained Catholic attitudes toward the Bible, it was the 1943 document, *Divino afflante Spiritu*. In contrast to earlier papal pronouncements, *Divino afflante Spiritu* was not one large protest against private readings and intuitive understandings of the Bible, independently reached. *Divino afflante Spiritu* gave the green light to modern methods of research, and in so doing it rejected those traditional Catholic notions which held the Vulgate (Latin) Bible of Saint Jerome to be the absolute depository of divine truth, the source, sole and authentic, of God's word. Pius XII's encyclical not only opened the door for a retranslating of the Scriptures, but it encouraged biblical scholars to return to the original languages of the Bible, the earlier, pre-Latin Aramaic, Hebrew and

Greek manuscripts. "The sacred books were not given by God to men to satisfy their curiosity or to provide them with material for study and research," said Pius XII in the encyclical, "but, as the Apostle notes, in order that these Divine Oracles might 'instruct us to salvation, by the faith which is in Christ Jesus' and 'that the man of God may be perfect, furnished to every good work.'" Leo XIII had made clear that the purpose of the Bible was not to teach scientific truth, and was therefore not to be judged as a scientific tract; Pius XII went much further, allowing that the time and place of composition of the various books and the character and literary style of the respective writers of the books were to be taken into consideration for a comprehensive, totally valid understanding of the texts.

One immediate effect of *Divino afflante Spiritu* was to grind to a halt a project of the U.S. Bishops' Committee on the Confraternity of Christian Doctrine, which aimed to produce a new translation of the Bible from the old Vulgate version. A totally new project was organized around guidelines recommended by the encyclical, and twenty-six years later was born the *New American Bible*.

Numerous other Bible translations were to appear under the impetus of renewed scholarly interest in the Bible, but it is interesting to note that at one point prior to the arrival of common or interconfessional Bibles only two modern English versions contained the so-called full Catholic canon: the *Jerusalem Bible* and the *New American Bible*.

Common or interconfessional Bibles are those produced in accordance with guidelines agreed on by the executive committee of the United Bible Societies and the Vatican's Secretariat for Promoting Christian Unity, and on the Catholic side they represent a response to Vatican II's Dogmatic Constitution on Divine Revelation (*Dei verbum*), and specifically the constitution's exhortation that "easy access to sacred scripture be provided for all the Christian faithful" (22) and that editions of the Bible be provided for all Christians, "with suitable comments" for the use of non-Christians and adapted so as to make the Bible useful to their situation (25). The problem of the deuterocanonical books and segments of apocrypha was solved by their grouping into what the *New Catholic Encyclopedia* termed "an Intertestamental cluster" between the Old and the New Testaments. The *Encyclopedia* also noted that, strictly speaking, the term "common Bible" does not apply to many Bibles used interchangeably by Catholics and Protestants, including the *Revised Standard Version* produced by Protestants between 1946 and 1952 and endorsed by Catholics in 1966. However, most of those who use the Bible, Catholics especially, no longer seem to be hung up on such niceties of ecclesiastical protocol as "approval by authority." For most, the Bible is the Bible.

Sensitive Translations

Along with the interconfessional Bible has come progress in the elimination of sexist language from the Bible.

Under pressure from feminists, the American bishops

several years ago approved studies testing English renderings of the New Testament against the original Greek texts. The result was the *Revised New Testament* of the *New American Bible,* which in 1987 began to find its way into the hands of the faithful. The new, so-called "inclusive" translation cleans away a lot of the chauvinist language of old translations by adopting contemporary American usages in certain gender contexts. For instance, the verse from Matthew 4:4, "Not on bread alone is man to live," has been revised to read, "One does not live by bread alone." Similarly, Matthew 16:23, "You are not judging by God's standards, but by man's," becomes "You are thinking not as God does, but as human beings do."

The changes in the Catholic-approved *Revised New Testament* of the *New American Bible* do not go as far as the revisions in a collection of Bible readings issued in 1983 by the National Council of Churches for experimental use, but they are a serious attempt to ovecome the male-centered language of the Bible that resulted from the use of "man" in the generic sense; thus, to an extent they meet objections about women being situated in a gender that is not theirs—specifically by being addressed as "man" or "sons," or bundled into the term "mankind." There are those who want a Bible whose language is even more inclusive than the version approved in 1987, and it is likely only a matter of time before it is theirs.

Other changes have been made to reflect other sensitivities of the times. The updated text, for instance, treats homosexuals less judgmentally. Thus it clarifies the reference to homosexuals in 1 Corinthians 6:9-10, where Paul speaks of those who will be excluded from the kingdom of God. The old text reads, "no adulterers, no sodomites, no thieves"; the new, "nor adulterers nor boy prostitutes nor practicing homosexuals." This is a change not merely of semantics; it reflects a whole new set of Catholic attitudes by distinguishing between sexually practicing homosexuals and those who have what is called a homosexual orientation. It is the former who are reprobated, not the latter.

The Bible is the Word of God, and that word cannot be changed. But obviously it is subject to nuances of understanding—dictated by time, if not also by place.

All this apparently helps, for the Bible is being rehabilitated to a degree among Catholics. According to the book *The American Catholic People* by George Gallup, Jr. and Jim Castelli (New York, 1987), the number of Catholics who said they had read the Bible within the last thirty days was up from twenty-three percent in 1977 to thirty-two percent in 1986. At the same time, however, only twenty-one percent of Catholics said that reading or studying the Bible was "very important" to them, in contrast to fifty-two percent of Protestants and eighty-five percent of those who described themselves as Evangelicals. The Bible is recovering its place of honor among Catholics, but obviously there is a distance to go before it is for Catholics the "catholic" book it was up to the Reformation.

15.

CANON LAW:
From Loose to Systematic, Detailed Code of Precepts

Spirit and Letter

CANON LAW is the sum of laws which regulate the Roman Catholic Church. It is the systematized legal structure which guides and coordinates church leaders and the faithful in the pilgrimage of faith and of service which is theirs by divine ordinance and individual baptism. Said more plainly, canon law is the practical expression of the church's existence as a visible society.

No entity of any appreciable size—political or ecclesiastical, corporate or private—can expect to run in methodical fashion, and aspire to be reasonably free of chaos and confusion, without a set of guidelines and regulations, a coordinated body of norms of some sort. The Catholic Church is no exception. The marvel is that, throughout the Western or Latin church at least, it actually managed to do so for some ten centuries.

Not that collections of ecclesiastical norms did not exist over all those years. Quite the contrary. For a variety of reasons, the church was slow in devising a legal code for itself, but once the need was recognized, collections of ecclesiastical laws were suddenly virtually countless.

RETROSPECT

But these early efforts at ecclesiastical law-making were replete with problems. They displayed a commonalty in that they were rooted in a shared inspiration and had connections with natural and divine law. But coherence and universality were lacking. Some were mere serial compilations of canons handed down by regional councils. Some were incomplete and not infrequently contradictory. Some were competitive; some partisan and self-serving, seeking, for instance, to strengthen one point of view or faction within the church against another—like the power of metropolitans and of synods against that of popes.

The church was slow in drawing up a structured legal code for itself for the simple reason that, again, like so much else of an organizational kind, a body of laws did not seem especially urgent. Early Christians lived in the popular belief that the Second Coming was imminent, or at most only a short time off, so why trouble with something that seemed so unnecessary as a complex body of laws? Besides, there was Roman law. This was an eminently fair code, and if any gaps showed up in the application to the life of the church, they could be plugged. Roman law seemed especially to make ecclesiastical sense in the era after Constantine, when emperors, as protectors of the church, also legislated on ecclesiastical matters.

Of course, the arrangement would prove suitable for only so long. Interests of popes and emperors would come into conflict. The influence of Roman law would deteriorate as the Roman Empire shrank. By contrast, the church would grow beyond all dreaming in numbers and geographical outreach. Most pertinently, its juridical concerns would become increasingly specialized, as its theological focuses broadened and refined. A shared body of law, even a body of law grouping civil and ecclesiastical canons into a single code, would no longer do. The church needed a systematized code all its own, and in time it developed one. Not completely independent of Roman law, however. Church law is a heritage of Roman law—in its approaches to justice, its teachings on contracts and pacts, its sense of the sacred and of priestly privilege, among other things. In fact, so derivative of Roman law is church law that for centuries the maxim of canonists was that when ecclesiastical law (*jus ecclesiasticum*) was silent, the church followed Roman law. The debt to Roman law remains large to this day.

Still, agreement in the church about the urgency of a separate body of ecclesiastical law did not bring one into existence immediately, nor even speedily. Between the end of the ninth century and the middle of the twelfth, no less than forty systematic collections of church law were on the books, of varying value and circulation. Each would contribute in its own way to the juridical renaissance that extended in the church from the mid-twelfth to mid-fourteenth centuries. Nonetheless, there was such a plethora of these collections, especially in the Western or Latin church, that some feared a loosening of ties and the formation of a number of individual churches in the West, such as existed in the East. This was not to happen. The Latin church would eventually settle on a single code of law, while the churches of the East would retain theirs. It is a situation that continues to this day. In fact, the very first canon of the revised Code of Canon Law promulgated by Pope John Paul II in 1983 states: "The canons of this code affect only the Latin church."

This chapter deals in the main with the development of the Latin Code of Canon Law. But the record begins in the East, for it is there that the church's canonical collections originated as the foundation of the discipline of their respective Christian communities.

The Cradle of Canons

The first collection of canons is thought to be that for the province of Pontus bordering the Black Sea in Asia Minor.

It comprised the twenty canons of the Council of Nicaea (325), the twenty-five canons of the Council of Ancyra (314), and the fifteen of Neocaesarea (314-325). The church at Antioch adopted this collection around 341, adding another twenty-five canons in the process. Local councils expanded the collection further, and the collection was sufficiently comprehensive by the time of the convoking of the ecumenical Council of Chalcedon in 451 as to provide a reference point for the discussions. The collection was hardly complete, however. Chalcedon wove some thirty canons more into the collection, and various other canons, including the eighty-five so-called "Apostolic Canons" and the four canons of the Council of Constantinople of 381, were picked up so that by the sixth century the church in the East had gathered the elements of a solid, methodical body of church law—several hundred articles governing hierarchical organization, social structure, worship, sacramental and liturgical rites, religious life, clerical and lay disciplines, and other aspects of ecclesiastical and institutional being.

Translated from the Greek to the Latin, the East's canonical collection enlarged the context for the development of the West's own system of canon law. Until then, the Western church had made do largely on the basis of local law based on usage and papal letters known as decretals. These were not drawn together into a single corpus until around the year 500 and the arrival in Rome of the Scythian monk Dionysius Exiguus. The decretals were born both of papal initiatives and in response to questions submitted to popes by various parties. The purpose in unifying them was obviously to enhance the authority of the pope by giving them the strength of law. Other areas of Western Christendom were developing codes of their own, but the Dionysian one acquired status such that Pope Adrian I (772-795) presented the collection to the future emperor Charlemagne in 774 as the canonical book of the Roman church. Known as the Dionysio-Hadriana canon, the collection soon became the code of the whole Western church—Anglo-Saxon regions excepted.

Because of distance, the churches of the Anglo-Saxon regions—England, Scotland, Wales and Ireland—were slower in coming into Rome's centralizing movement. But they made their contribution nonetheless to the development of canon law, the Irish church most especially. Through the legion of missionary monks that fanned out across the continent, the Irish church spread a system known as Penitentials for the guidance of confessors in assigning penances for sins owned to in the confessional. A Roman Penitential did not exist. In many places the Irish Penitential, with its catalogue of sins and corresponding scales of penances, became the guiding norm, and so remained for a long period of time. Along with the Penitentials of the other insular churches, the Irish Penitentials proved a historic influence on Western civilization, helping shape many moral codes and customs of the larger society.

Other systematic collections of canon law were taking shape in the meantime, achieving currency across North Africa and in areas of Italy, Spain, France and Germany.

Also appearing was the famous code known as the False Decretals. These were the so-called pseudo-Isidore forgeries, and they came into circulation between 847 and 857. The False Decretals joined spurious letters of popes of the first three centuries to historically authentic decretals of later periods to comprise a skillful intermixture of the false and the true, and a convincing document overall. The False Decretals did not greatly influence or modify canon law. Mostly they were concerned with the stability of ecclesiastical geographical units, such as dioceses and provinces, and the rights of bishops and clergy against the encroachments of temporal power. From some points of view, the False Decretals, rather than being subversive or corrupting, were laudable in that they served positive canonical purpose. But they were forgeries, and once they came under suspicion they were doomed. They influenced much, however, before disappearing.

The False Decretals, for one thing, helped point up the need for stronger controls, vested in some central authority, by accenting the dangers of canonical free-lancing, then in vogue among the various churches of the West. The False Decretals thus contributed in their oblique way to progress towards canonical unity. In so doing they also quickened the movement in the Western church, and notably throughout Frankish regions, toward centralization of authority around the see of Rome.

Finally, and probably as could be expected, the False Decretals wrote *finis* to the last of the chronological collections of canon law—that is, the last in which the canons were listed in the order in which they appeared, rather than according to some thematic or classified order. For in probing the authenticity of the decretals, scholars agreed to the need for some more systematic presentation of the church's canons than seriatim additions tacked one upon another. In other words, the church needed a coherent, codified body of laws, a workable system of interpretive texts, which drew conclusions as it countered objections relating to the subject matter.

A Coherent Code

Such a process did indeed develop between the end of the ninth century and the middle of the twelfth, and it led to the corpus of canon law *(corpus juris canonici)* of the Camaldulesian monk Gratian.

Stimulated by the vigor of intellectual life in Bologna, with its coincidental focus on civil law, Gratian took the existing mass of canonical texts of wide origins and differing periods, and applying Abelard's dialectical *Sic et Non* (Yea and Nay) method, he produced the code that was to become the foundation of the classic law of the church. Thus Gratian's *Concordia discordantium canonum,* or *Decretum,* came into being about 1140.

Gratian demonstrated that, just as a civil society could have its corpus of law, so could an orderly system of ecclesiastical jurisprudence be drawn up for a church. His methodology involved the synthesizing of patristic, conciliar and papal teachings into a body of law covering organization (the hierarchy, clerical discipline, excommunication, etc.), social structure of the Christian society (matrimony, usury, the interrelation of religious and secular societies, etc.), and liturgical order (belief, the sacramental system, worship, etc.). Gratian's *Decretum* was never officially received by the church as its authentic collection of laws, but from the reign of Alexander III (1159-1181) until the twentieth century it served as a basic manual of the Roman Curia.

Not that there were not other developments in canon law in the meantime. Gratian's *Decretum,* basic as it was, was still tentative and fragmentary on a number of issues, and accordingly was in some respects a work of transitory character. Its incompleteness sparked a surge of new canonical writings, commentaries in the form of glosses, and new compilations intended to complete the work. The supplements resulted in the accumulation of a body of material as considerable as the *Decretum* itself, and this led in turn to supplementary collections of canon law. Pope Gregory IX (1227-1241) sponsored the first of these, and others followed under Gregory X (1271-1276), Nicholas III (1277-1280), Boniface VIII (1294-1303) and Clement V (1305-1314). Meanwhile, the code moved more and more away from a presentation of solutions for particular problem cases to the articulation of a hard body of abstract law. The net result was the solidification of a living, uniform body of law, one that strengthened under the twin influences of centralized ecclesiastical authority and a closely regulated society. The ecclesiastical law which this corpus included came to constitute the classical law of the church, and even now is commonly called by this name.

With canon law established as a science and the distinction made between it and theology, schools of canon law began to flourish—in France at the University of Paris; in England at Oxford, Northampton and the cathedral schools of Exeter and Lincoln; in Spain at Palencia, Salamanca and Valladolid; in Italy at Padua, Vercelli, Siena and Piacenza, as well as Bologna of course. Canonical literature became a species of its own, spawning works under such headings as *commentaria, summae, quaestiones, repetitiones, consilia, responsa,* etc. Periodically there had been talk of "closing" the body of law, but this was never to eventuate. External circumstances —schisms, the Reformation, papal and conciliar decisions, acts of the increasingly busy Vatican congregations, the discovery of the new world, social changes, seemingly endless scientific breakthroughs—made unrealistic any hope of the code's ever being carved in stone. To this day the church's code of law, however specific, retains about it certain elements of fluidity.

In the aftermath of the Reformation, the Council of Trent (1545-1563) ordered a revision of all the church's official books, canon law included. So far as canon law was concerned, the revision was to anchor the church more firmly in the papacy. But old canon law was not abolished. Again, it was supplemented and renewed, its focus strongly on the position and duties of clerics, the governance of ordinations, benefices and patronages, the place of religious orders, synods, behavioral matters, criminal proceedings, penitential discipline and marriage —the last in special detail.

"A Thousand Perplexities"

The curious thing is that the laws enacted by Trent and those issued later by various dicasteries of the Roman Curia were never digested into a single collection.

Thus the church eventually had to cope again with the very situation it had earlier: "an immense pile of laws piled on top of other laws." Once more there was confusion. Obsolescence and lacunae in many laws quickened problems of discipline and observance, and increasingly there were calls for an updating of the code. The calls were insistent by the nineteenth century, with hopes strongly linked to Vatican Council I (1869-1870), as a petition of a group of French bishops confirmed. "It is absolutely clear," they said, "and has for a long time past been universally acknowledged and asserted, that a revision and reform of the canon law is necessary and most urgent. As matters now stand, in consequence of the many and grave changes in human affairs and in society, many laws have become useless, others difficult or impossible to obey. With regard to a great number of canons, it is a matter of dispute whether they are still in force or are abrogated. Finally, in the course of so many centuries, the number of ecclesiastical laws has increased to such an extent, and these laws have accumulated in such immense collections, that in a certain sense we can well say: We are crushed beneath the laws, *obruimur legibus*. Hence arise infinite and inextricable difficulties which obstruct the study of canon law; an immense field for controversy and litigation; a thousand perplexities of conscience, and finally contempt for the laws."

But Vatican I adopted a different agenda. It focused on universal papal primacy and papal infallibility—canon law issues, to be sure, but not the sum of canon law. In point of fact, a revision of canon law from beginning to end was a matter so vast as not to lend itself particularly to conciliar action. Besides, Europe was on the brink of war, and this along with attendant pressures did not make feasible something so time-consuming as a wholesale revision of the church's canons. As it was, the decisive vote on papal infallibility came only one day before the breakout of the Franco-German war of 1870-1871.

RETROSPECT

The Council hastily adjourned and was never to reconvene.

It was left then to Pope Pius X (1903-1914) to resurrect the issue, and this he did at the very beginning of his reign, when he named a commission under Cardinal Pietro Gasparri to collect and reform all ecclesiastical laws. The work took twelve years to complete, and the result was a new Code of Canon Law grouped into five books, substantially imitating the institutes of Roman law with respect to persons, actions and things. The arrangement of the laws was different from anything that had existed before, and so was their form, articles being expressed in briefer, more succinct terminology. But the old disciplines were retained. As various portions of the code were completed in 1912, 1913 and 1914, they were sent to the bishops and superiors of major religious orders for their review. The whole was then collected into a body of law officially called the *Codex iuris canonici,* Code of Canon Law. Pius X, later to be sainted, did not live to see the new code into law. It was Benedict XV (1914-1922) who promulgated the new code in the constitution *Providentissima mater ecclesia,* on Pentecost, May 27, 1917. It took effect the following Pentecost, May 19, 1918.

It was thought that the 1918 Code of Canon Law would stand for an indefinite, open-ended period of time. But within just a few decades the world had so changed, and with it so many external and internal customs of the church, that a modernization was necessary. Pope John XXIII set the modernizing process in motion on January 25, 1959, the historic day closing the annual

Octave of Prayer for Christian Unity when he revealed plans for a Roman synod and a worldwide ecumenical council to cardinals assembled at St. Paul's Outside-the-Walls, an event he was to recall six months later in the encyclical *Ad Petri cathedram.* The revision would take some ten years longer to accomplish than the previous one, and John XXIII would be long dead by the time the new code was ready for promulgation. But he would be remembered as its initiator. The new code would be promulgated on January 25, 1983—the anniversary, twenty-four years to the day, of John's announcement—with glowing references to his "predecessor of happy memory" by the reigning John Paul II.

Postconciliar Revisions

This latest modernization of canon law proved to be an especially complex process, for the revision process had to span a council and no fewer than four papacies—John XXIII, Paul VI, John Paul I and John Paul II.

The process was never in danger of being jettisoned. Paul VI in fact announced on June 22, 1963, the very first day after his election, that he would continue the work begun by his predecessor, and that determination carried forward through the papacies to follow.

The truly serious work on the new code began after the Council and proceeded according to formulae outlined to commission members by Paul VI on November 20, 1965—namely, that canon law flows from the nature of the church; that its purpose was to be viewed in terms of the care of souls and salvation; that a reform was needed in order to adapt church law to changed circumstances. Paul stressed that the task was not simply to reorganize old laws into some more orderly arrangement, as in the instance of the so-called Pio-Benedictine Code of 1918, but rather to reform old norms to accommodate them to a new mentality and new needs, even if the old law was to be the foundation for the revision.

And so the work proceeded. Bishops around the world were asked to recommend experts on canonical law for work on the commission. They saw draft texts and were invited to make suggestions for their improvement. But the real work was done in Rome, the process ultimately engaging the labors of 105 cardinals, 77 archbishops and bishops, 73 secular presbyters, 47 religious presbyters, 3 religious women and 12 laity from 5 continents and 31 countries as commission members, consulters and collaborators of one sort or another.

The result was a revised code of 1,752 canons, nearly 700 fewer than the old code of 2,414. The canons were grouped into seven books of specific themes or norms as follows: General Norms (Canons 1-203); The People of God (Canons 204-746); The Teaching Office of the Church (Canons 747-833); The Sanctifying Office of the Church (Canons 834-1253); Temporal Goods of the Church (Canons 1254-1310); Sanctions in the Church (Canons 1311-1399); Procedures (Canons 1400-1752). The collection was then reviewed by John Paul II, and

John Deedy

hardly perfunctorily so; he made changes of his own, one of which, of course, was the rescinding of a canon reducing the number of holy days of obligation. The new code was finally promulgated by the pope as the new fundamental law of the church on January 25, 1983. It took effect November 27, 1983.

The church's intention, as made clear by John Paul II, is that the new code perpetuate the spirit and further the work of Vatican II. But the code is in no way intended as a substitute for faith, grace, charisms and especially charity in the life of the church and of the faithful. "On the contrary," said the pope in the document of promulgation, "its purpose is rather to create such an order in the ecclesial society that, while assigning the primacy to love, grace and charisms, it at the same time renders their organic development easier in the life of both the ecclesial society and the individual persons who belong to it."

But streamlined and improved as the new code was, there apparently was some lingering of affection for the old. John Paul II put an end to that in a talk to the Roman Rota on January 26, 1984. ". . . [It] cannot be forgotten that the period of *drafting* is over," the pope declared with emphasis, "and that now, the law, even with its possible limitations and defects, is a *choice* already made by the legislator after careful reflection and . . . [it] therefore demands full adherence."

This does not mean, of course, that the church's Code of Canon Law cannot be revised, in whole or in part, at some future date. Once again, nothing is clearer from history but that the letter of the church's code is not carved in stone. But any revision is for the church's tomorrows to determine. Right now, the church's law is the law. In the Western or Latin church, that means the law promulgated in 1983 by John Paul II. As stated earlier, Eastern Rite churches have their own canon law.

16.

PAPAL INFALLIBILITY:
A Doctrine Born of the Evolutionary Process

A New Variable

WHEN Baltimore's Cardinal James Gibbons returned from a visit to Rome after Vatican I and toward the end of the last century, he was reportedly asked by a newsman if the pope was really infallible. "All I know," replied Gibbons, "is that he kept referring to me as 'Jibbons.'"

The point of the story pivoted of course on the pronunciation in the Italian language of the letter "g" as "j" (the pope at the time was the Italian, Leo XIII, a native of Carpineto). It was one of many such yarns—most of them no doubt apocryphal—circulating at the time with reference to infallibility. Another had a visitor asking Leo's predecessor, Pius IX, what it felt like to be infallible. Pius is said to have answered, "I do not know whether I am fallible or infallible. But one thing I am sure of, I'm *in fallimento* [bankrupt]!"

There was nothing irreverent about these particular jests. Mostly they reflected the fascination that the notion of papal infallibility held even on the kindly disposed. The fascination was to be expected. The Catholic

RETROSPECT

Church had been around going on to 2,000 years, but it was not until 1870 that the pope, its head, was formally declared to be infallible, absolutely so, when in the exercise of his office as pastor and teacher he pronounced on matters of faith and morals.

The pronouncement seemed a radical departure from the past, and was bitterly criticized in many quarters, particularly Protestant ones. The proclamation remains to this day a Catholic-Protestant ecumenical stumbling block.

But, in fact, the church had historically exercised its authority with the confidence of its being infallible. The declaration of papal infallibility may have telescoped the infallibility concept in a new and narrow context, but there was no question that from the beginning the church considered itself free of error in faith and morals—and acted accordingly. Tertullian ridiculed the idea that the church could possibly be wrong; Saint Polycarp was so intolerant of the mere suggestion of error that in one street encounter he purportedly denounced the maverick Marcion as "the firstborn of Satan"; and what else could the anathemas, inquisitions and ecclesiastically approved tortures of other days be rooted in but the conviction that right resided in the church, and with those who were its properly authorized instrument?

Yet reactions to the 1870 declaration of papal infallibility—whether of anger, or sport, or whatever—had to be expected. For however much church leaders could appeal to Christ and the Scriptures, and to tradition, in defense of their understanding and interpretation of infallibility, the reality was that the equation now was different. If there had not been a certain dogmatic development—and there certainly seemed to have been one—then there definitely was a new mode of exercise of the power of infallibility—through the centralization of the power in the hands of a single person. It wasn't always this way.

The Rise of Certainty

The church's claim to infallibility is essentially scriptural, being deduced from such passages as Matthew 28:18-20 ("All power is given to me in heaven and on earth. Go therefore, teach ye all nations, baptizing them in the name of the Father, and of the Son, and of the Holy Spirit; teaching them to observe all things whatsoever I have commanded you; and know that I am with you all days, even to the end of the world"), and chapters 14, 15 and 16 of the Gospel of John.

Doctors of the church and various councils added the weight of authority to the claim, but the basic difference then was this: rather than belonging to a single person, infallibility was vested in the collective body of bishops acting in concert with the pope, who was in effect the chief bishop, their head and center. This was logical, and a simple enough procedure when the church was a neat, compact organization, its leaders all within easy geographical reach of one another. It was only when the church started to expand to distant corners of the then-known world that complications arose.

RETROSPECT

The exercise of authority in the early church, in sum, was very much a collegial thing, and the notion that infallibility might reside in a single individual was altogether foreign. It was a notion that belonged in fact to the pagan hubris surrounding the old Roman emperors, and which the first Christians were anxious to repudiate. As said, the church obviously believed itself to be infallible. But from the Councils of Nicaea to Chalcedon to Florence to Trent, the principal way of exercising its infallibility—whether in confirming the symbols and formulas of faith, condemning heresies, or casting out the reprobates—was through ecumenical or general councils of the episcopate.

Ecumenical councils are still regarded as infallible expressions of the church in action—the *sensus ecclesiae,* mind of the church, taking form and shape in assemblies convened or at least authorized by the pope, *ante* or *post factum.* But ecumenical councils were and remain rare events; there have been only twenty-one in the church's 2,000-year history. But rare or not, infallibility is now far more popularly associated with the pope than with councils.

Certainly, such has been the case since 1870 and Vatican Council I's formal declaration of papal infallibility. At the same time, it is true that as far back as the reigns of Damasus I (366-384) and of Leo the Great (440-461) popes consciously cultivated the aura of the papacy's infallibility. Damasus stressed the link between Peter and the Bishop of Rome, a thought fostered further by such sainted successors as Siricius (384-399) and Innocent I

(401-417). As for Leo, he assumed for himself and his successors for all time the title of supreme pontiff, *pontifex maximus,* which had just lately been discarded by the Roman emperors. It was Leo, too, who first made the claim to a plenitude of power, *plenitudo potestatis,* and with that claim the ground was prepared for the eventual locating of all cognitive power and all authority relating to faith and morals in the unerring and unerrable person of the pope. Even without conciliar confirmation, it was a power that proved remarkably impervious to the caprices of history, the concept surviving even the collapse of the theocratic world order, the presumably idyllic ecclesiastical period that ended with the reign of Boniface VIII (1294-1303). The Reformation dealt a blow to the concept of an unerring church head, but not in Roman Catholicism, where the faithful continued to look upon the pope as preserved from error, whether he was formally defined as infallible or not.

Several factors converged to make formal definition of papal infallibility a Catholic imperative. A remote factor was Gallican, Febronian and Josephian conciliarism, centered respectively in France, Germany and the Austrio-Hungarian Empire. Conciliarism held the authority of general church councils to be above that of any person, including the pope himself, and it resisted Roman or papal centralism in favor of greater autonomy for national churches. The threats which these varieties of conciliarism presented to Rome were more theoretical than real by the middle of the nineteenth century, but one can readily see why Rome would be anxious to establish a bulwark against the possibility of any future resurgence.

A more proximate cause was the French Revolution and the waves of secularism which followed in its wake, flooding society with what church leaders saw as an ocean of liberalism and materialism. It was a situation that contributed initially to what amounted to a challenge to modern civilization, Pope Pius IX's Syllabus of 1864, *Quanta cura,* and ultimately to a Catholic commitment to exert a firmer moral control over the state of affairs in the wider social community.

But how was the latter to be accomplished? The prestige of the papacy was experiencing an eclipse with the deterioration of the Papal States, and the pope was coming to account less and less in the determination of events in the ecumenical and secular societies. The situation cried in Rome for correction, and Pius IX gave thought to the calling of a general council whose object would be "to discover with God's help the necessary remedies against the many evils which oppress the church." The church had not convened a council in some three hundred years, and to many it seemed an opportune time for a forceful reaffirmation both of Catholic Christian principles and of papal primacy.

Vatican I

In an unusual display of collegiality, thirty-six bishops of Italy, France, Spain, Austria, Hungary, Germany, Belgium and England were polled on the plan.

Not only did they support the idea, but eight returned

John Deedy

memoranda favoring an explicit declaration of papal infallibility. Only the unerring voice of the church actualized in the person of the pope, it was argued, could put an end to the spiritual confusion that gripped much of the world. It was further contended that a declaration of papal infallibility would correct what many church leaders felt was the great oversight of the Council of Trent—its failure to condemn the fundamental error of reformers; namely, their denial of the hierarchical structure of the church and the church's authority to teach unerringly.

So Vatican Council I was convened on December 8, 1869, and though by now papal infallibility was a hotly debated topic both inside and outside the church, it was not among the topics (*schemata*) officially scheduled for deliberation. To be sure there were chapters on primacy and the pontifical magisterium, but papal infallibility itself was not added until later, and with a certain hesitation on the part of the council presidents. Once on the floor, debate was intense, many holding that the moment was not opportune for declaration of such a doctrine—a contention which spawned the reverse logic that a declaration had become opportune for the very reason that under the pretext of inopportuneness the concept of papal infallibility was itself being attacked. The infallibility chapter went through several drafts and a seemingly endless number of amendments (the fourth draft alone drew one hundred and forty-four amendments) before a final text was agreed upon. Thus was born the dogmatic constitution *Pastor aeternus* and the decisive passage:

RETROSPECT

"We teach and define . . . that the Roman Pontiff, when he speaks *ex cathedra,* that is, when in the exercise of his office as pastor and teacher of all Christians, he defines, by virtue of his supreme apostolic authority, a doctrine of faith or morals to be held by the whole church—is, by reason of the divine assistance promised to him in blessed Peter, possessed of that infallibility with which the Divine Redeemer wished his church to be endowed in defining doctrines of faith and morals; and consequently that such definitions of the Roman Pontiff are irreformable of their own nature, and not by reason of the church's consent."

The last phrase, it might be noted, put to rout the rearguard—those who held that infallibility was a collective power residing in the church at large and its councils rather than a single individual.

Despite all the controversy, the vote on *Pastor aeternus* at the solemn session of July 18, 1870—Pope Pius IX himself presiding—was decisive. Four hundred and thirty-three voted *placet* ("it pleases") and only two *non placet* ("it does not please"). The lone official dissenters were Bishop Luigi Riccio of Caiazzo in the then Kingdom of Naples and Bishop Edward Fitzgerald of Little Rock, Arkansas. However, sixty-one of the Council Fathers conveniently absented themselves from the critical session, submitting written objections, then leaving Rome on the eve of the vote. (In fairness, some had good reason to make a hasty exit, for European political tensions were high, and indeed the very next day the Franco-Prussian War erupted.)

259

John Deedy

Once the infallibility decree was voted though, Riccio and Fitzgerald, and all of the sixty-one whose chose for whatever reason not to vote, made their peace with its teaching. In a few places, notably Germany and Austria, some bishops were slow in signifying acceptance by publishing the decrees of the Council in their dioceses, but within a year or two all had done so. The episcopal lines might have bent, but there were no breakaway bishops. The church, however, did lose some from the ranks. A number of prominent priests and professors were irreconcilable, and they formed themselves into a so-called Committee of Bonn. Out of that group grew the schismatic church known as "Old Catholics," a church which still exists, though generally without great influence or impact. By and large, the Roman Catholic Church escaped major fall-out from the infallibility decree.

Adherents and Dissidents

The infallibility decree accomplished much of what proponents had hoped it would. Certainly, it solidified the spiritual and ecclesiastical power of the papacy at a critical point in its history, and directly or otherwise this would eventually re-enhance the authority of the pope in the wider world community.

Two months after the adoption of *Pastor aeternus,* the Papal States were swallowed up in the Italian Risorgimento and the temporal authority which had belonged to the papacy for a millenium in effect was gone forever.

RETROSPECT

The pope was now a purely spiritual leader. But primacy and infallibility strengthened that dimension of the papal office—to such a degree, in fact, that the loss of temporal authority was to prove benefit rather than bane.

Actually, to the extent that problems were spawned by the definitions of primacy and infallibility, they were mainly of a procedural kind, and stemmed mostly from Vatican I's failure to situate the papacy in the broader context of the church. The episcopacy and the power that bishops might possess by virtue of episcopal collegiality hardly entered into the Council's discussions. This opened doors for a radical centralization of ecclesiastical power in the papacy. Primacy and infallibility crept from matters of faith and morals to issues of all kinds, and from the pope to his Curia. Bishops were more and more reduced to functionaries of Rome, managers whose principal responsibility was to perform loyally and communicate papal teaching faithfully.

Vatican Council II (1962-1965) would seek to correct this disequilibrium with a reformulation of the principle of collegiality—the proposition that the bishops of the church in union with, but also subordinate to, the pope share in the supreme teaching and pastoral authority in the church. Vatican II's initiative would lead to the creation of the Synods of Bishops and the institution of consultative procedures of various kinds. But not a whole lot has changed. Collegiate power is on the books. Obviously it will be accepted and honored by popes, as they are elected, but, as is already apparent, with their individual understandings of what collegiality means. Papal primacy and papal infallibility remain principles that are thoroughly strong in Roman Catholicism.

But neither principle is home free, totally relieved of challenge and the possibility of change. Each concept continues to be studied and probed by theologians—as by Hans Küng, the controversial Swiss priest-professor who is a member of the faculty of the University of Tubingen in Germany. Küng alleges that the church's understanding is quite wrong, certainly in the matter of papal infallibility. Essentially, Küng's thesis is that there is no serious exegetical, historical or theological ground for the doctrine of infallibility; that infallibility belongs only to God; and that the church's legitimate spiritual claim is rather to "indefectibility or perpetuity in the truth." What this means, in Küng's words, is that "the church remains in the truth, and this is not annulled by the sum total of individual errors." In other words, the church can and does err through the pope (e.g., on Galileo, usury and, in Küng's opinion, birth control), but the church remains the community of the faithful, assured of surviving all upheavals, for the message of Christ will endure and Christ will remain "with her in the Spirit and thus keep her through all errors and confusions in the truth." Küng formalized his theories in the book *Infallible? An Inquiry* (New York, 1971).

Of course, Rome would have none of this theorizing, and there was little delay in making this known to Küng. Küng was put under immediate pressure to withdraw his opinions on papal infallibility, as well as on other points of dogma, among them the Virgin Birth and the divinity of Christ. When he refused, his ecclesiastical theological credentials were lifted. Under a compromise reached in 1980, Küng was able to remain on the faculty at Tubingen, but he was no longer responsible to the Catholic theology department in the state-run university, and he could no longer be involved in examining candidates for the priesthood.

Authority in Writing

Obviously, Rome is unqualifiedly committed to the proposition of papal infallibility.

At the same time it has to be conceded that Rome has not exactly flaunted the doctrine or the power of infallibility. Infallibility, in fact, has been directly invoked but once in the years since its promulgation in 1870, and that was in 1950 by Pope Pius XII in defining the dogma of the Virgin Mary's Assumption into heaven. Indeed, most popes seem wary in their approach to the doctrine of infallibility. Paul VI, for instance, in 1970 allowed the one hundredth anniversary of Vatican I's promulgation of papal infallibility to pass without official notice, and he did not specifically invoke infallibility in making his weighty and contentious statement on artificial birth control. Rather he chose the vehicle of the papal encyclical, and gave the Catholic Christian world *Humanae vitae*.

Encyclicals are a primary method for implementing the church's teaching authority, but it is a matter of debate precisely how binding they are. Certainly they are authoritative statements, but are they infallible? Pius XII addressed the subject in the encyclical *Humani generis* of August 12, 1950:

"Nor must it be thought that what is contained in encyclical letters does not of itself demand assent, on the pretext that the popes do not exercise in them the supreme power of their teaching authority. Rather, such teachings belong to the ordinary magisterium, of which it is true to say 'He who hears you, hears me' (Luke 10:16); for the most part, too, what is expounded and inculcated in encyclical letters already appertains to Catholic doctrine for other reasons. But if the supreme pontiffs in their official documents purposely pass judgment on a matter debated until then, it is obvious to all that the matter, according to the mind and will of the same pontiffs, cannot be considered any longer a question open for discussion among theologians."

The fact is, however, that rather than Pius XII's being the last word on a topic, encyclicals and their subject matter remain very much open for discussion, and from all ideological sides. If progressives and liberals did not like *Humanae vitae,* and were most outspoken in their opposition, neither did hardline conservatives like John XXIII's *Mater et magistra* (1961), as was typified by the *National Review*'s celebrated term of rejection, "Mater, si, Magistra, no"—mother, yes; teacher, no. The tradition of disagreement and dissent from encyclicals continues.

Many on both the ideological left and right objected to John Paul II's equating of Western capitalism and

RETROSPECT

Soviet-style Marxism in the 1988 encyclical on the social concerns of the church, *Sollicitudo rei socialis.*

The general attitude appears to be that encyclicals are important documents expressing the mind of the church as reflected in the thinking of the reigning pope, but that the contents of encyclicals do not become dogma per se merely by fact of their being put forth in an encyclical. This is an attitude more reflective of the conclusion of the 1913 *Catholic Encyclopedia:* "The degree to which the infallible magisterium of the Holy See is committed [in an encyclical] must be judged from the circumstances, and from the language in the particular case."

Status Quo

Whatever the Catholic understanding of all this, infallibility remains an ecumenical impediment, although interchurch commissions have been at work on the issue.

A Lutheran-Catholic commission of the 1970s, for instance, situated infallibility "in the theological categories of promise, trust, and hope rather than in the juridical categories of law, obligation, and obedience," in a meeting of minds which some thought advanced the possibility of reunion under some type of "universal primacy" exercised by the "see of Rome." Once again, Rome was not buying.

In *The Papacy in Transition* (New York, 1980), Patrick Granfield cited four areas of clarification and explanation concerning infallibility which underlie much Catholic ecumenical thought: (1) papal infallibility must be seen in the context of the entire church, which church is also infallible; (2) an infallible teaching only affords a partial and inadequate insight into the mystery of God, so therefore there is a continual need to interpret and reformulate dogmas, in order to discern their meaning more accurately; (3) every infallibility definition is historically conditioned by such elements as language, the limited context of faith and knowledge in the given situation, and by changeable thought patterns of particular periods; (4) recognition that the ultimate trust of Catholic Christians is in Christ and the Gospels, not in the doctrine of infallibility, whether of Scripture, church or pope. "These four observations help theologians to ground their discussions more soundly, as well as to develop a more acceptable ecumenical base," Granfield observed.

There is no indication, however, that Rome is ready to embrace those points or others which are likely to change inherited formulas and current operative modes of papal primacy and infallibility. Perhaps there is anxiety lest the authority of the pope be diminished; perhaps there is concern that a restatement of infallibility might open for reexamination large chunks of Catholic faith whose basis is ecclesial rather than scriptural, such as the doctrines of the Virgin Birth and of Mary's Assumption. Whatever the considerations, and they would be many, the exercise of infallibility in the church is likely to be for the indefinite future what it has been since the promulgation of *Pastor aeternus* in 1870. But this is quite a different exercise of authority from that which was known in the more collegial early church.

17.

CANONIZATION:
The Saints Come Marching in, in Numbers Awesome

Adoration to Veneration

IT IS A holy and wholesome thought to honor the dead, and people have been doing so since primitive times in recognition of illustrious deeds of bravery or other great services of particular individuals.

Some ancient people did not even wait until death had claimed the hero to do their consecrating. They apotheosized their hero—that is, raised him or her to the rank of a god—during the person's very lifetime. Emperors, for instance, were accorded divine honors. Some refused the honors; most accepted them as nothing less than what was due one of their exalted rank.

The Catholic practice is to reward confirmed sanctity with beatification and canonization of the hallowed dead, a process that evolved over many centuries and which at one time did not involve distinction as to rank. There was no marked difference, in other words, between beatification and canonization.

In the view of some writers of old, the Catholic practice of honoring the heroes of Christian history with beatification and canonization—these would be the church's blesseds and saints, respectively—traced back to the custom of pagan apotheosis. It was a nettlesome contention in many Catholic circles, and one which drew the fire of Pope Benedict XIV, in what is termed "his masterly treatise," *De servorum Dei beatificatione et beatorum canonizatione*. But the defense was a considerable time in being formulated. Benedict reigned from 1740-1758.

In fairness, there was from the beginning a distinct difference between pagan apotheosis and Christian canonization. For one thing, the Christian hero was never adored or worshipped. Adoration and worship belonged to God and God alone. Christian scholars defined that as *latria*. The Christian hero, by distinction, was to be venerated—an act called *dulia* in the instance of saints and blesseds; *hyperdulia* in the case of the Virgin Mary, because of her "greater excellence." The honoring came as no accident of birth, as with some of the pagans apotheosized. The church honored only those whose lives had been marked by the exercise of heroic virtue, and then only after this fact had been indisputably confirmed, or theoretically so.

Canonization—beatification too—is now an involved, infinitely detailed procedure overseen by its own special Vatican curial office, the Congregation for the Causes of Saints. But the sainting of those of heroic virtue was once a fairly simple process, rooted mainly in cumulative public acclaim rather than bureaucratic findings—as for example the sainthood of Flavianus, which was confirmed in 451 during the eleventh session of the Council of Chalcedon, the Council Fathers exclaiming: "Flavianus lives after death! May the Martyr pray for us! "

To be sure, martyrs were always special, as one could see from the epistle circulated in the early church of Smyrna with respect to Saint Polycarp, who was martyred February 23, 155. "We have at last gathered his bones, which are dearer to us than priceless gems and purer than gold," said the epistle, "and laid them to rest where it was befitting they should lie. And if it be possible for us to assemble again, may God grant us to celebrate the birthday of his martyrdom with gladness, thus to recall the memory of those who fought in the glorious combat, and to teach and strengthen, by his example, those who shall come after us."

Martyrs, obviously, were the perfect Christians. They were instant saints, their supreme sacrifice providing visible, irrefutable proof of their love for Christ and his church. There was no question in the church's mind but that they were indefectibly united with Christ in heaven. Thus they were honored, but in ways that differed from the usual commemorations of the dead. As the Polycarp epistle made clear, their memorial days were to be celebrated. The person was in heaven, virtually certifiably so. Memorial days of the sainted thus became feast days, times for thanksgiving and celebration. The church's calendar of feasts was crowded early on with feasts of the martyred.

John Deedy

Local Authority

The blood of martyrs nourished the seeds of the faith. But martyrs were not the sum of the story, the only heroes.

What of the many who had defended the faith and suffered for it—confessors of the faith, they were termed—but whose lives were closed not in martyrdom but Christian peace? What of ascetics and others who lived lives of distinguished virtue after the Roman persecutions were over, when dying for the faith was no longer a likelihood? What of those who excelled in doctrinal learning and theological skills—those called doctors of the church? What of the great missionary priests and bishops, who brought the faith to distant lands? What of those who distinguished themselves by their austerities, their remarkable devotion, their charities? Saints there were among those people too, but with nothing so explicit as a martyrdom to set them apart and define their sanctity, who was to decide whether their lives were so holy that they should be officially honored as saints?

In a decentralized church, the answer was the bishops, and specifically the bishop of the area where the holy one had borne his or her witness. The bishop had the advantage of proximity and familiarity. He could observe the record and determine from close study whether the particular person merited so-called public *cultus*. If the determination was affirmative, the honor was strictly a local one, however. From earliest times, it was only the bishop of Rome, the pope, who could decree a *cultus* deserving of acceptance in the universal church.

The problem with local determination of sainthood was that the system was vulnerable to enthusiasms, partialities and worse. Abuses of several kinds inevitably crept in. Fervor was known to overwhelm rationalities. Laxness and carelessness were suspected of resulting in the recognition of "saints" whose qualifications were dubious. There was even talk in some instances of the perpetration of outright fraud.

The net consequence was that Rome eventually moved to restrict the authority of local bishops to pronounce on sainthood. But that was not until towards the close of the eleventh century. Several popes, among them Urban II (1088-1099), Calistus II (1119-1124) and Eugenius III (1145-1153), began to gather to Rome the authority to determine who was to be sainted and who not. But the old ways did not die easily or quickly, not even after Alexander III (1159-1181) in 1170 declared that bishops could not institute the *cultus* of a new saint without the authority of Rome. Local bishops still continued to canonize. It was not until 1634 that Urban VIII (1623-1644) brought the matter to an end with a bull reserving exclusively to Rome the right to canonize.

Popes are now central to the canonization process, but it is plain they were slow in arriving there. Indeed, except to confirm declarations of canonization, popes for centuries were relatively detached from the process. The first papal canonization for which positive documents exist is not found until the reign of Benedict VI (973-974) and the elevation of Saint Udalricus. That was in 973.

Still, the intimate involvement of popes in the canonization procedure did not translate immediately to great systematization of the process. In the twelfth and thirteenth centuries there were numerous pronouncements of sainthood by popes, but the methodology was casual, some would say careless, certainly by modern standards. Procedural norms would eventually be developed, but at first guidelines of detailed kind were lacking, and authenticating investigations scanty. In many instances, inquiries into the life and holiness of the candidate for canonization took place soon after the person's death. Testimonies were gathered on the spot from those acquainted with the individual, and these inquiries were often as speedy as the decision whether to canonize or not. Time intervals were not built into the system to protect against rash or impulsive conclusions. Saint Peter of Castelnau, for instance, died January 15, 1208, and was canonized March 12 of the same year.

The wonder is that the process worked as well as it did. Some of the church's greatest saints were raised up during this period. They included Saint Thomas of Canterbury, who died in 1170 and was canonized in 1173; Saint Francis of Assisi, who died October 4, 1226, and was canonized July 19, 1228; Saint Anthony of Padua, who died June 13, 1231, and was canonized June 3, 1232.

Pope Gregory IX (1227-1241) laid the groundwork for a more systematized canonization process in 1234, one which succeeding popes were to build upon. Sixtus V

RETROSPECT

(1585-1590) placed the process within the competency of the Congregation of Rites in 1588, and this resulted in further standardization of norms. The process as it came down to modern times was settled during Urban VIII's pontificate. Urban also was responsible for a considerable pruning of the calendar of saints, decreeing that in cases that had not involved the Holy See, an immemorial public *cultus* had to be shown in order for the person to be continued on the calendar. He fixed "immemorial" at 100 years. The time was 1625. Thus for a *cultus* to be honored, it had to date back to 1525. Gone were many saints, including some who were regarded as martyrs and confessors.

Blessed States

In conjunction with revisions, as mentioned, came the distinction between beatification and canonization. Previously there was no marked difference between the two. Henceforth, they would be two wholly separate ritualistic actions.

Generally speaking, the difference between beatification and canonization is the difference between local (or restricted) and universal veneration of one whose life is marked by holiness and confirmed by the working of miracles. Beatification was, and remains, the penultimate step before sainthood.

Essentially, beatification is the church's authorization of a public *cultus* honoring an individual, but except in extraordinary cases, as happened with Rose of Lima and

John Deedy

Stanislaus Kostka, the cult is limited to a locale or region; said another way, it is the church's permission to venerate a person of known holiness, but with certain restrictions established as to place, community and liturgical solemnity. Canonization, on the other hand, involves a universal precept. It is the church's solemn and definitive statement that a plenitude of honors belongs to the individual everywhere in the church. The person beatified is called blessed; the person canonized is known as saint.

Traditionally, canonization has been regarded as an infallible exercise of the church's authority. Saint Thomas Aquinas, for instance, said of canonization: "Since the honor we pay the saints is in a certain sense a profession of faith, i.e., belief in the glory of the saints (*qua sanctorum gloriam credimus*), we must piously believe that in this matter also the judgment of the church is not liable to error." The consensus was that the same infallibility did not extend to beatification.

The ordinary or common procedure for advancing the cause of one invested with "fame of sanctity" was for the bishop of a diocese to initiate a process of inquiry at a decent interval following the person's death. The bishop would establish a tribunal for the interrogation of witnesses, examination of writings and other documents pertaining to the person's life, study of miracles and other extraordinary events involving the person's life or memory. At one time bishops were free to initiate this process entirely on their own authority, but in 1969 Paul VI decreed in the *motu proprio Sanctitas clarior* that diocesan bishops (or their equivalents) must first consult

274

with the Holy See before introducing a process. The Holy See accordingly now decides whether sufficient grounds exist for going ahead with an action, the deciding being done by the Congregation for the Causes of Saints, which was created out of the Congregation of Rites in 1969 by Paul VI. Pope John Paul II restructured the congregation and refined beatification and canonization procedures further with his apostolic constitution of January 25, 1983, *Divinus perfectionis magister.*

The process proceeds on the local level with special attention paid to the writings of the candidate to authenticate purity of doctrine. Examination is also made of miracles worked through the candidate's intercession. Martyrs are not subjected to the same intense examination as others, the "fame of martyrdom" being sufficient to open most doors to the honors of the altar. But if miracles are not required of martyrs, they are of others, who are expected to produce miracles as signs of God's approval of their cause—traditionally, two to begin with, then two more when the process turned from beatification to canonization. At least that was the practice. As mentioned in the essay dealing with miracles, the insistence is less rigorous nowadays on a specific number of miracles, miracles being harder to certify unequivocally with the advance of science.

Divinus perfectionis magister, for instance, does not demand a specific number of miracles for the advancement of a cause. Miracles nonetheless fit into the process. They are looked to and respected as the ultimate proof of God's approval on the person and life of the future beatus or saint. Since 1983, however, one miracle has sufficed for the advancement of a cause.

The preliminary investigations completed on the local level, the process then passes to Rome, where the procedure pretty much follows that of a suit at law. There is the supreme judge, in this instance the pope himself. There is the postulator, or representative of the petitioners, whose charge it is to furnish arguments and proofs in the candidate's behalf. And finally there is the co-called promoter of the faith, *promoter fidei,* a prosecutor of sorts, whose duty it is to present *animadversiones*—that is, raise objections testing the solidity of the petitioners' case. He is better known as the *advocatus diaboli,* or devil's advocate.

The promoter of the faith, or devil's advocate, is rather a late addition to the processes of beatification and canonization. The first mention of the office is not found until the pontificate of Leo X (1513-1521), and then it was united with that of the fiscal advocate. Clement XI (1700-1721) regarded the two functions in the one office as incompatible, and named Prospero Lambertini, one of the most distinguished jurists of the day, to formulate an autonomous office of general promoter of the faith. Lambertini did his work well, and in due course was elected pope. He became Benedict XIV, the very same who, as noted earlier, defended the beatification and canonization processes against the pagan-apotheosis linkages.

Incidentally, beatification and canonization are not now, and never were, a joined process. To be sure, canonization is the ultimate goal of every cause that is introduced, but a cause passes from one step to the other—that is, from beatification to canonization—only if after beatification further events of a miraculous kind are called to attention, continuing or stimulating renewed interest in the venerated person. The cause is then resumed, with the process of inquiry for canonization proceeding along much the same lines as those for beatification.

Papal Prerogative

Popes are not irrevocably bound by the process of canonization. They can dispense from the usual formalities, and have commonly done so by a method known as equivalent canonization. (The same power applies with respect to beatification.)

Equivalent canonization is a pope's definitive declaration on behalf of a person for whom a canonical process has not been introduced, but with whom a public *cultus* has long been connected, traditionally for more than 100 years. There is no fixed procedure for equivalent canonization, although the historical section of the Congregation for the Causes of Saints is presumed to confirm for the pope the authenticity of the cult, the virtue of the subject, and miracles worked through his or her intercession. Many saints have come onto the calendar through this process, among them Saints Norbert, Bruno, Peter Nolasco, Raymond Nonnatus, King Stephen of Hungary and the eleventh century pope, Gregory VII. Pope John XXIII (1958-1963) exercised the prerogative in 1960 in

John Deedy

canonizing Saint Gregory Barbarigo, a Venetian (like himself, coincidentally), who was a bishop at age 32, a cardinal at 35, a participant in five papal conclaves, three times as a front-runner for the papacy, and who died in 1679.

Similarly, this papal prerogative was used in 1983 by Pope John Paul II, when he bypassed usual procedures and issued on his own initiative a decree beatifying Fra Angelico, the fabled Florentine painter and Dominican friar of the early Renaissance. John Paul II, in fact, has been one of the busiest canonizers and beatifiers of Christian history, raising 254 to the sainthood and 305 to the ranks of the blessed in his first ten years as pontiff. The surge is explained both by John Paul II's propensity for group elevations (e.g., the 117 Vietnamese martyrs of the eighteenth and nineteenth centuries; the 103 Korean martyrs of the last century), and by the 1983 ruling reducing the number of required miracles to one. The most immediate effect of the latter action was to clear way for causes on hold while awaiting a further miracle. One can expect the pace of canonizations and beatifications to slow, however. As Archbishop Traian Crisan, secretary of the Congregation for the Causes of Saints, said in 1989, "We need to be careful. Like anything that is done every day, it loses its value."

The essential portion of the canonization decree, as articulated by the presiding pope, is as follows:

"For the honor of the holy and undivided Trinity; for the exaltation of the Catholic faith and the increase of the

Christian life; with the authority of our Lord Jesus Christ, of the Blessed Apostles Peter and Paul, and with our own authority; after mature deliberation; with the counsel of many of our brothers.

"We decree and define that (name) is a saint and we inscribe (him or her) in the Catalogue of Saints, stating that (he or she) shall be venerated in the universal church with pious devotion.

"In the name of the Father and of the Son and of the Holy Spirit. Amen."

The official list of the canonized and beatified is contained in the *Roman Martyrology* and related materials issued after its last publication. Butler's unofficial (1956) *Lives of the Saints* contains 2,565 entries, but there have been scores of canonizations since then. Once done, a formal, solemn canonization is an irrevocable act, and not subject to revision. Mistaken zeal and confused identities might have landed some early Christians on the calendar of saints, but in the opinion of modern authorities so many safeguards are now built into the system as to make that unlikely anymore—although, to repeat, this confidence was tested in 1985, when the book by Giordano Bruno Guerri, *Poor Saint, Poor Assassin: The Story of Maria Goretti,* contended that Maria Goretti had not died in 1902 resisting advances against her virginity, but on several occasions had yielded to her killer's sexual advances in order to save her life. The church convoked a commission, which reconfirmed Maria Goretti's sanctity and revalidated the decision to canonize her.

Incidentally, baptized babies who die in infancy are not canonized, the reason being that they have not reached the age where they could perform the necessary deliberate actions demonstrating heroic virtue. The church's reasoning complements its insistence that the sainted not only be intercessors before the throne of God, but also that they leave behind lives that stand as models of perfection for imitation by others. Obviously, babies dying in infancy are hardly likely to be role models. True, the church accords special honors to the Holy Innocents, the infants who died at the hands of Herod's soldiers seeking to kill the child Jesus (Matthew 2:16-18). These infants, however, fall into a special category because of their unique role in the Savior's life story.

Reforms and Innovations

As might be presumed, beatification and canonizations are expensive processes, costs beginning with the drawing up of rescripts and continuing through to the lavish ornamenting of the site of the final solemn ceremonies of elevation, usually Saint Peter's Basilica.

In the deinflation period of the early century, costs were calculated at $20,000 for a beatification, with another $30,000 involved in the step to canonization. These large figures help explain why for a time at least so many of those honored were priests, religious sisters or personages of national repute; their causes could be supported by the resources of a diocese, a religious order or a nation. Efforts have since been made to control expenses connected with the processes, but beatification and canonization remain costly propositions.

Efforts have also been made to democratize the processes, or at least universalize them more in terms of the honored. One result has been the breaking of the dominance of persons of the Western church, and the introduction to the church's calendar of saints such as the Ugandan martyrs of 1886-1887 (Saint Charles Lwanga and Companions) and beatified such as the Korean martyrs of 1866 (Saint Simeon Berneaux and Companions), honored in 1964 and 1968, respectively.

Another innovation, one credited largely to John Paul II, is a return to a practice common in the eleventh and twelfth centuries, when popes traveled more freely than they had previously, and indeed were ever to do again until the age of the airplane. That practice is to preside at canonizations in the home locales of the persons being honored. Thus on a 1987 trip to Cologne, John Paul II beatified Edith Stein, a German Jew who converted to Catholicism and died at Auschwitz. A few days later, in ceremonies at Munich, he beatified Father Rupert Mayer, a Jesuit imprisoned three times for resisting Nazi rule.

John Paul II has also acted to accent unmistakably the central place of the papacy in the beatification and canonization processes. Though the pope's place had indeed been central to sainthood procedures since the Middle Ages and the general collecting of authority into Rome

John Deedy

itself (including that of beatification and canonization), only in recent times were the guidelines for these procedures spelled out by the Code of Canon Law.

The Code of Canon Law effective from 1918 to 1983 described the norms for beatification and canonization in Canons 1999 to 2141 of Book 4. The revised code approved January 25, 1983 by John Paul II eliminates those canons, but for one. It states succinctly in Book 7, Canon 1403, that "The causes of the canonization of the servants of God are regulated by special pontifical law," then in a legalistic subparagraph adds that the prescriptions of the code "are applicable to the aforementioned causes whenever the pontifical law refers to the universal law or when it is a question of norms which affect those causes from the very nature of the matter." This is consistent with the recommendation of a 1968 subcommittee studying the new Code of Canon Law that the norms for the processes of beatification and canonization be treated apart from the code itself.

Canonical instructions on the processes have thus dropped from forty-two to a single one in the new code. But there is the pope, and there is "special pontifical law," *peculiari lege pontifica.* Beatification and canonization continue, accordingly, as Catholic Christian traditions. The letter of the law is much the same. It is only the oversight that is different. *Le plus ca change. . . .*

18.

FAST AND ABSTINENCE:
What's Good for the Body
is Good for the Soul

Discipline or Sin?

WHEN THE church dropped its Friday abstinence rule, cartoonists had a field day.

One artist's rendition sticks strongly in memory. It depicted two devils consulting with one another in the bowels of hell, flames licking away at a number of people in the background. The cartoonist had one devil asking the other: "What are we going to do with all those people who are here for eating meat on Friday?"

Insignificant changes in policy can have surprisingly large effects, and perhaps no single post-Vatican II change had more of an impact on Catholics collectively than dropping the so-called fish-on-Friday regulation. For here was a change that touched most Catholics of the world in a direct and immediate way. Spain and Portugal enjoyed a centuries-old papal exemption from the law of Friday abstinence, but not the rest of Christianity. The overwhelming number of Catholics had been brought up on the principle that eating meat on Friday was not just a sin. It was a mortal sin. Then suddenly one day in 1966 the eating of meat on Friday was not a sin after all. How could something that was a mortal sin one day be no sin at all the next?

I have heard Catholics contend, in defense of the church's theoretical continuity of tradition, that the eating of meat on Friday was never a sin, mortal or otherwise, and that Friday abstinence from meat was merely a discipline that individual Catholics in their pious zeal somehow or another got confused with sin.

This is an old argumentative tactic, one encountered frequently in defensive Catholic strategies, to explain away change by denying that any change has in fact occurred. The denial may hold up as accurate in some few instances, but not so far as the old Friday abstinence rule is concerned. The Gilmary Society's 1913 *Catholic Encyclopedia,* complete with *nihil obstat* and *imprimatur* from John Cardinal Farley of New York, and once the definitive source of Catholic information, was unequivocal on the obligation to abstain from meat on Fridays: "Texts of theology and catechisms of Christian doctrine indicate that the obligation of abstaining forms an element in one of the Commandments of the Church. Satisfaction for sin is an item of primary import in the moral order. Naturally enough, abstinence contributes no small share towards the realization of this end. As a consequence, the law of abstinence embodies a serious obligation whose transgression, objectively considered, ordinarily involves a mortal sin. The unanimous verdict of theologians, the constant practice of the faithful, and the mind of the church place this point beyond cavil. They who would fain minimize the character of this obligation so as to relegate all transgressions, save such as originate in contempt, to the category of venial sin are anathematized by Alexander VII."

There are those who contend—not illogically—that beyond all the changes wrought by Vatican II no single development in the modern church had more of an effect on the psyche of the individual Catholic than the revising of Friday abstinence laws, as nothing more clearly demonstrated that the church could change not only its mind on a matter of seeming consequence, but also its teaching on an aspect of salvation theology that had affected the lives of Catholics generally. To be sure, Friday abstinence had assumed an importance out of all proportion to dogmatic validity. But the rule was on the books, and again the common teaching was that deliberate violation of the rule could lead to eternal damnation. It was as plain as that. Understandably, any tampering with so explicit a precept as Friday abstinence would cause shock and confusion, certainly for a time. And indeed it did.

On the other hand, Catholics should have been able to handle change of the most radical sort in this area, as within the lifetimes of most Catholics dramatic changes had already taken place in the church's complex code of fast and abstinence—the laws of fast specifying the amount of food or drink that could be taken on certain days or within certain hours; the laws of abstinence regulating the eating of flesh meat or the use of meat juices as nourishment on given days. Admittedly, most of those changes had involved the code of fasting rather than that of abstinence, and violations which disqualified persons from a privilege rather than the consigning of their soul to eternal damnation. Yet those preliminary changes were startling nonetheless, as they replaced ecclesiastical disciplines that had been in place for centuries.

Reforming the Code

The first of these changes involved the ruling that the taking of water no longer broke the eucharistic fast.

For centuries eucharistic fast regulations required Catholics in good health and normal life situations to fast from midnight in order to receive communion. In the normal course, there were no exemptions, not even in instances of the small sip taken while half-asleep in the middle of the night. Catholics took the rule with dead seriousness. More than one person was scratched as a child from his or her First Communion ceremony because of a drink of water unconsciously taken, say, on a trip to the bathroom at three o'clock in the morning. That iron rule went by the boards with *Christus dominus,* Pope Pius XII's apostolic constitution of January 16, 1953, declaring that water did not break the eucharistic fast—though one still had to fast from food from midnight. The papal document provided further that under certain circumstances other liquids (alcohol excepted) could be taken up to one hour before mass and communion, as by those who had to journey a long distance to mass or who were engaged in heavy, energy-sapping work prior to mass.

RETROSPECT

Those relaxations, together with the special provisions governing reception of communion at increasingly popular evening masses, then paved the way for *Sacram communionem,* Pius XII's *motu proprio* of March 19, 1957, reducing the eucharistic fast to three hours from solid food and one hour from liquids, alcohol again excepted. As in *Christus dominus,* a three-hour fast from alcoholic beverages was required. At the close of the third session of Vatican II, November 21, 1964, Pope Paul VI further reduced the time period of the eucharistic fast to one hour, the point at which it stands today.

The bombshell was still to come, however. It exploded February 17, 1966, in the form of the apostolic constitution *Poenitemini,* Paul VI's document abrogating obligatory Friday abstinence, reducing the number of days requiring fast and abstinence under obligation to two (Ash Wednesday and Good Friday), and introducing a number of other changes in the church's dietary disciplines, such as the age at which the church's abstinence laws began to apply to children. Previously it had been the completion of one's seventh year; Paul changed that to the completion of the fourteenth year.

Certain confusions were bound up with *Poenitemini,* perhaps inevitably so in light of its sweeping nature. The major one concerned Friday abstinence. Though one was no longer going to go to hell for eating meat on Friday, one was expected nonetheless to respect the day as one of penitence, the basic requirements of which consisted, in Paul's words, of "prayer—fasting—charity," with peoples of the world's richer nations expected to practice

John Deedy

self-denial and charity on behalf of "their brothers who suffer in poverty and in hunger, beyond all boundaries of nation and continent." Said another way, Catholics were still expected to do something of a penitential nature on the ordinary Fridays of the year, and it was left to the individual episcopal conferences to decide what. The French bishops actually reinstated the practice of Friday abstinence in 1984, but extended the abstinence options from meat to tobacco or alcohol. In the United States, works of penance are encouraged in place of the old Friday abstinence law, and abstinence from meat is required not just on Ash Wednesday and Good Friday, but on all Fridays of Lent.

Early Observances

There is nothing unique about the Catholic Church's insistence on periods of fast and abstinence.

From time immemorial fasting has been regarded as spiritually salutary, a method both for cleansing the inner self and atoning to divine power for failures or inadequacies of self. Persons of all religions observe laws of fasting. In the Old Testament, fasts were commonly observed at times of public calamity and on occasions of grief and misfortune. In the New Testament, Christ fasted for forty days and forty nights in the desert (Matthew 4:1-11), and he recommended the fasting discipline to others, even bothering to prescribe the spirit in which a fast should be undertaken in order to be of value: "When you fast, you are not to look glum like the hypocrites do.

They change the appearance of their faces in order that others may see that they are fasting. I assure you, they are already repaid. When you fast, see to it that you groom your hair and wash your face. In that way no one can see you are fasting but your Father who is hidden; and your Father who sees what is hidden will reward you'' (Matthew 6:16-18).

The early church honored the recommendation. Fasting was observed on Wednesdays and Fridays as a matter of practice, and many abstained from certain foods as well, particularly from flesh meats. In time abstinence became linked to Friday as a commemoration of the passion and death of Christ. The Wednesday fast was shifted to Saturday around the year four hundred, and days of fasts were multiplied to include the vigils of major feast days, and periods of repentance (Lent) and petition (Rogation Days).

Interestingly enough, there was no such thing in the early church as a eucharistic fast. Communion was often received after the communal meal, or agape, to which people had assembled. It was not until the fourth century that fasting from food and drink before receiving communion became common. Saint Augustine noted the impulse to fast before communion, and speculated that this growing and by then almost universal practice was of divine inspiration. The eucharistic fast was formally enacted into universal church law with the Council of Constance in 1414-1418, the Council declaring that except for cases of necessity, such as danger of death, the Eucharist was neither to be consecrated nor to be received by anyone not fasting. Previously, local councils had regulated the length and extent of the fast. Now the rule was to abstain from all food and liquids, including water, from the previous midnight.

As for days of fast and abstinence, the requirements were much more rigorous in the early centuries than they were to be later. For instance, abstinence from meat meant abstinence from all meat products and food items derivative of flesh animals, such as milk, eggs, butter and cheese. By the ninth century, however, milk, eggs, and milk products, cheese and butter included, were pretty much exempted from dietary proscriptions through the twin forces of local custom and repeated dispensations.

In the meanwhile, the number of fast days steadily increased, though the increase was never so great in the Western church as it was in the East, where not only the traditional Lent of forty days was observed, but three other "Lents" as well: the Lent of the Holy Apostles, June 16-28; Mary's Lent, August 1-14; and a Lent preceding Christmas, December 15-24. (Lent is a Teutonic word that originally meant no more than the spring season.) The Greek church once knew as many as one hundred and eighty fast days in a year's time. The number eventually was scaled back, but nonetheless the requirements of fast and abstinence were more stringent in the Eastern churches than in the Western, and remain so to this day.

Still, the fast and abstinence laws for a long time were only relatively easier in the Western church. As late as 1917, general law of the Western church required fasting on all days of Lent, except for Sundays; on Wednesdays, Fridays and Saturdays of the year's four Ember weeks; on the vigils of the feasts of Christmas, Pentecost, Assumption and All Saints. Furthermore, abstinence was required on all Fridays and Saturdays throughout the year.

Exemptions and Privileges

The law was not carved in stone, however. Dispensations were obtainable.

In 1837, for instance, the Fathers of the Third Provincial Council of Baltimore obtained from Rome a dispensation from the requirement to fast on the Wednesdays and Fridays of Advent, Friday abstinence of course remaining in effect. Then three years later, in 1840, the fathers of the Fourth Provincial Council of Baltimore obtained a ten-year dispensation from the law of Saturday abstinence, a dispensation subsequently renewed for twenty years by Pope Gregory XVI (1831-1846).

Pope Leo XIII (1878-1903) granted further relaxations in 1886, but fast and abstinence were still serious business in the Catholic Church. Lard and meat drippings, for instance, could now be used in the preparation of foods, and people could shift about the order of meals, thus doing away with the old necessity of taking the principle meal at noon. However, meat and fish—seemingly a dietary luxury—were never allowed at the same meal, even on Sundays, long a traditional day of dispensation in the church from the obligation of fasting.

John Deedy

When the turn of Benedict XV (1914-1922) came, he granted bishops the privilege of transferring the Lenten law of Saturday abstinence to any other days of the week, except for Ash Wednesday and the Fridays of Lent. The effect of his ruling was to free up Saturday diets, but retain the custom of two days of abstinence each week of the Lenten season.

In 1941, Pope Pius XII (1939-1958) anticipated in a real way the sweeping relaxations that were to come from Paul VI in 1966, when he granted to bishops the power to dispense entirely from the laws of fast and abstinence except on Ash Wednesday and Good Friday. Restrictions, however, were subsequently placed on that faculty. In 1949 the Holy See handed down the ruling that abstinence must be observed on all Fridays of the year, and fast and abstinence on Ash Wednesday, Good Friday, as well as on the vigil of Christmas and the Feast of the Assumption.

It became more complicated year by year. But what made the church's laws of fast and abstinence difficult to keep straight—and for some hard to take seriously—was that there were exemptions within exemptions, dispensations within dispensations.

One such was the so-called workingmen's privilege, originally granted in 1895, which permitted the taking of flesh meat once a day on many days of abstinence, though never on Fridays. In the United States, the indult —which applied incidentally not only to "workingmen" but also to their families—was renewed periodically before being dropped in 1951 as dated and outmoded.

292

Travelers also qualified for exemptions. In 1965 the Holy See dispensed railroad travelers from the obligations of abstinence, including on Fridays, "in view of the difficulty that the railroad companies have in preparing meatless meals." Similarly exempted that same year were travelers on the forty-three U.S. airlines affiliated with the Air Transport Association.

Even the eucharistic fast law was not all that fast, particularly around midnight, when daylight-saving or standard time could be used to extend the hours when food or drink could still be taken without the fast-from-midnight rule being broken. When that manipulation no longer served, one could invoke what an old pastor of mine used to call "sun time." I never exactly figured out what that was, though it seemed to have something to do with living on the edge of a time zone; in other words, though the clocks read the same in Boston and Pittsburgh, it was actually earlier in Pittsburgh because the sun was moving from East to West, and if you were in Pittsburgh you had an extra half-hour—or was it forty-five minutes?—of lead time. It could be, as noted earlier, very complicated.

Further Modifications

The American bishops acted in 1951 to eliminate ambiguities and confusions, drawing up a set of uniform norms governing fast and abstinence and making them applicable to all dioceses and archdioceses of the country.

Still there was nothing simple about the new norms. The regulations required big paragraphs of explanation, and still were not tamper-proof or above change. They were modified by the bishops themselves in 1956, then again in 1957 and 1959 as the Holy See shifted around days of fast and abstinence that are no longer on the books. In 1957, for instance, the Congregation of the Council, since reconstituted as the Congregation for the Clergy, transferred the fast and abstinence requirement connected to the vigil of the Assumption to the vigil of the Immaculate Conception, and in 1959 Pope John XXIII (1958-1963) granted permission to shift the Christmas vigil fast and abstinence then in force from December 24 to December 23. Then, of course, came Paul VI's apostolic constitution of February 17, 1966, *Poenitemini,* and its total reorganization of ecclesiastical disciplines relating to fast and abstinence. *Poenitemini*'s major innovation was to allow episcopal conferences to substitute other forms of penitence, and especially works of charity and exercises of piety, for the fast and abstinence hitherto required of Catholics on given days. Thus went the old custom of abstaining from meat on the ordinary Fridays of the calendar.

Poenitemini, incidentally, did not affect fast and abstinence disciplines of the Eastern churches. *Poenitemini* left to the individual patriarchs, together with the synod or governing authority of the individual rites, the right to determine fast and abstinence codes in accordance with the conciliar decree on Eastern rites, *Orientalium ecclesiarum.* In effect this continued a 1949 decree of the Holy See that the laws of fast and abstinence were to be observed in the Eastern churches "if and as it is in effect in their respective rites.'' The situation varies from church to church, but as a rule of thumb, the laws of fast and abstinence remain more demanding in the Eastern churches than in the Western church.

As for the Western church, not everyone was happy about the big change in the fast and abstinence code—the lifting of obligatory Friday abstinence from meat, and thus the passing of what had become the Catholic custom of fish-on-Friday. Leaders of the fishing industry protested the change mightily, and so did Boston's Cardinal Richard Cushing, who saw the relaxation as a mortal threat to the economic welfare of the Catholic fishermen of Gloucester, a major fishing port on Cape Ann in the northern corner of his archdiocese. These industry-related protests turned out to be without merit, of course, as within a few years changes in dietary habits made fish more popular a dish than ever it had been in the past. No longer was fish penitential fare. Indeed, the elements of supply and demand combined with other factors (e.g., cholesterol counts and similar health considerations) to make fish the luxury or more expensive dish that meat generally used to be. Ironically, soon afterwards advances worldwide in fishing technologies rendered some fish endangered species.

A Matter of Personal Conscience

Modern changes in the church's laws of fast and abstinence do not mean that official viewpoints have changed about the need for penance symbolized by those laws.

John Deedy

They indicate only that emphases have changed. The church is less legalistic, more understanding; less demanding, more exhortatory. This is so even for the most solemn of days and seasons. The U.S. bishops, for instance, detail their Lenten regulations, reminding that the obligation to fast and to abstain from meat still binds on Ash Wednesday and Good Friday, and that the Fridays of Lent are to be observed as days of abstinence. But at the same time they concede that in this matter Catholics enjoy freedom of conscience to excuse themselves, although not lightly so. ("No Catholic Christian will lightly excuse himself from so hallowed an obligation . . .") The bishops' emphasis now is on voluntary fasting and on good works in the love and imitation of Christ, among them solicitude for the sick, the poor, the underprivileged, the imprisoned, the home-bound, the lonely, the discouraged, the minority person of race, color or creed, the stranger.

In not linking disregard of fast and abstinence in a direct way to sin, as had ever been the case in the past, the bishops adopt an approach initially set forth in *L'Osservatore Romano,* the semi-official Vatican daily. Immediately after *Poenitemini*'s promulgation in 1966, *L'Osservatore* featured an article by Father William Bertrams, S.J., of the canon law faculty of the Gregorian University in Rome, declaring that individual violations of the new penitential laws of fast and abstinence were not grave, a judgment he based on use of the word "substantial" in the papal document. In Bertrams' view, *Poeni-*

temini was saying that it was "substantial observance" that was important, not absolute, unwavering observance, as in the past.

Still, doubt lingered over the meaning of the pope's statement that "substantial observance [of the obligatory days of penance] binds gravely"—such doubt in fact that on February 2, 1967, the Vatican was forced to issue the clarification that "substantial observance refers not to the individual days of penance but to the sum total of penitential days."

Whether the clarification helped or not, this much was certain: the new tradition removed from the laws of fast and abstinence two old, indispensable props in the lives of Catholics, namely blind habit and that inhibiting element known as "pain-of-sin." It meant that now Catholics had choices of their own to make. Then as now this brings Catholics face to face with what has been called that enigmatic and inescapably Christian phenomenon, the philosophy of penance.

Historically the church has always taught that penance is a virtue, a supernatural moral virtue, but it invariably framed its teaching in the context of satisfaction for an offense against God and firm purpose of amendment of one's living habits. Lost almost entirely was the possibility of penance also being an intuitive act of worship, an element in the persistent and instinctive search for that elusive thing called Christian confraternity through the acknowledgments, not so much of personal fault, but of responsibility for what is happening to others—the neighbor near at hand as well as the stranger far distant in the world community. It is this responsibility which the new discipline seeks to emphasize.

As for fast and abstinence, there will always be those who view the practices negatively, as neurotic exercises inhibiting of personal potential and intuition. If there is any reason to fast and abstain, detractors would say, it is because the practice is good for bodily health. Supporters of the discipline would not dispute the therapeutic good to be achieved through a proper and balanced system of fast and abstinence. But supporters would add that fast and abstinence also enhance personal qualities of constraint, discipline, toleration and perspective— enhancements which ultimately benefit the soul as well as the body. This is undoubtedly part of what the church has in mind in its current encouragements involving fast and abstinence.

19.

EDUCATION:
An Old Tradition in a Challenging Today

The Light of Learning

ONE of the church's proudest boasts is its historical role in the field of education. There is nothing idle about the boast.

From their beginnings, monasteries and Catholic religious communities generally were centers of learning and of culture. Thus when education was systematized and the modern university was born in the Middle Ages—a development spurred by the revival of interest in learning that followed on the retreat of the Dark Ages—the church inevitably was destined to be an influential part of the movement. Of the eighty-one universities that dotted Christendom prior to the Reformation, no fewer than thirty-three held exclusive papal charters, and the other forty-eight without exception were strongly Catholic in character; namely, the fifteen with imperial or royal license, the twenty with combined papal-imperial/royal license, and the thirteen that developed independently of official charter.

The scenario would be much the same when popular education was developed on the primary and secondary

299

levels for the masses of people. The church would be in the forefront of the development.

The church's pre-eminence in education would continue for centuries. But times and fortunes would change as others, notably the state, began to assume responsibilities that were once consigned or left by default totally to the church. Gradually the church's role passed from that of soloist to one player among many in a score that became more and more widely orchestrated, and branched into specialized fields beyond the church's purview, such as the natural sciences. (No longer was theology the mistress of sciences.)

To be sure, the church was never completely elbowed out of education, but in many places its influence was to wane, or at least suffer diffusion. The challenge was, and indeed continues to be, not to regain (much less enlarge) those centuries-old educational frameworks of reference, but rather to maintain and hold fast to what remained of an educational system at once unique, founded in great and holy idealism, and nurtured at large personal and financial sacrifice. As said, it is a challenge that persists, and nowhere is that challenge greater than in the United States, where the Catholic educational system, from primary through university levels, is larger, if not also stronger, than anywhere else in the world.

The Humble Beginnings

The Catholic university system began in the United States with the founding of Georgetown University in

1789, not by the Jesuits, but by a group known as the Catholic Clergy of Maryland, Inc.

The beginnings were humble—the school was known as an academy and it opened in 1791 with a solitary student: William Gaston of North Carolina, a future associate justice of the state's supreme court. In 1805, Georgetown was entrusted to the care of the Jesuits, a move of historical importance, as it would go far toward helping establish the Jesuits as the primary (though hardly the exclusive) educators in the United States on the college and university level. There are some two hundred and thirty-two Catholic colleges and universities in the United States, according to recent statistics. Only twenty-eight of them are Jesuit, but they include some of the largest and most prestigious. Of the 551,466 students enrolled in American Catholic colleges and universities in 1989, some 200,000 were in Jesuit institutions, including those in adult and continuing-education programs.

However, the best known of American Catholic colleges and universities—the one which, in Father John Tracy Ellis' words, has found a secure place in the hearts of all Americans—is Notre Dame, founded in 1842 by the Congregation of the Holy Cross, and operated still by that order. Notre Dame is associated in some minds with athletics, football most especially. But, returning to Father Ellis, "none has had a brighter record of achievement in education for Christian manhood, than the University of Notre Dame."

The comment appears in Ellis's *Documents of American Catholic History* (Milwaukee, 1962), and with the passing of time his use of the word "manhood" would become misnomer as well as anachronism, for the University of Notre Dame is now coeducational. But, conceding Ellis' literal accuracy, Notre Dame was long a strictly male bastion—as indeed were so many American Catholic colleges and universities. The reality is that before the gender revolution, Catholic education on advanced academic levels in America tended to develop along separate and often less than equal lines. In fact, the first Catholic women's college did not come into being in the United States until 1896, about a generation after Vassar received its charter. That institution was the College of Notre Dame of Maryland, in Baltimore.

At two hundred and thirty-two, the number of Catholic colleges and universities is large—though the number was even larger before the religious attritions of the 1960s and early 1970s took their institutional toll. The number stood at two hundred and fifty-four, at the time Ellis put together his book. The upheavals of those years seem well behind American Catholic colleges and universities, but for most the struggle for survival is as great as it ever was. If yesterday the problem was a kind of academic anarchy, today it is financial pinch. Costs have soared and there seem no upward limits. How to survive?

For some, the answer had been to take refuge in a kind of institutional limbo. Some Catholic colleges and universities in several states—New York is a good example—have reconstituted themselves as independent entities in order to sidestep constitutional complications and more easily meet eligibility requirements for receiving public funds. The common procedure in such cases is for the Catholic institutions to reconstitute themselves as independent institutions by the legal incorporation of the resident religious community as separate from the educational institution. The college or university is then run by a newly devised board of directors which includes religious, but is mostly laity, chosen usually from across the ideological spectrum.

By and large, the maneuver is a charade, a *pro forma* legal exercise, by which the status of the institution is changed in letter of law but not in denominational or religious character. At the same time, however, the action is not without certain intramural implications, particularly given Vatican concerns about ensuring the traditional identity and role of the Catholic college and university through insistence on academic orthodoxy and the primacy on campus of the teaching authority of the magisterium. The legal arrangement entered into by some Catholic colleges and universities sets up potential conflict situations on any and all issues serious enough to involve the interests of Rome. Among the questions are, who does the adjudicating, and when push comes to shove, whose deciding authority is decisive? Is it that of Catholic Church officials, or is it that of government bureaucrats, educational accrediting agencies, or the courts?

These are murky grounds for church and state, town and gown. They are also questions not to be dismissed lightly, for more is involved in the answers than pride and prestige. Principle weighs in heavily—and so, alas, does subsidy, large subsidy. Catholic colleges and universities in the United States receive a half-billion dollars annually in federal and state aid for such things as study and research projects of nonreligious kinds, dollars which in the short run may not affect survival, but which for many institutions translate in direct contexts to the difference between excellence and mediocrity.

Protecting the Faith

In place alongside American Catholic institutions of higher learning is an ambitious Catholic primary and secondary educational system, once a booming apostolate but now come upon hard times.

Catholic commitment to this system, and to primary schools especially, dates from the very beginnings of an American hierarchy. The issue engaged the concern of John Carroll of Baltimore, the first American bishop. Immediately after the Revolutionary War he envisioned a system in which Catholics and non-Catholics would be united in the construction of an elementary educational system that would be mutually satisfactory from religious perspectives. Undaunted when it became clear that such a system was impossible, he addressed a pastoral letter to American Catholics emphasizing the necessity of a "pious and Catholic education of the young to insure their growing up in the faith." That was in 1792. Carroll's theme was picked up by the Plenary Councils of Baltimore. The First Plenary Council of 1829 pronounced: "We judge it absolutely necessary that schools should be established, in which the young may be taught the principles of faith and morality, while instructed in letters." The Second Plenary Council of 1832 renewed the decree, and the Third of 1884 got tough. It ordered the establishing of a parochial school in every parish within two years, except in those instances where a bishop granted a delay on account of severe difficulties (*ob graviores difficultates*).

Different urgencies characterized the development of Catholic colleges and universities from those of diocesan schools. (Private Catholic schools were to come later.) The former came into being to help Catholics compete on the highest intellectual levels with others in the community; the latter, on the other hand, had as their essential purpose the safeguarding of the faith of Catholic school children. The Congregation de Propaganda Fide, the Vatican agency overseeing the United States, then a missionary territory, made this plain in fusing the decision for an extensive parochial school system. In an 1875 instruction, the congregation excoriated the American public school system as "most dangerous and very much opposed to Catholicity," and added that nothing was more "needful" to protect the faith of young Catholic Americans than "the establishment of Catholic schools in every place—and schools no whit inferior to the public ones."

The objective of an exclusively Catholic, totally comprehensive parochial school system was more idealistic than realistic, even in days of low educational costs and high vocational rates, which provided teachers at bargain prices. The objective was complicated further by non-Catholic suspicions that Catholic parochial schools were somehow subversive, and thus not deserving of public support. Archbishop John Ireland of St. Paul addressed these objections in a speech at the 1890 convention of the National Education Association, capped with the proposal that parochial schools be absorbed into the public school system, with provision made for the teaching of religion. The proposal of "State Schools Fit for Catholic Children" was roundly attacked from all sides. Non-Catholics viewed Ireland's proposal as a ruse by which Catholics would gain control of the public school system; many Catholics, including some in Rome, saw the proposal embodying a threat to the integrity of Catholic education. Pope Leo XIII wondered what was going on, and Cardinal James Gibbons of Baltimore came strongly to Ireland's defense.

Alternatives lacking, the building of a Catholic school system went forward, American Catholics generally united in the effort on behalf of their system, the largest by far of its kind in the country, but with questions being raised from other quarters. Some questions struck at the heart, challenging the very right of private schools to exist, including (especially is the more accurate word) those schools which were Catholic. The issue was joined when the state of Oregon in 1922 enacted legislation compelling all children between the ages of eight and sixteen to attend public schools. The Sisters of the Holy Names of Jesus and Mary went to court, joined by Hill Military Academy, and the case went all the way to the Supreme Court. In 1925, the Court ruled unanimously in favor of the sisters, saying that the state could not interfere "with the liberty of parents and guardians to direct the upbringing and education of children under their control."

Church, State and School

The decision affirmed the right of Catholic schools to exist.

It did not gain them that which they came increasingly to need, a measure of tax support. This was an issue that was to dominate much of the 1950s and 1960s, but it is one with roots in the early nineteenth century, when Catholic authorities first began to press the matter, only to encounter objections that aid to parochial schools violated constitutional provisions of separation of church and state. The issue was different from that involving grants which went to Catholic colleges and universities for specialized projects having nothing to do with religion; aid to parochial schools was regarded as a direct subsidy to a religious denomination, since parochial schools were theoretically religious counterparts to public schools. If Catholics insisted on subsidized education for their children, the reasoning went, then let them send them to public schools, where everything was free. Catholics have their answers to objections such as these, and some have been persuasive enough to gain for Catholic school children certain marginal benefits. But the door to public aid is still pretty much shut tight.

Curiously, it wasn't always this way—or at least not to so extreme a degree. In the early nineteenth century Detroit Catholic schools qualified for their share of public funds, and as late as 1855 the two Catholic schools in Lowell, Massachusetts, were recognized as part of the city's school system. Arrangements benefiting Catholic schools were fairly common until mid-century, before being routed in the century's latter decades by movements which were Americanist or religiously prejudiced, depending upon the individual's reading. A common allegation at the time was that a sincere Catholic could not be a totally loyal citizen of the United States, because of a divided allegiance between Rome and the U.S., a dichotomy allegedly fostered by Catholic schools.

It should be said that not all Catholics were dismayed by the refusal of public funds, some Catholics being convinced that federal and state aid could be accepted only at cost to the independence and integrity of Catholic schools. The rationale was that federal and state aid came forever with conditions, and therefore its acceptance risked at least the partial de-Catholicization of Catholic schools. Nor was that a period-piece argument. Boston's Cardinal Richard Cushing said during the tense mid-twentieth century controversies over federal and state aid that he wouldn't accept it for his schools, even if he could get it. He didn't have much of a chance of getting it anyway, not even with a Catholic in the White House who happened also to be a close personal friend. When President John F. Kennedy in 1961 proposed his 2.3 billion dollar program of federal assistance for education, a revolutionary proposal containing large-scale aid for public schools, there was not one penny in the package for private or parochial schools.

Yet, despite handicaps of finance, the Catholic parochial school system grew astonishingly. Archbishop Martin J. Spalding of Louisville (1810-1872) called the American Catholic school system "the greatest religious fact in the United States today," adding the observation that it was "maintained without any [public] aid by the people who love it." His was hardly overstatement.

The Catholic school system was a large fact of American life. By 1910 this school system comprised some 31,000 teachers instructing 1,237,251 students in 4,845 parish schools—a service worth, it was said, more than $100,000,000 to the public treasury. Educational costs were placed at $15,000,000 annually. These were astronomical numbers in their day, and yet the system was still to peak. It did so in the mid-1960s, when some 5,600,000 pupils were at desks in more than 13,000 Catholic schools, under instruction by nearly 200,000 teachers, the majority of them religious sisters, a seemingly bottomless vocational resource. Then matters began to change. There were vast declines over the next twenty years. Some 4,000 Catholic schools closed over twenty years' time, so that by 1989 Catholic school enrollments were down to 2,261,298 pupils (almost twelve percent of that enrollment non-Catholic) in 8,904 schools—impressive numbers still, but nowhere near what they were.

What happened? Many things at once.

End of an Era

Demographics were a major factor.

Suburban migration left many Catholic schools without their old constituencies, and in place after place this forced a decision either to close the schools or keep them open and serve people of a different religious background. Many opted for the latter alternative, which helps explain the sizable non-Catholic composition in schools that were once virtually one hundred percent Catholic. At the same time, suburban migration relocated many Catholic families in neighborhoods where Catholic schools did not exist—and where they were never to be built for a variety of reasons, ranging from economics to what some see as a lack of will on the part of clergy, even though Catholic lay commitment to parochial schools seemed as strong as ever.

A second major factor was the sudden drying up of that seemingly inexhaustible labor pool, the teaching sister. Vocations fell off; sisters left the religious life; many who stayed moved into apostolic careers other than teaching. The net result was that by 1989 there were 83,252 fewer sisters teaching in Catholic schools from the 104,441 recorded at their peak in 1964, roughly a 75 percent decline. Their places were taken by laity, whose numbers jumped correspondingly—from 75,103 in 1965 to 130,793 in 1989. However welcome and competent the lay teachers, the heavy overload of lay teachers affected budgets radically, and for some schools fatally. Salary scales for lay teachers are less than their counterparts in public education, but they are considerably higher than they had traditionally been for sisters. Sisters, in fact, had long received only token wages.

A third factor, one cited regularly by sources like the *New York Times,* is fallout from Vatican II. As *Times* reporter Deirdre Carmody wrote April 4, 1988, in covering the annual meeting of the National Catholic Education Association, its eighty-fifth, enrollment declines in Catholic schools resulted "in part" because the Council de-emphasized preaching about obligations. "After the mid-1960s," she commented, "pulpit exhortations about parental responsibility for children's Catholic schooling were virtually ended." This is true, but one is forced to ask what good "pulpit exhortations" would have been when Catholic schools did not even exist in most of the suburban neighborhoods to which Catholics were relocating.

There is controversy to this day whether the American Catholic leadership defaulted in its responsibilities in not foreseeing the possibility of Catholic-family relocation, and not acting decisively in the matter of schools once suburban migration became a pronounced fact. However one argues, this much is certain. Times are tough for the Catholic elementary and secondary schools that continue on. As Carmody remarked, the American Catholic school system must grapple with such problems as how to pay competitive salaries to lay teachers, who now comprise eighty-one percent of the teaching staff; how to deal with the needs of students who are members of minority groups, and who now make up twenty-two percent of Catholic school enrollments (half of these students are non-Catholic, thus raising questions of ecumenical kinds); the religious welfare of that twelve percent of the Catholic school population which is non-Catholic; and finally, in Carmody's words, "how to persuade parents in affluent suburban areas, who face expensive mortgages and are paying hefty local school taxes, that they should spend extra money to send their children to parochial school, if they can find one in the area."

Pessimists say that wholly satisfactory answers to questions such as these do not exist, that the battle to save parochial schools is in its rear-guard phase, and pretty much lost. But not everyone is ready to concede the point. Pennsylvania's Catholic bishops, for instance, recently remarked that education in the United States is in a period of "unprecedented crisis." But they were speaking of public as well as private education, and so far as Catholic education was concerned they were pledging its continuance in that state. Their logic, summarized in a 1988 joint statement, echoed a conviction that has infused the Catholic educational apostolate from the beginning: Catholic education is an education of the heart and the mind; it is the development of the "whole child," the "total person"; it is more than the mere inculcation of civic virtues, such as the typical American ones of freedom, honesty, personal and social responsibility, equality, free and fair competition, cooperation and the like; Catholic education is a learning experience in an atmosphere that reflects the lived values of the Catholic faith.

The rhetoric may be stilted and idealized, but it is beyond question that, all practical problems aside, Catholic education has been a great success. The proof is in the product. Studies consistently show Catholic school students scoring significantly above the average on national tests, on both the elementary and secondary school levels. The dropout rate among students in Catholic high schools, from sophomore through senior years, is markedly lower than the national average: three percent, compared to fourteen percent for public schools and twelve percent for private schools. And eighty percent of those who attend Catholic high schools go on to college or other kinds of post-secondary education.

Whether such impressive data will rekindle commitments akin to what existed in the late nineteenth and early twentieth centuries is uncertain. Much militates against the likelihood of a reborn Catholic school system on yesterday's scale, beginning with costs and the reluctance of government to be of any great direct help. In a 1988 talk to Catholic educators, the Reagan administration's education secretary, William J. Bennett, urged that they seek out the worst students—"the poor, the disadvantaged, the disruptive, the dropout"—then come hat in hand, as it were, and "ask society for fair recompense" for their efforts. One has to be skeptical about

John Deedy

Bennett's "carrot" proposal. Catholic schools already have their share of problem students, and in some communities are in fact already doing what Bennett suggests. To some, Bennett seems to want Catholic schools to solve a nettlesome public school problem, with the guarantee of nothing concrete in return except maybe more constitutional challenges to whatever compensatory aid is provided, if indeed they get any aid at all.

Catholic parochial and secondary schools will nonetheless survive in the United States, and of course so will Catholic colleges and universities—although the latter's future seems probably more secure than the former's, for there seems no upward limit in tuition charges that Catholics are willing to pay for a college or university education. By contrast, very many Catholics still expect primary and secondary education to be free or, by way of compromise, of nominal cost, the school's levying but modest tuition charges. Actually, the latter isn't so far from the situation which in fact exists; most Catholic-school primary and secondary fee schedules are loss propositions for the sponsor, or at best break-even enterprises.

This is not, in sum, a scenario for great growth, but with the collaborative effort of the Catholic community it is one that should enable Catholic education in the United States to continue at current levels. This may be more than consolation; it may be gain in itself.

20.

BURIAL RITES:
In the End, Not Quite as in the Beginning

Rites of Passing

DEATH HAS never been a pretty business. It isn't now, although, in social contexts, events relating to death are handled far better than they were.

At least many of the old taboos are gone. Generally speaking, the dead are not rushed out of sight and presence as was once the case, and old suspicions—such as death leaping from corpse to person, or deaths occurring in multiples of three—have largely been put to rest.

But the business of death was long pretty grim. Persians of old, for instance, believed that rigor mortis was caused by the evil spirits which invested the corpse, and that anyone who touched the corpse was rendered "powerless in mind, tongue and hand." In ancient Greece and Rome, corpses were buried by night, lest they pollute the sunlight. The Navahos destroyed the dwelling in which a person died, as a safeguard against the pollutions of death. People of the Solomon Islands, likewise concerned about pollutions, hung the dead person's arms on the person's dwelling and let the place go to rack and ruin.

John Deedy

Extreme and extravagant policies? Yes and no. The ancients had no informed scientific knowledge of infection, but they knew bodily corruption when they saw it—or more particularly when they smelled it—and they took guard, particularly in warm climates where, inevitably, decomposition was accelerated by the heat. There was thus an unconscious but solid logic to many of the old practices. Nor were practicalities always despised. That Navaho dwelling, for instance. If it was an imposing one, the dying person was moved to a makeshift hut. Let death come to the person there, so that the imposing dwelling could be spared ruin.

Time, sophistication and ever-increasing scientific knowledge in the care of the dead and the preservation of corpses from putrefaction—an art carried to high perfection by the ancient Egyptians and eventually adopted elsewhere—gradually changed most of the dark practices of ancient times.

Religion played a part in the change, too, including the Christian religion—though not dramatically so. Although later Christian ages were to connect a pious symbolism to the rites of burial generally, the fact is that many of those rites were derivative of the practices of others. With burial rites, as with so much else, early Christians tended to follow local customs that were not patently idolatrous. This applied from the laying out of the body to the final kiss of farewell. Nonetheless, not everything in Christian burial rites is borrowed. Some of the burial customs of modern times, including a few now common to purely secular rites, are of Christian origin or have been refined by Christianity.

The tradition of the wake, for instance, derives from the three-day "watch"—the interval of respect and prayer for the deceased that even in pre-Christian times was the occasion for friends to condole with close survivors of the departed. Tradition became mandate, when an instruction of the early *Rituale Romanum* ordered that a proper interval (*debitum temporis intervallum*) be allowed to lapse between the moment of death and the burial, especially in cases of those stricken unexpectedly. The purpose was to leave no doubt that life was really extinct. Obviously, not fully accepted by the church as infallible confirmations of death were such methods peculiar to the day as hammer taps to the forehead (if the corpus did not respond, dead he or she was), or mirrors held to mouth and nostrils for traces of moisture that indicated a presence of breath. At the same time, the Christian wake perpetuated certain pagan customs, some of which have carried to modern generations, such as lighted candles around the bier and the all-night watch. Both practices had their origin in a desire to protect the corpse against assaults from evil demons.

Another custom of Christian inspiration was that of the chanting of psalms on a person's death. It was introduced as a religious activity, to be sure. But the chanting was also intended as a substitute for the outcries of mourning, the explosions of emotion, the so-called *conclamatio,* that in some societies accompanied the closing of the eyes and mouth of the deceased upon ascertainment of death, a demonstration which some churchmen regarded as pagan and distortional of the Christian understanding of death as the doorway to eternal life.

Nonetheless, some pagan customs were slow in dying in the church. One source (the 1911 *Encyclopedia Britannica*) has Saint Boniface, the eighth-century English apostle to Germany, commending the self-sacrifice of the Wend widows, who in his day burned themselves alive on their husbands' funeral pyres. The Wends were a Slavic people in Saxony and adjoining parts of Prussia. The immolation of widows, self-induced or otherwise, is now thoroughly reprobated in Christianity. But it has continued in other cultures and among other religions. It was a problem, in fact, just recently in India among members of a fundamentalist sect. On the whole, Western civilization—when it wasn't at war or otherwise homicidally engaged—brought a dignity to dying, and so in the process did Christianity.

Respect for the Dead

Infusing Christian attitudes toward death, and specifically toward the corpse, were two basic propositions:

(1) That burial of the dead was a corporal work of mercy, a basically religious function—so basically religious, indeed, that in early Christian times workers in the trade were chosen with great care and in some places even regarded as *clerici,* clerics. Today we call them under-

takers (those who "take" one "under"), but the more common designation in early Christianity was *fossores,* from the Latin *fodere,* to dig. Interestingly enough, *fossores* comprised one of Christendom's first organized lay groups.

(2) The other basic Christian proposition connected with death was that the body—or corpse now—was a holy and sacred thing, and that death was merely an interval, a resting period, before the body's resurrection in the Lord, according to the very professions of the Nicene Creed: "I confess one baptism for the remission of sins, and *I believe in the resurrection of the body,* and the life of the world to come. Amen." The body/corpse was to be respected, because it would rise again.

Actually, the issue passed well beyond mere respect. Burial of the dead was considered so profound a spiritual activity that the twelfth-century *Decretum* of Gratian stipulated that no fee whatsoever was to be connected with the function, and that to exact a fee was to be guilty of simony. It was a stipulation that in Western societies helped promote the popularity of burial confraternities, such as the "Misericordia" of Florence, whose members performed not only the burial tasks associated now with undertakers, but also the duties of an ambulance corps, like rushing to accidents and the homes of the ailing, then conveying to hospitals not just the dead but those in need of medical attention. It might be noted, in passing, that one of the principal works of the famous guilds of the Middle Ages—those associations which presaged the modern labor union—was seeing that their members went seemly into the hereafter, with proper burial rites and the added guarantee of a specific number of memorial masses.

On the other hand, though the *Decretum* specified that no fees were to be connected with the burial liturgies, gifts to the church were permitted—partly in acknowledgment of the trouble taken by the clergy, and partly for the spiritual benefit of the deceased, for it was a constant Christian teaching that it was holy and wholesome to honor the dead. Inevitably, therefore, "gifts to the church" often translated to gifts to the individual clergyman. This was easily accommodated by the recipients. The gifts were classified under the heading of "stole fees," offerings provided on special occasions and intended for the personal support of the clergyman performing the rite. Official church policy was thus preserved from taint, for the performance of the rite was never to be made conditional upon payment of a fee. The gift qualified as a free-will offering.

Again, this general policy was bound with respect for the corpse as a holy and sacred thing. This respect, in turn, was nothing more than the logical extension of the basic Christian belief that the body was created in God's image, that it was the co-instrument of the soul in a shared life in Christ, and that it was destined for personal, glorious resurrection on the final day of judgment —that day when, according to Catholic belief, the body is to be reunited with the soul to share in eternal reward or be meted punishment according to God's assessment of the person's life on earth.

Earth to Earth

For reasons associated with all of the above, Christians have maintained their own Christian burial grounds from earliest times—the catacombs being the first and perhaps the best known of them.

Incidentally, so far as origin is concerned, the Christian catacombs have little to do with the Roman persecutions, popular impression notwithstanding. Underground burial chambers and passages were the custom of the region in those times. There were some 500 miles of underground catacomb passages in and about the city of Rome alone, not all of them Christian by any means.

Nonetheless, it is true that the catacombs served as convenient meeting places for Christians, including for worship. This was especially so before Christians got their own churches built. The catacombs thus were early churches of a sort, places where believers could gather and where liturgies could be held away from inquisitive eyes. The tombs of the martyrs held a particular attraction for early Christians. The martyrs were the first heroes of the faith, and their tombs were used as altars for the celebration of mass. It was a practice subsequently memorialized by the custom of including relics of saints in the altar stones set in the formal table of liturgical worship in churches around the world.

John Deedy

From the beginning, Christians wanted their own burial grounds. The importance of specifically Catholic burial grounds was dramatized early on by accusations brought by Saint Cyprian (200?-258) against a Spanish bishop. The bishop was charged with associating with members of a pagan funeral confraternity and, more seriously, with burying his sons in a cemetery over which pagans had charge. The bishop was deposed.

So insistent was the church of yesterday on exclusively Christian burial places that it once required every parish to have its own cemetery, where this was permitted by the secular government. Of course, as the population exploded and as Christianity in some countries established itself as an urban religion, the ideal of individual parish cemeteries had to give way to more practical arrangements, like large cemeteries serving wide areas of the Catholic population. The community Catholic cemetery thus became standard. Yet remnants of the old ideal can be glimpsed in the quaint cemeteries one finds in the churchyards of many country parishes. "God's Acre" next to "God's House." Longfellow said the term "God's Acre" was an "ancient Saxon phrase." The fact is that it is a modern borrowing from Germany, and some would say a presumptuous one. A cemetery-association convention speaker caused a sensation in 1918 when he linked the phrase to one of the day's great villains, exclaiming, ". . . . Someone as deficient in modesty as the Kaiser in his hallucination of an alliance with God, as expressed in the supposed partnership of *Me und Gott,* in looking after the destiny of the world and its inhabitants, has possessed someone to take God into partnership in providing a burial place for the human dead."

But if not exactly "God's Acre," cemeteries are sacred places, and Catholic ones are conducted as the privileged resting spots for those dying in communion with the church—although not so exclusively privileged as once upon a time. They're easier to get into, in other words. But there are still exclusions. Unless there has been some sign of repentance before death, Christian burial—ecclesiastical funeral rites included—is supposed to be denied notorious apostates, heretics and schismatics; those who choose cremation as an act of defiance or ridicule of the Christian faith; and other manifest sinners whose lives were such that the granting of ecclesiastical privileges would be a cause of scandal to the faithful. With respect to the last, just a few years ago the Archdiocese of New York denied public ecclesiastical funeral rites to a notorious gangland figure who died a spectacular victim of mob violence, lest the faithful be scandalized. (Private services were allowed later.)

Tough as the rules are, they were once a lot tougher, even for those far less notorious than some gangland character. The toughness goes back to Pope Leo the Great (440-461). He decreed in 448 that the church could not hold communion in death with those who in life were not in communion with it (*equibus viventibus non communicavimus mortuis communicare non possumus*), and over the centuries his instruction came to be applied with such rigidity that even into the twentieth century the remains of non-Catholic spouses and infants of Catholic parents who died before being baptized were consigned to unblessed parts of Catholic cemeteries. Thus, families united in life were separated in death. These strict provisions could be waived by bishop's permission or circumvented in other ways so that the remains of the non-Catholic spouse or the unbaptized baby could be laid to rest in the family plot in blessed ground—and regularly were. Nonetheless the exclusions were on the books, and not always in some mere *pro forma* way. They were strictly applied in some places. Generally, however, the measure was that of leniency, particularly as the church moved further into the twentieth century.

The reverse of the coin was the consignment of Catholic remains in a non-Catholic cemetery. Was it even possible? For instance, what if there were no Catholic cemetery around, or what if the deceased were a Catholic but the family burial plot was in a non-Catholic cemetery? Could anything be done? It could. Bishops could allow the Catholic party to be buried in the family's plot in the non-Catholic cemetery, just as in certain unusual circumstances, such as the absence of satisfactory Catholic cemetery facilities, they could permit Catholic burials in non-Catholic cemeteries. But in such instances it was the custom for the graves to be blessed according to the approved Catholic rite. From a Catholic point of view, the result, in effect, was a cemetery within a cemetery.

Loosening the Restrictions

Quaint as the old rules might seem to some, many of them are still on the books—but, once again, applied by the church with great leniency.

RETROSPECT

It is a leniency that extends to the rites of liturgy as well as to the privileges or rights of commital. The leniency is reflected in the new Code of Canon Law, as indicated by Canon 1183, sections 2 and 3, which read:

"The local ordinary can permit children to be given ecclesiastical funeral rites if their parents intended to baptize them but they died before their baptism.

"In the prudent judgment of the local ordinary, ecclesiastical funeral rites can be granted to baptized members of some non-Catholic church or ecclesial community unless it is evidently contrary to their will and provided their own minister is unavailable."

A similar leniency—a more psychologically informed understanding is perhaps a better way of wording it—applies with respect to those who die as suicides. The Scriptures condemned suicide as a most atrocious crime, and as early as the fourth century the church was refusing Christian burial to those who died by their own hand. Even as late as 1918, the church carried in its Code of Canon Law a stipulation (Canon 1240, section 3) specifically forbidding Christian burial to "those who, in full possession of their faculties, have killed themselves." The qualifying clause, "in full possession of their faculties," clued that ecclesial logic had begun to fall in line with that of psychiatrists and medical authorities, that a mental derangement of at least temporary duration could have contributed to the individual's act of self-violence. Still, there were those in authority who could be unbending.

It's different today. At present, medical examiners are

less judgmental in determining reason (as distinct from cause) of death, and thus issue death certificates allowing the possibility of the deaths occurring because of accident or mental instability. The documents are commonly accepted by church officials as proof of mitigating circumstances allowing permission for Christian burial. The new Code of Canon Law (1983) no longer automatically denies ecclesiastical burial to those hitherto classified as suicides. The word "suicides" isn't even used in the Code.

Neither, incidentally, is there reference in the new code to duelists, a group once also automatically excluded from the privileges of Christian burial. In this instance, the reason very likely is that dueling has passed from common practice virtually everywhere as a method of defending one's honor or reputation, evening scores, or whatever.

Cremation is another once-reprobated practice that has undergone something of a re-evaluation. As mentioned, the statute is still on the books: Christian burial is denied those choosing cremation over inhumation (common interment) "for reasons opposed to the Christian faith" (Canon 1184, number 2). But so many elements of an extenuating kind have entered into decisions affecting funeral arrangements—considerations of personal and practical, hygienic and financial kinds—that the church is no longer so adamantly opposed to cremation. The church "earnestly recommends that the pious custom of burial be retained" (Canon 1176, number 3), but at the same time it now allows that the traditional Christian practice of inhumation may be difficult or even impossible for some families. For instance, there may be a lack of cemetery space in the region, or cremation may be more affordable. Cremation is, in the normal course, a far less expensive procedure than inhumation.

Certain ecclesiastical restrictions are in force, however, in instances of cremation, one being that the cremation must take place apart from the church's formal liturgical services of burial, and remain apart. In other words, the ashes ("cremains," as the ashes are called in such circumstances) are not to be brought into the church for the funeral liturgy. Many persons—among them, Father Michael J. Henchal, columnist for *The Church World* of Portland, Maine—have proposed to the bishops a change in church law which would permit such a practice. The proposal lost in 1987, but proponents promise to keep trying until a change is made. As Henchal wrote, "I'll try again, until, as we did with communion in the hand and communion from the cup, for example, we eventually win over enough support to change the law."

The changes in regulations affecting suicides, cremations and the like have been consequential, to be sure. But far and away the most dramatic changes of recent times in the rites of Catholic-Christian burial must be accounted those of mood and tone.

The Death of Death

In keeping with the instruction of Vatican II that burial rites "should evidence more clearly the paschal character of Christian death" (Constitution on the Sacred Liturgy, 81), liturgical emphases have been redirected so as to reflect those of the early church.

Though now as then death is an occasion of sadness, the liturgy frames the event as one also of glorious triumph in the Lord. It was this very element of triumph that in the early church never failed to amaze pagans. Pagan burial rites featured instrumental music, professional mourners, actors and buffoons, and rituals of purification for those who looked on the corpse, lest the ghost of the dead had infiltrated the body of the viewer. By contrast, Christians substituted triumphal marches signifying belief in the resurrection and triumph over death (the procession at today's funeral services is likely a remnant of them). They sang joyous psalms, such as Psalm 100 ("Sing joyfully to the Lord, all you lands; / serve the Lord with gladness; / come before him with joyful song"). Finally, the funeral liturgy featured a eucharistic celebration, at which all who could joined in receiving the sacrament.

Over the centuries most of the joyous and triumphal aspects of the death rites were to be lost. In the early Christian ages, the Alleluia was regarded as singularly proper for funerals, particularly in the East. Not so in the West, where by the eighth and ninth centuries the Alleluia and Gloria had both disappeared from the liturgies for the dead. Funerals became extremely somber occasions. Priests donned black vestments. The choir abandoned joyous psalms for mournful dirges. Then, when communion-time arrived at the funeral mass, only the celebrant received. The people remained in the pews.

With the return since Vatican II to early liturgical emphases, it is quite different today. White vestments—traditionally restricted to funerals of infants and children dying before age seven—may now be used in the offices and masses for the dead, whatever the age of the deceased. Violet (purple) or black vestments have not been totally discarded, but the white option is popular, and has been going on more than twenty years. Similarly, if music is included in the liturgy of the dead, it is apt to be much less gloomy or ponderous than before. As for the funeral mass itself, when communion-time arrives, the aisles crowd with communicants, the same as at Sunday services. The funeral mass, in sum, takes on aspects of the community liturgical banquet.

Since the revised liturgical rites went into effect November 1, 1971, the general objective has been to orient burial liturgies toward paschal or resurrection themes. Thus the funeral mass—the Mass of Christian Burial, in official liturgical parlance—is also known as the Mass of Resurrection. The paschal candle is carried in the entrance procession, and when it comes time for the homily, preachers are directed by the church's official Sacramentary to include an expression of praise and gratitude to God for his gifts, particularly the gift of Christian life to the deceased, and to relate Christian death to the paschal mystery of the Lord's victorious death and resurrection and to the hope of eternal life. To

John Deedy

help underscore "the fellowship of all Christ's members," and the consolations of hope, the Sacramentary suggests that the first and second readings of the funeral liturgy be read by relatives or friends of the deceased person.

The scriptural bases for these emphases are rooted in the main in Paul's First Epistle to the Corinthians, the letter embodying Paul's conviction that in the resurrection of Christ is the Christian's assurance of eternal life.

As Father John L. McKenzie remarks in his book *Source* (Thomas More Press, 1984), "Paul is insistent that both Christ and the believer rise to a new life and not to a resumption of the life which is terminated by death." It had to be, for what attraction to the Christians addressed by Paul was there in a resumption of the old life? The life those Christians knew was mostly one of disease, destitution, oppression and persecution. Paul promised something better, and so does the new liturgy. It is the life of Christ. In McKenzie's words, "Christians are invited to unite themselves with Jesus in his life and death, and thus to give their own life and death a redeeming value." The offer ultimately is the hope of absolute and complete human fulfillment.

The bottom line, then, is the word of Paul in 1 Corinthians 15:53-55. The exquisite King James version of the Scriptures delivers it thus:

"For this corruptible must put on incorruption, and this mortal *must* put on immortality.

"So, when this corruptible shall have put on incorruption, and this mortal shall have put on immortality, then

330

shall be brought to pass the saying that is written, Death is swallowed up in victory.

"Oh death, where *is* thy sting? Oh grave, where *is* thy victory?"

BIBLIOGRAPHY

Abbott, Walter M., S.J., general editor. *The Documents of Vatican II.* New York: Guild Press, American Press and Association Press, 1966.

Casey, William P. *God's Acre.* National Catholic Cemetery Conference, 1951.

Catholic Encyclopedia. New York: The Gilmary Society, 1913.

"A Catholic Home Encyclopedia," supplement to *The Holy Bible.* Chicago: The Catholic Press, Inc., 1950.

Cogley, John. *Catholic America.* New York: Dial Press, 1973.

Coulson, John, editor. *The Saints: A Concise Biographical Dictionary.* New York: Hawthorne, 1958.

Daniel-Rops, Henri. *The Protestant Reformation. Volumes 1 and 2.* Garden City, New York: Image Books, 1963.

Deedy, John. *American Catholicism: And Now Where?* New York: Plenum, 1987.

Deedy, John. *The Catholic Fact Book.* Chicago: Thomas More, 1986.

Delaney, John J. *Dictionary of American Catholic Biography*. Garden City, New York: Doubleday, 1984.

Deretz, J., and A. Nocent, O.S.B. *Dictionary of the Council*. Washington and Cleveland: Corpus, 1968.

Ellis, John Tracy. *Documents of American Catholic History*. Milwaukee, Wisconsin: Bruce, 1962.

Ellis, John Tracy. *American Catholicism*. Second edition, revised. Chicago: University of Chicago Press, 1969.

Encyclopedia Britannica. Eleventh edition. New York: Encyclopedia Britannica Co., 1911.

Encyclopedia Britannica. Fifteenth edition. 1987.

Fesquet, Henri. *The Drama of Vatican II*. New York: Random House, 1967.

Fogarty, Gerald P. The Vatican and the American Hierarchy from 1870 to 1965. Wilmington, Delaware: Foy, Michael Glazier, 1985.

Foy, Felician A., O.F.M., editor. *Catholic Almanac*. Huntington, Indiana: Our Sunday Visitor, 1985.

Granfield, Patrick. *The Papacy in Transition*. Garden City, New York: Doubleday, 1980.

Greeley, Andrew M., et al. *Catholic Schools in a Declining Church*. Kansas City: Sheed & Ward, 1976.

Greeley, Andrew, and McManus, William. *Catholic Contributions: Sociology & Policy*. Chicago: Thomas More, 1987.

Hardon, John A. *Christianity in the Twentieth Century*. Garden City, New York: Doubleday, 1971.

Hardon, John A. *Christianity in the Twentieth Century*. Garden City, New York: Doubleday, 1971.

Hughes, Philip. *The Church in Crisis: A History of the*

RETROSPECT

General Councils, 325-1870. Garden City, New York: Image Books, 1964.

Hughes, Philip. *A Popular History of the Catholic Church.* New York: Macmillan, 1962.

Jedin, Hubert. *Ecumenical Councils of the Catholic Church.* New York: Deus Books, Paulist Press, 1961.

John, Eric, editor. *The Popes: A Concise Biographical Dictionary.* New York: Hawthorne, 1964.

McKenzie, John L. *Source: What the Bible Says About the Problems of Contemporary Life.* Chicago: Thomas More, 1984.

Martos, Joseph. *Doors to the Sacred.* Garden City, New York: Doubleday, 1981.

Morrow, Louis LaRavoire. *My Catholic Faith.* Silver Jubilee Edition. Kenosha, Wisconsin: My Mission House, 1961.

Murphy, Francis X., C.SS.R. *The Papacy Today.* New York: Macmillan, 1981.

New Catholic Encyclopedia. New York: McGraw-Hill, 1967.

Pegis, Anton C. *Basic Writings of St. Thomas Aquinas.* New York: Random House, 1945.

Smith, George D. *The Teaching of the Catholic Church.* Volumes 1 and 2. New York: Macmillan, 1948.

Vaillancourt, Jean-Guy. *Papal Power.* Berkeley, California: University of California Press, 1980.

* * *

No one particular Bible translation has been used in this book. Where possible, biblical quotes familiar to my religious-educational training have been given preference over more recent, approved renderings of the passage concerned. Inevitably this means a certain reliance on the Douay version of the Bible (now considered archaic, though Catholics of my generation grew up on it), and in a few instances on the King James version of the Bible (which once upon a time we weren't supposed to read for fear of losing our immortal souls).

INDEX

INDEX

INDEX

Council of Baltimore (1832), 305

Council of Baltimore (1837), 291

Council of Baltimore (1840), 291

Council of Baltimore (1852), 166

Council of Baltimore (1884), 153, 166, 305

Council of Carthage, 113

Council of Chalcedon, 239, 255, 269

Council of Constance, 289-90

Council of Constantinople, 239

Council of Elvira, 133, 130, 133

Council of Florence, 227, 255

Council of Lyons, second, 69

Council of Nicaea, 78, 135, 159, 239, 255

Council of Neicaesarea, 239

Council of Orange, 69

Council of Riez, 69

Council of Rome, 113

Council of Toledo, 113

Council of Turin, 113

Conciliarism, 265

Constantine, emperor, 36, 67, 146, 161, 209, 237

Corpus Christi, feast of, 165, 167

Cremation, 326-7

Crisan, Traian, archbishop, 278

Crusades, 98

Cushing, Richard J., cardinal, 89, 294, 308

Cyprian, saint, 322

Damasus, pope, 226, 255

Daniel, 206

Dante, 231

Decent, bishop, 74

Decree of Gratian, 161, 319-20

Decretals of Gregory IX, 161

Deretz, J., 108

Devil, 212ff

"Devil's Advocate," 276

Devotional exercises, 174ff

Divino afflante Spiritu, encyclical, 231-2

Divinus perfectionis magister, apostolic constitution, 275

Divorce, 49, 60, 61

Dollinger, Johann von, 121

Dominican order, 2, 33, 69, 181

Dominic, saint, 181-3

Dueling, 326

Dulles, Avery, S.J., 9

Easter, 158-9, 165

Easter duty, 42

Education, 299ff

Ellis, John Tracy, Father, 301-2

Epiphanius, saint, 19

Epiphany, feast of, 160, 165, 167

Eucharist, 48, 54, 63, 66, 71ff, 93, 200

Eugenius II, pope, 271

INDEX

INDEX

Holy Orders, 48, 63, 76ff
Holy Spirit, gifts of, 70
Holy Week, 11
Homosexuals, 234-5
Hubert, saint, 180
Hugh of Saint-Cher, 99-100
Hugh of Saint Victor, 69
Humanae vitae, encyclical,
  263
Humani generis, encyclical,
  264
Hundred Years War, 101

Immaculate Conception, 21,
  25, 166, 175, 294
Indulgences, 95ff
  types of, 98-9
  "Doctrine of . . .,"
    apostolic constitution,
    108
  "Handbook of . . .,"
    (*Enchiridion
    Indulgentiarum,* 1968),
    109
Infallibility, 43, 246, 252ff
Innocent I, pope, 52, 74,
  227, 255
Innocent II, pope, 117
Ireland, John, archbishop,
  306
Irenaeus, 17
Isaiah, bishop, 87
Ishmael, 206

James I, king, 225
Janney, Russell, 85
Jerome, saint, 131, 205-6,
  226, 231

Jesus 15ff, 20, 49ff, 79ff,
  98-9, 128, 133, 162, 181,
  200, 207, 213-4, 280,
  288-9, 330
  as the "new Adam," 17
Jesuits (Society of Jesus), 24,
  187, 301
John, the baptizer, 66, 81,
  162
John, the evangelist, 16-7, 33,
  207, 218, 22
John XXIII, pope, 26, 125-6,
  169, 247-8, 264, 277, 294
John Chrysostom, saint, 52,
  56, 132
John of the Cross, saint, 89
John Nepomucene Neumann,
  saint, 185
John Paul I, pope, 248
John Paul II, pope, 29, 60,
  111, 123-5, 137, 143, 168,
  172, 239, 248-51, 264, 275,
  278, 281
Jophiel, angel, 208
Joseph, saint, 162, 167, 175,
  180-1, 207
Julius II, pope, 102
Justin, saint, 17

Kennedy, John F., 309
King Stephen of Hungary,
  saint, 277
Korean martyrs, 278, 281
Küng, Hans, Father, 262-3

Lambertini Prospero
  (Benedict XIV), 276
Lateran Council I, 117

INDEX

INDEX

INDEX

344

INDEX

INDEX